UNDERSTANDING
COMMUNITY

ver

WITHDRAWN

Also available in the series

Understanding social citizenship (second edition)
Themes and perspectives for policy and practice
Peter Dwyer

"A second edition of this excellent book is most welcome. Dwyer's understanding of social citizenship is second to none and this new edition provides an updated discussion and assessment of all the practical and theoretical issues that students need to know about this important area of study." Nick Ellison, University of Leeds

PB £19.99 (US$32.95) **ISBN** 978 1 84742 328 3 **HB** £65.00 (US$85.00) **ISBN** 978 1 84742 329 0
280 pages June 2010
INSPECTION COPY AVAILABLE

Understanding theories and concepts in social policy
Ruth Lister

"This is an admirably clear and comprehensive account of the theories and concepts of contemporary social policy. Excellent and essential for undergraduate and postgraduate social policy and social theory courses." Fiona Williams, Professor of Social Policy, University of Leeds

PB £19.99 (US$34.95) **ISBN** 978 1 86134 793 0 **HB** £60.00 (US$80.00) **ISBN** 978 1 86134 794 7
328 pages June 2010
INSPECTION COPY AVAILABLE

Understanding human need
Hartley Dean

"Hartley Dean's book certainly meets a need: he expertly summarises debates over what human needs are, how they relate to happiness and capabilities, and what they entail for human rights and social policies. An invaluable book." Ian Gough Emeritus Professor of Social Policy, University of Bath

PB £21.99 (US$34.95) **ISBN** 978 1 84742 189 0 **HB** £65.00 (US$89.95) **ISBN** 978 1 84742 190 6
240 pages February 2010
INSPECTION COPY AVAILABLE

Understanding social welfare movements
Jason Annetts, Alex Law, Wallace McNeish and Gerry Mooney

The book provides a timely and much needed overview of the changing nature of social welfare as it has been shaped by the demands of social movements.

PB £19.99 (US$35.95) **ISBN** 978 1 84742 096 1 **HB** £65.00 (US$99.00) **ISBN** 978 1 84742 097 8
304 pages June 2009
INSPECTION COPY AVAILABLE

For a full listing of all titles in the series visit www.policypress.co.uk

SOCIAL POLICY
ASSOCIATION

www.policypress.co.uk

INSPECTION COPIES AND ORDERS AVAILABLE FROM:
Marston Book Services • PO Box 269 • Abingdon • Oxon OX14 4YN UK
INSPECTION COPIES
Tel: +44 (0) 1235 465500 • Fax: +44 (0) 1235 465556 • Email: inspections@marston.co.uk
ORDERS
Tel: +44 (0) 1235 465500 • Fax: +44 (0) 1235 465556 • Email: direct.orders@marston.co.uk

UNDERSTANDING COMMUNITY

Politics, policy and practice

Peter Somerville

First published published in Great Britain in 2011 by
The Policy Press
University of Bristol
Fourth Floor, Beacon House
Queen's Road
Bristol BS8 1QU
UK

t: +44 (0)117 331 4054
f: +44 (0)117 331 4093
tpp-info@bristol.ac.uk
www.policypress.org.uk

North American office:
The Policy Press
c/o International Specialized Books Services
920 NE 58th Avenue, Suite 300
Portland, OR 97213-3786, USA
t: +1 503 287 3093
f: +1 503 280 8832
info@isbs.com

British Library Cataloguing in Publication Data
A catalogue record for this book is available from the British Library.

Library of Congress Cataloging-in-Publication Data
A catalog record for this book has been requested.

ISBN 978 1 84742 392 4 paperback
ISBN 978 1 84742 393 1 hardcover

Cover design by Qube Design Associates, Bristol
Front cover: photograph kindly supplied by www.alamy.com
Printed and bound in Great Britain by Hobbs, Southampton
The Policy Press uses environmentally friendly print partners

FSC
www.fsc.org
MIX
Paper from
responsible sources
FSC® C020438

Contents

Detailed contents

List of boxes, figures and tables

Boxes

Figures

Tables

Preface

The original idea for this book came to me from a series of lectures that I deliver to final year undergraduate students. The purpose of these lectures was (and is) to use ideas about community to understand how social policy is formulated and implemented across a wide spectrum of issues. Much, if not most, social policy literature tends to assume that social reality consists of what appear to be almost two dimensions: on the one hand, structures, processes, institutions, systems, etc, and on the other hand, perspectives, ideologies, values, etc. In fact, however, these two dimensions are inextricably intertwined, and a focus on community as both idea and practice serves to reveal this.

Having decided, then, to focus on community and signed a contract with the publishers, I had already written a few chapters before I stumbled upon what appeared to have the potential to be the unifying theme that I was looking for — one that embodied both the ideal and potential realisation of community as meaningful interconnectedness. This was the idea of a beloved community, derived from Martin Luther King. According to this idea, the ideal of community can only be achieved through the actual flourishing of all of its individual members. I then used this deceptively simple idea to evaluate a range of policies and practices and indeed a variety of kinds of community. I leave the reader to judge how successful (or not) I have been in making this evaluation.

The reader should also be forewarned that, in the concluding chapter, I attempt to explain the spiritual meaning of community (as conveyed in the expression 'community spirit') as an imagined wellspring of social action. Following what is perhaps now the mainstream literature on spirituality, I make an important distinction between desire and attachment: desire is an attribute of the ego (or soul), while attachment is to do with connections that exist even in the absence of desire. To try and make more sense of this, I have used concepts from Buddhism, since the Buddha's teachings reflect my own concerns with achieving meaningful interconnectedness through the cessation of desire. The flourishing of humanity as a whole occurs precisely through this free (that is, free from desire) communion among all human beings. And lest this seem impossibly utopian, I also argue that it is no more utopian than what is currently expected by governments from their citizens.

List of acronyms

ASBO	Anti-Social Behaviour Order
BME	Black and minority ethnic
CCTV	closed-circuit television
CED	community economic development
CEN	Community Empowerment Network
CIC	Commission on Integration and Cohesion
CLG	Communities and Local Government
COF	Citizens Organising Foundation
FIP	family intervention project
HAZ	Health Action Zone
HHW	Hill Holt Wood
JRF	Joseph Rowntree Foundation
LEA	local education authority
LGTB	lesbian, gay, transgender and bisexual
LMS	Local Management of Schools
LSP	Local Strategic Partnership
MINCy	mixed income community
NDC	New Deal for Communities
NESS	National Evaluation of Sure Start
NGO	non-governmental organisation
NHS	National Health Service
NMP	neighbourhood management pathfinder
PB	participatory budgeting
PCT	primary care trust
RDA	Regional Development Agency
SSLPs	Sure Start Local Programmes

one

The nature of community

Overview

This chapter argues that community is a phenomenon that:

- can be *expressed* through networks of sociability
- *interpellates* individuals as members of the same collectivity
- involves the possibility of mutual *recognition* of such membership.

Through a consideration of the work of Durkheim, Bourdieu, Habermas and others, the chapter explores the nature of this social phenomenon.

The meaning of community

'Community' is a very familiar word, frequently found on the lips of politicians and professionals, as well as members of the general public. As they say, however, familiarity breeds contempt, and community is no exception, with the term being dismissed by many as too vague, woolly or even ideological. This book will argue that the concept of community does need to be taken seriously but its meaning is complex, multidimensional and essentially contested.

As good a starting point as any here is Day (2006, p 24), who identifies three core elements of the meaning of community (see also Butcher, 1993): 'a particular way of organising social relationships, a general (and desirable) quality of sociability and mutual regard, and a summons to undertake joint mutual action'. Let us consider each of these elements in turn.

First, what is distinctive of community as a way of organising social relationships? Many commentators have conceived communities as *networks* in which people relate to one another through cooperative interaction, involving forms of mutual trust, affinity and obligation. Such networks are contrasted with other ways of organising social relationships, for example, through market exchange or command-and-control systems. While communities do typically consist of networks, however, a community does not seem to be the same thing as a network. To take an obvious example, the internet is a network, and one can also identify internet communities of all kinds, but this does not mean that the internet is a community. Moreover, it is not clear why communities should be organised only through networks – why should it not be possible for communities to be hierarchically organised or constructed on the basis of rules of contract? The answer, of course, is that such modes of organisation would appear to conflict with our understanding of what we feel to be the 'real' meaning of community. So what is this 'real' meaning, which is expressed through networks but is not to be identified with networks?

This leads us on to Day's second element of community, namely quality of *sociability* and mutual regard. The meaning of sociability may seem obvious but is in fact complex and deeply mysterious. For Bourdieu and Wacquant (1992, p 119), sociability is the ability and disposition to sustain networks of 'more or less institutionalised relationships of mutual acquaintance and recognition'. The beauty of this definition is that it not only identifies the nature of the networks that express community (as relations of mutual acquaintance and recognition) but also the relationship that community as sociability has to those networks (as an ability and disposition to sustain them). A sustainable community becomes at once a truism because a community that cannot be sustained cannot be a community at all. Community as sociability is therefore understood as involving networks of actors who sustain those networks through a certain style of interaction.

Misztal (2000, p 81) throws important light on the nature of this style of interaction. She argues that sociability is one of three main styles of human interaction (the others being civility and intimacy) and involves a balance between *informality*, with actors having freedom to choose, shape and model the main features of their particular relationships, and *formality*, with reliance on universal and more or less codified norms such as ethical codes and occupational rules. In developing sociable relationships, and thereby creating and sustaining community, actors choose whether and how to interact with others, but their choices are determined, in part, by the roles that are available to them to play in particular situations. (This point will be taken up further in discussing Bourdieu's concept of habitus.)

Communities can therefore be understood, to some extent, as *networks of sociability*, which can take an unlimited number of forms and be created in an unlimited number of contexts. Thus far, however, this is to understand community only in a descriptive sense, as an empirically identifiable object. Day's third element of community, in contrast, sees community prescriptively, as a call to action. Butcher (1993) sees this as the active or instrumental meaning of community – community as collective agency, an invocation of a capacity for collective action. Community therefore connotes not only a certain kind of potential (the capacity of a network for sustaining and sustained interaction) but the actualisation of that potential through named courses of action. The importance of the concept of community is not that it explains anything but that it is *ideological* in the sense defined by Althusser (1970, p 30): '*all ideology hails or interpellates concrete individuals as concrete subjects*'. What this means is described in *Box 1.1*.

Box 1.1: Interpellation

Interpellation or hailing can be imagined along the lines of the most commonplace everyday police (or other) hailing: 'Hey, you there!' Assuming that this takes place in the street, the hailed individual will turn round. By this mere 180-degree physical conversion, he becomes a *subject*. Why? Because he has recognised that the hail was 'really' addressed to him, and that 'it was *really him* who was hailed' (and not someone else). Experience shows that the practical telecommunication of hailings is such that they hardly ever miss their man: verbal call or whistle, the one hailed always recognises that it is really him who is being hailed. And yet it is a strange phenomenon, and one which cannot be explained solely by 'guilt feelings', despite the large numbers who 'have something on their consciences'.

Source: Althusser (1970, p 31)

'Community' is therefore a word that serves to interpellate individuals as members of a certain collective, who consequently feel obliged to act in a certain way. The interpellation works to the extent that individuals have a disposition to act cooperatively and the roles they are called upon to perform are consistent with this disposition.[1] The real power of the ideology of community, however, stems from its capacity to interpellate individuals *irrespective of their participation in networks*. Where networks connecting its members are absent, the community can be represented as an *imagined* one, as in Anderson's (1983) interpretation of nations as 'imagined communities'.[2]

Community, therefore, is something that can be *expressed* through networks of sociability but is not necessarily to be *identified* with such networks. At least part of the core meaning of community seems to lie in a capacity to interpellate individuals to act cooperatively as members of the same collectivity. Not only can individuals cooperate without necessarily being sociable (civility may be sufficient, involving recognition but not necessarily acquaintance), but they can 'cooperate' in some sense (that is, their actions can be coordinated in some way) without even interacting. Clearly, they must be linked in some way for cooperation to occur, but these links may be highly mediated and largely, if not entirely, imagined. At bottom, therefore, community is (embodied or imagined) connectedness among individuals.[3]

But what makes individuals act cooperatively or be connected? In deciding how to act, each individual has to balance their own dispositions against prevailing rules and norms, but the logic of their action is rarely one of rational calculation, particularly insofar as they are subject to interpellation, but also because the nature of informality precludes the application of decision rules (Misztal, 2000). The work of Bourdieu has thrown some light on this point. In *The Logic of Practice* (1990), for example, Bourdieu argues that the social world is to be understood in terms of practices that are objectified in two ways. The first involves bodily experience and activity, and is more informal: 'a spontaneity without consciousness or will' (Bourdieu, 1990, p 56). This objectification is known as '*habitus*', which can be understood as a durable way of going on in the world that is adapted to that world but is not produced by following any set rules (Bourdieu, 1990, p 53).[4] The second is more formal and involves fields, with '*field*' being defined as 'a network, or a configuration, of objective relations between positions' (Bourdieu and Wacquant, 1992, p 97). The term 'habitus' therefore refers to the everyday balances that individuals and groups draw between informality and formality, which form the basis for community in its active sense, while 'field' denotes a system of organised social relations and institutions.

In the example of hailing described in ***Box 1.1***, the habitus of the individual being hailed is one in which they recognise certain calls as being addressed to them, even though they are not being addressed formally or by name, while the field has to do, in part, with the system of relations between police and citizens. A less trivial example of a habitus, perhaps, would be the well-established processes by which individuals are interpellated to traditional gender roles, so that these roles assume the character of what Duncan and Edwards (1999) have called 'gendered moral rationalities'; here the field could be patriarchal structures of various kinds (Walby, 1990). In this chapter, I will be focusing on the habitus (plural) of class, particularly the habitus (singular) of the working class, where individuals are interpellated as wage labourers, and the field is construed primarily in terms of labour market structures.

The relationship between habitus and field is particularly important for understanding community, and for understanding social life generally.

Bourdieu (1990, p 57) argues that habitus is what makes it possible to inhabit institutions and make them work. He cites the example of property, where possession enables the possessor to participate in property-related institutions, for example giving, exchanging, lending, borrowing and economic institutions generally: 'An institution, even an economy, is complete and fully viable only if it is durably objectified not only in things, that is, in the logic, transcending individual agents, of a particular field, but also in bodies, in durable dispositions to recognise and comply with the demands immanent in the field' (Bourdieu, 1990, p 58). A community is therefore a group of individuals, bodily located within a habitus, who are adapted and who adapt to the constraints imposed on them (and possibly the opportunities afforded to them) by the structures of a particular field. Here a community is seen as something historically formed, dynamic and continuously changing.

The relationship between habitus and field is indeed conceived by Bourdieu as dialectical:

> It is in the dialectic between class conditions and 'class sense', between the 'objective' conditions recorded in distributions and the structuring dispositions, themselves structured by these conditions, that is, in accordance with the distributions, that the continuous structure of the distributions reappears, now transfigured and misrecognisable, in the discontinuous structure of hierarchised life-styles and in the representations and recognitions that arise from misrecognition of their objective truth. (Bourdieu, 1990, p 140)

This is a difficult statement, but it seems to me to be of crucial importance. Bourdieu sees the relationship between habitus and field primarily in terms of social class, and secondarily in terms of culture. Individuals are positioned in relation to a social system, for example, as workers, managers, self-employed, capitalists or whatever, and their dispositions reflect these positions; these dispositions in turn result in hierarchies of social distinction (Bourdieu, 1984) and in illusions about the real basis for these hierarchies.[5] For Bourdieu, therefore, a community is primarily class based (and secondarily culture based), and communities of different classes or cultures have different kinds of habitus, which relate in different ways to fields, where fields are understood as sets of institutions characteristic of a particular social system such as capitalism.

Bourdieu's distinction between habitus and field echoes earlier distinctions made, for example, by Tönnies between *Gemeinschaft* and *Gesellschaft*, by Durkheim between mechanical and organic solidarity, and by Habermas between lifeworld and system. In the case of Tönnies (1988), *Gemeinschaft* is defined as 'a lasting and genuine form of living together', undertaking 'coordinated action for a common good'. This is contrasted with *Gesellschaft*, which is sometimes translated as 'association', and refers to an arrangement where individuals engage in 'artificial' relations for their own ends, for example, through the market (trade associations) or the state (political associations). The use of the terms 'genuine' and 'good' here clearly signal that *Gemeinschaft* is regarded as a condition that is to be valued and desired, so the possibility of communities that lack value or desirability is excluded a priori. This approach is reminiscent of Anselm's proof of the existence of God, that is, God must exist because he is perfect, so cannot lack existence as this would mean that He was not perfect. In this case, the argument is that community must work for a common good, so if there are communities that do not do this, they cannot be 'true' communities.

This is therefore an idealisation of community, which results in a somewhat crude, unnecessary and unconvincing dualism. The downside to this has been pointed out by Iris Marion Young (1990, p 235):

> The ideal of community, I suggest, validates and reinforces the fear and aversion some social groups exhibit toward others. If community is a positive norm, that is, if existing together with others in relations of mutual understanding and reciprocity is the goal, then it is understandable that we exclude and avoid those with whom we do not or cannot identify.

Durkheim (1984) was critical of Tönnies' idealisation of community but retained the gist of the latter's dualism, based as it was on a distinction between pre-modern and modern societies. Durkheim introduced the concept of *social solidarity* to denote social integration or cohesion – the ties that bind individuals to one another, that is, the connectedness among individuals that has been argued above to be the core meaning of community. He identified two kinds of solidarity: *mechanical* solidarity, in which individuals identify with those who have similar characteristics to themselves, often based on kinship and/or on living and working together; and *organic* solidarity, in which individuals are dependent upon one another as a result of the division of labour, where different individuals perform different specialist tasks, each of which is required for the survival and well-being of all.

This distinction is important because it recognises that individuals can be tied together in different ways – not only through embodied or imagined networks of sociability (mechanical solidarity) but also in ways that may have nothing at all to do with sociability or interaction of any kind and *may not even be imagined or felt by the participants*. It raises the question of the nature of our obligations to those on whom we depend but who fall outside what we might regard as our communities. This is an issue to which I shall return in discussing the nature of political community (namely, the issue of cosmopolitan obligation). The main point to note for now is that Durkheim's achievement was to show that there exist forms of connectedness among individuals that are embodied in some sense but do not require interaction among those individuals and do not even require interpellation in Althusser's sense. Arguably, however, such organic solidarity cannot be described as community because it lacks the sense of a definite group of persons or sentient beings who can act or be together.[6]

What Durkheim achieved was to draw a distinction between two kinds of connectedness: what Lockwood (1958) later called 'social' integration, which characterises community, and 'system' integration, which is an attribute of modern societies. Clearly, this formulation has similarities with Bourdieu's distinction between habitus and field. Durkheim, however, saw the two forms of solidarity as characteristic of different kinds of society and so did not attempt to see how they were related, whereas Bourdieu saw habitus and fields as dialectically related, and more or less integrated, within social practices. He talks of an 'immediate adherence that is established in practice between a habitus and the field to which it is attuned' (Bourdieu, 1990, p 68). This occurs 'whenever the practices of the group show very little dispersion and when each member helps to impose on all the others, willy–nilly, the same constraint that they impose on him' (Bourdieu, 1990, p 110). This condition is characteristic of what Bourdieu (1990, p 111) calls 'strongly integrated communities'.

Where does this leave our thinking about community? Bourdieu teaches us that communities cannot be considered in abstraction from their historical and social context. Community is about connectedness among persons, and the connectedness has to be meaningful to the persons concerned – there has to be a substantive grouping or collectivity with which those persons can be identified (by themselves and by others), with the possibility of recognition of one another as being members of it. The nature of those persons, however, and how they are connected to one another, seems to depend on the character of particular habitus and fields and on how each habitus relates to its corresponding field. This point will become clearer below, for example in the discussion of working-class habitus.

Habermas' binary opposition of lifeworld and system seems very like those of both Tönnies and Durkheim. Lifeworlds are seen as symbolic structures of taken-for-granted meanings, produced through communicative action (understood as action oriented towards establishing agreement among individuals). Systems are seen as ordered connections among social consequences, produced through rational, purposive action (understood as being strategic and instrumental). The concept of lifeworld encompasses not only patterns of meaningful interaction but collective representations such as Durkheim's 'conscience collective' and Parsons' 'societal community', which is understood as the structured set of norms and institutions that sustains and is sustained by the interaction order of the lifeworld (Scott, p 241). This sounds like Bourdieu's habitus but it is not because it is conceived as a society-wide sphere of social integration, posited in opposition to a sphere of system integration. For Habermas, the lifeworld is primary but systems emerge as societies become more organised in terms of the social division of labour. This separation of the system sphere from the lifeworld sphere is what makes Habermas' conceptualisation seem more like Durkheim's distinction between mechanical and organic solidarity. Habermas goes further than Durkheim, however, in arguing that, in late capitalism, the instrumental rationality of its political economy 'colonises' the lifeworld, precipitating a succession of crises (economic, rationality, legitimation).

For Habermas, therefore, the lifeworld appears to include community, but the objectification of this lifeworld in society as a sphere of social integration results in distortion of a most peculiar kind. As many commentators have noted, the separation between communicative action and rational action is highly problematic (see, for example, Fraser, 1989; Honneth, 1991; McCarthy, 1991; Cook, 2005). Systems come to be seen as beyond the (rational) control of human beings located in the lifeworld, particularly as the political system 'colonises' the lifeworld in its production of mass loyalty (McCarthy, 1991, p 127). In reality, however, as May and Powell (2008, p 172) succinctly express it, following Fraser (1989): 'strategic action is neither analytically, nor practically, distinct from a horizon of shared meanings and norms'. In other words, Habermas' dualism of lifeworld and system lacks either empirical or analytical foundation.

Habermas therefore misrepresents the mechanisms by which communities are produced and sustained. Communities are not produced exclusively by certain types of action – although communication is of course indispensable for their existence.[7] Communities are like the lifeworld in that they are symbolic structures but they are also structures of production and power. Habermas' work is nevertheless important for understanding the nature of community. He helps us to see that *communities are not systems* and that community as meaningful (mutually communicated) interconnectedness can characterise *society as a whole*. This does not mean, however, that community cannot contain systems (for example, in the sense described earlier, organised through networks, recognition systems and coordination systems) or that community does not permeate the institutions of what Habermas calls 'system' (for example, the state and the market). Rather, what it means is that modern society is a complex unity of community ('lifeworld') and non-community ('system'). On the one hand, meaningful connectedness among persons embodies and reflects all the 'system' characteristics (in this sense, communities are always within the 'system', not outside of it). On the other hand, persons are connected with one another in other ways that are not necessarily meaningful to them (for example, through the division of labour – functional interdependence – in which they are not connected as persons but only through the roles they perform). There is therefore the possibility of research, education and other forms of action that will make these connections more meaningful to those concerned, so extending the scope for community.[8]

Returning to Bourdieu, it can be argued that Habermas' work can be used to clarify the discussion of habitus and field. Like the lifeworld, habitus can be construed as social relations that are revealed through the practices of everyday life. Unlike the lifeworld, however, habitus are plural: each one is a specific set of embodied relationships to material conditions. Similarly, like Habermas' system, fields are constituted as relations among social positions (relations between social relations). Unlike system, however, fields vary according to the nature of the habitus (plural) – the specific dispositions of the actors, forms of capital deployed, balances of informality and formality, and systems of recognition, interpellation, coordination and symbolic representation.[9] Above all, a habitus has a particular character of connectedness that actually constitutes a field as meaningful – indeed, the 'system' quality of the field is to some extent a product of the connectedness within the habitus (singular) to which it is related. The relationship between habitus and field is therefore one of greater or lesser social/system integration. This point will be illustrated later in this chapter in relation to working-class communities.

Community, therefore, can be expressed in a variety of ways: through systems of recognition and cooperation; as mechanical solidarity; and as a product of communicative action. None of these, however, does sufficient justice to the significance of the concept. Community is perhaps best understood as meaningful connectedness within habitus, more or less integrated with a field, and *a* community is then an embodied or imagined group of persons who are so meaningfully connected, for example, through forms of communication, recognition and/or shared identity. This is how the term 'community' will be used in the rest of this book.

Attributes and dynamics of community

Communities enjoy a rich variety of attributes, typically expressed in the form of binary oppositions: strong/weak, homogeneous/heterogeneous, integrated/segregated, cohesive/fragmented, united/divided, open/closed, inclusive/exclusive. The boundaries of communities can be rigid or flexible, permeable or impermeable, clear or fuzzy, stable or unstable. To be a member of a community is to have a certain status, but the nature of that status varies according to the habitus and can also vary within the habitus itself.

Reference is often made to communities of place, communities of interest and communities of identity. 'Community' here means something like living in the same area (place), or having common concerns or other characteristics in common with others. Sharing the same residence, interests or identity, however, does not in itself constitute community. One can easily imagine groups of people living in the same neighbourhood or having the same interests (for example, occupations, values) or perceiving themselves in the same way (for example, in terms of culture, religion, nationality, sexual orientation or whatever) but who do not make up what we would call a community. They may be organised around a particular place, interest or identity, but they can be called a community only when the members of the group recognise what it is they have in common – and this is, at the very least, their membership of a clearly recognised group.

A *strong* community can be regarded as one in which either the connections among the members are strong or the community as a whole is powerful. These two meanings are quite distinct but commonly confused in practice.[10] In the first case, what seems to be involved are 'strong ties' (Granovetter, 1973) among the members, which connote deeply felt, lifelong commitments and obligations to one another. In this sense, the strength of a community can be measured in terms of the breadth and depth of such ties among its members – the greater the proportion of members who have these ties, and the more binding these ties are, the stronger the community. In practice, such ties derive mainly from kinship and close friendship (relationships of intimacy – Misztal, 2000). Strong ties can also arise indirectly, however, through strong, shared attachments to a particular identity, culture, place or sense of habitus (compare Durkheim's concept of mechanical solidarity). This occurs, for example, in the case of Bourdieu's 'class sense', and numerous studies of local communities have also found evidence of such attachments (echoing Tönnies' concept of *Gemeinschaft*) (for reviews of the literature, see Crow and Allan, 1994; Day, 2006). It seems that strong ties arise mainly from the habitus itself, with the dispositions of community members being shaped through their experiences and choices over extended periods of time. Community members can therefore be tied to one another directly, through a sense of mutual obligation, or indirectly, through having a mutually recognised common identity or status, for example, related to class, culture, neighbourhood, city, nation or whatever.

The use of terms such as 'ties', 'bonds' and 'obligations' is perhaps a little unfortunate, as it suggests restrictions on personal freedom. Communities certainly can be experienced as oppressive and stifling, but meaningful connectedness does not have to be like this. Žižek (1993), for example (as reported in Clarke et al, 2007, p 99), paints a more positive picture: 'the bond that holds a given community together is the way in which we share our enjoyment. What we fear most is the theft of that enjoyment by others. Our enjoyment is made up of all kinds of things, ways of life, mythologies. It is the way in which we imagine our community to be and therefore is often based on a nostalgic attraction to another way of life that never really existed or has been lost.' Community is therefore based on the joys of shared experiences and imaginings, as remembered, retold and typically embellished over the years. Members of a community are brought together primarily through a shared life, and the acceptance of obligations is an integral part of this process.

The second sense of 'strong community' is one in which the community is empowered, so that it acts in such a way that it makes a difference to its habitus and to society more generally. This seems to me primarily a matter of the *resources* that the community can command, how *united* the community is in its purpose to deploy those resources, and the *organisational capacity* (particularly strategic capacity) of the community to deploy those resources effectively. Middle-class communities may often seem stronger than working-class ones because they have greater resources at their disposal and are more organised in the sense of having more and larger organisations – even though working-class communities may be stronger in the first sense (with more of their members having strong ties within the community). This issue will be discussed further in the next chapter.

Communities are not necessarily held together by strong ties alone. Granovetter (1973) also introduced the concept of weak ties. These have more of the character of acquaintanceship and 'thin' sociability (Somerville, 2009a), and are not necessarily deeply felt or lifelong. They are nevertheless important for ensuring that communities are strong in the second sense, for example, by facilitating access to resources, enabling the community to be integrated and cohesive (with all of its members being connected together) and increasing its capacity for coordinated action. Again, this will be discussed further in the next chapter, but it can be noted here that strong ties of community members to a shared habitus can and do coexist with weak ties of many of those members to one another. Where ties are generally weak, however, both among community members and between those members and their habitus, a community is unlikely to be stable.

A *homogeneous* community is one in which the members enjoy more or less the same bundle of statuses, at least as perceived by the members themselves. This may be because all members hold to the same gender and occupational roles, follow similar everyday practices, share similar narratives and beliefs about the world and their place in it, enjoy similar leisure pursuits, and express similar attitudes on a wide range of issues. Historical evidence of the existence of such communities is found in the community studies mentioned above, for example, mining communities. Such communities are now commonly referred to as 'monocultural'. In contrast, *heterogeneous* (or multicultural) communities are those whose members vary in their everyday practices, identities, beliefs and attitudes.

It might seem reasonable to suppose that homogeneous communities would be likely to be stronger, at least in the first sense defined above. This is because people who have more in common with one another are more likely to associate with one another and to develop deep and lasting friendships, and so on, and of course they are also tied together by recognition of their common identity, culture, sense of place, and so on. However, homogeneous communities are not necessarily strong in the second sense, because they may lack significant resources, they may be internally divided (particularly along lines of gender and generation) and may lack effective organisation; they may lack all four forms of Bourdieu's capital (economic, social, cultural and symbolic).

Conversely, it might be supposed that heterogeneous communities would be likely to be weaker in the first sense, because people from different cultures (which may amount to different, possibly homogeneous, communities) are likely to engage less often in meaningful interaction and are less likely to recognise one another as having the same identity. In practice, however, people's identities are often multiple and fluid, and they may give priority to different identities at different times and in different contexts. A more heterogeneous community may turn out to be stronger in the second sense because its variety of cultures (or communities) can function as a resource that makes it more outward looking and more adaptable to change, and it may be stronger even in the first sense if its adaptation to change involves increased meaningful cross-cultural contact. Scherer's (1972) study of the highly heterogeneous community of Harlem, for example, suggests that the basis of a strong community (of place) may be not so much a shared culture as a shared experience of living in a particular area, with open access to community resources, reinforced by regular mutual recognition. Similarly, Wallman's (1984) study of Battersea, another highly heterogeneous community, clearly shows how shared attachment to a locality can overcome the potential barriers posed by differences of skin colour and language.

Based on studies of Catholic and Protestant communities in Northern Ireland, Hewstone et al (2007, p 104), following Allport (1979, p 287), have identified three conditions under which contact across cultures (or communities) becomes meaningful: the contacts have equal status; there is a common goal to which they can aspire; and the contact situation is legitimated through institutional support. Unity of purpose has already been identified above as necessary for a strong community in the second sense, and equality of status is clearly essential to heal divisions within or across communities. In the absence of these conditions, interaction between different communities can produce antagonism rather than cooperation. For example, Seabrook (1973) reports how in Blackburn in the 1960s the Asian community began to take on some of the characteristics of the white working class while simultaneously, through economic decline and disintegration, the white working class suffered a loss of these qualities. The white community projected onto the Asian community the demoralised and disintegrated state it was experiencing in the form of hostility towards the Asian community. Similarly, Hoggett (1992, p 352) reports that the Bangladeshi community in Tower Hamlets 'has many characteristics – extended and extensive kinship networks, a respect for tradition and male superiority, a capacity for entrepreneurship and social advancement – which the white working class in the area have lost'.

How are such findings to be explained? It seems to me significant not only that the rise of one community was perceived to be associated with the decline of another but also that the change in its fortunes was due to competition in the labour market. The cultural similarities between the two competing communities noted by Seabrook and Hoggett merely served to accentuate the differences between them (for example, skin colour, religion, language, dress, food, music and so on).[11] Both communities are working class, but the white community sees its territory as belonging historically and exclusively to it. In relation to the East End of London, this is clearly expressed by Wemyss (2006, p 228): 'white, working-class people were normalised as being the natural and historically legitimate occupiers of East End spaces in the discourses of the local and national media. They were at the top of the "hierarchy of belonging".' This hierarchy of belonging is therefore an example of Bourdieu's (1990, p 140) 'discontinuous structure of hierarchised life-styles' mentioned earlier. Essentially, the two communities inhabit the same habitus but the white working class does not recognise the legitimacy of the 'other's' inhabitation of that habitus – or, insofar as it accepts that the other community has a certain status within the habitus, it perceives it as a lower one, involving weaker entitlements and weaker or smaller territorial claims.

The use of the term 'belonging' is also significant. Hierarchies of status within the working class, based on skill, education and so on, as well as race, are nothing new, but here it is claimed that a certain territory or space 'belongs' exclusively to a particular group (or at least that the group enjoys certain superior rights or privileges in relation to that territory), which is identified by its position within a hierarchy of cultural distinction. Such a claim is an example of what Bourdieu calls 'misrecognition' and is of course entirely illegitimate. It serves to highlight the problems in interpreting communities as forms of belonging – the use of the latter term signals exclusivity (of ownership), and communities are not necessarily exclusive.

A strong community that encompasses both senses of the term, therefore, is one that is both strongly and weakly interconnected, and is also resourceful and capable of united action, irrespective of any differences within the community. Unfortunately, it is difficult to find examples of such communities in the literature because researchers have tended to focus on communities whose resources are relatively few. It is important to note, however, that a strong community is not necessarily a 'good' one, in the sense of being law abiding or just. In this respect, heterogeneous communities may have an advantage because, to build such a community, the condition of equality of status requires that action across the community be fair and be seen to be fair.

The terms 'cohesive community' and 'community cohesion' have been widely used in government literature since the 2001 disturbances in Bradford, Oldham and Burnley. Following the report of the Commission on Integration and Cohesion (CIC, 2007), the then Labour government combined 'community cohesion' with 'integration' to arrive at what it called 'a vision of an integrated and cohesive community' (see **Box 1.2**).

Box 1.2: An integrated and cohesive community

Our vision of an integrated and cohesive community is based on *three foundations:*

* People from different backgrounds having similar life opportunities
* People knowing their rights and responsibilities
* People trusting one another and trusting local institutions to act fairly

And *three key ways of living together:*

* A shared future vision and sense of belonging

- A focus on what new and existing communities have in common, alongside a recognition of the value of diversity
- Strong and positive relationships between people from different backgrounds.

Source: CLG (2008a, p 10)

Analysis of this 'vision' reveals that it encompasses much of what has been identified above as characteristic of a strong heterogeneous (or culturally diverse) community. 'Similar life opportunities' is identifiable with equality of status, which Hewstone et al (2007) argue is essential for the meaningful cross–cultural contact that leads to more united communities (see also Orton, 2009). Trust across the community and its institutions is just part of what is meant by meaningful interconnectedness, which defines community itself. 'Strong and positive relationships' presumably refers to sociability, which is essential for community in its embodied form. A respect for what groups within a community do and do not have in common is an inevitable part of the process of mutual recognition, which again is essential for community as meaningful interconnectedness. Knowing one's rights and responsibilities follows simply from recognising oneself as a member of a community. Finally, 'a shared future vision and sense of belonging' is taken from the Parekh Report (CFMEB, 2000), which was concerned specifically with national community. This element of the 'vision' is arguably inappropriate, not only because of the use of the term 'belonging', as criticised above, but also because it is not clear why the members of any community should all have the same vision of the future.[12]

Overall, the 'vision' seems rather banal as a guide to political action because it has nothing to say about the substantial divisions both within and between communities in Britain and how these might be resolved. One understands that the previous government, much like the current Conservative-Liberal Democrat coalition government, would want to see strong diverse communities, and much of what characterises such communities may well be unobjectionable, but this 'vision' does not convince because it is so far removed from where we are in Britain today. We might be persuaded, or more prepared to be persuaded, by a vision that began with a more honest and realistic appraisal of the social problems that we face. Even putting these criticisms on one side, however, the concept of an integrated and cohesive community, as expounded by the Labour government, seems skewed. In comparison with the concept of strong community developed above, an integrated and cohesive community may lack resources, for example, and is silent about how strong and weak ties are to be balanced within it. The 'vision' is therefore lacking in substance, an empty signifier that serves to over-simplify, obscure and depoliticise complex community issues. At bottom, the concept of an integrated and cohesive community is ideological in Althusser's sense: it is an illusion that alludes to the reality of how social divisions are experienced, it is where the field of state action meets the habitus of community – in a process of what could be called systematic misrecognition.

A final issue concerning the attributes of community is that of how open or closed they are, how inclusive or exclusive. This issue is quite different from that of their strength or diversity or cohesiveness, and there is no necessary connection between the two types of issue. One might expect, perhaps, that more homogeneous communities would be likely to be more closed and exclusive (for a well-known example, see Elias and Scotson, 1994), while heterogeneous communities would be likely to be more open and inclusive (as in Wallman, 1984). Overall, however, the relationship between the strength of a community and its openness or inclusiveness is not at all straightforward.

The issue being raised here can be represented as having to do with the *boundaries* of a community, which may be expressed in terms of the criteria for membership of that community. Some communities have relatively strict conditions that people have to meet in order to qualify as members of the community, while others are more lax. Whether a community counts as open or closed, inclusive or exclusive, therefore depends upon how permissive or stringent its membership criteria are. The issue is that of the *boundedness* of the community as defined by its rules for membership. It is *not* that of the *bondedness* or connectedness of the community members. The strong bondedness of a community may indeed be a foundation for strong boundedness (for example, because it enables the community to enforce stricter membership rules[13]), but boundedness itself is not the same thing as bondedness.

It is this point that a number of writers appear to have failed to grasp. Mooney and Neal (2009, p 18), for example, state: 'Communities are defined through difference and against one another.' This statement assumes that a community is necessarily exclusive but, as we have seen, this is not the case. The boundaries of a community, even a strong community (or especially a strong community) do not have to be rigidly defined – they can be flexible, permeable, porous or fuzzy. Also, members of one community can be members of others, and they can have strong or weak ties with members of other communities. Mooney and Neal confuse the definition of community with the identification of an attribute that characterises certain kinds of community, this attribute being that of boundary assertion and exclusion of the 'other'.

To support their argument, they select an example of a community that appears to be both strongly bonded and strongly bounded, namely, Ordsall in Salford. This is a community of place where the key criterion for membership is residence within the neighbourhood and the boundary of the neighbourhood is clearly demarcated in physical terms (Mooney and Neal, 2009, p 20 – but see the original research by Walklate and Evans, 1999).[14] They simply assume that bondedness and boundedness must go together. They are right, however, to suggest that strongly *bounded* place communities are likely to be problematic, because boundary maintenance is related to territoriality, which Kintrea et al (2008) show is a matter for serious concern.

Territoriality is defined as 'a situation whereby control is claimed by one group over a defined geographical area and defended against others' (Kintrea et al, 2008, p 9). People living in an area engage in territorial behaviour when they have a sense of ownership of the area, seeing it as their area, their community. This takes us back to the concept of belonging, which was criticised earlier: 'young people feel their estates or inner urban areas are the places that they belong to and, in turn, the places belong to them' (Kintrea et al, 2008, p 49). For these people, therefore, their community is a strongly bounded community of place. The boundaries of their area are clearly visible to all, and there is no ambiguity about who is or is not a member of their community – residential location is the key factor, though 'heavily overlain or paralleled by other divisions between groups' in some areas (particularly divisions on grounds of ethnic origin) (Kintrea et al, 2008, p 5). Kintrea et al (2008) explore the nature of these strongly bounded communities in six urban areas (Glasgow, Sunderland, Bradford, Peterborough, Bristol and Tower Hamlets) and conclude that territoriality is both an effect and a cause of violence and disadvantage: 'Territoriality appeared to be a product of deprivation, a lack of opportunities and attractive activities, limited aspirations and an expression of identity' (Kintrea et al, 2008, p 5), and it also resulted in severe restrictions on young people's freedom of movement and access to opportunities and facilities: 'negative impacts were reported on young people's potential, access to education, leisure and relationships' (Kintrea et al, 2008, p 6).

Like Mooney and Neal (2009), however, Kintrea et al (2008) are less clear about the difference between boundedness and bondedness. They write, for example:

> While the hypothesis underlying the research is that territoriality is problematic for the life chances of the young people caught up in it and for the neighbourhoods that experience it, we recognise the potentially positive nature of territoriality as

an expression of mutual support and community attachment. Territoriality leading to isolation and violence is the dark side of place attachment. (Kintrea et al, 2008, p 9)

This quote relies on a concept of attachment to community, which can be either positive or negative. It suggests that territoriality is actually negative (as the dark side of such attachment), but potentially positive (as the bright side of such attachment). The problem with this formulation is that their research does not appear to have identified anything positive about territoriality ('we saw no evidence of positive social impacts of territoriality among young people' – Kintrea et al, 2008, p 41). As we have seen earlier, attachment to a shared habitus can be strong or weak, and strong attachment is what makes for a strongly connected or bonded community. A shared habitus can be symbolically represented by a place, but strong attachment to that place does not have to be expressed through claims of exclusive ownership. Again, therefore, it can be seen that strong bondedness does not have to lead to strong boundedness. Attachments are not simultaneously inclusive and exclusive, as if inclusivity and exclusivity were two sides of the same coin. My attachment to Manchester, for example, in no way detracts from the attachment that others might have to Manchester, nor do I wish to place any bounds on who might legitimately have such an attachment. Territoriality, therefore, cannot be justified or excused on the grounds that it is an expression of community attachment.

Having distinguished between bondedness and boundedness, the question can now be posed as to how they might be interrelated – a question that was effectively suppressed by the fusion of the two. Kintrea et al's (2008) research suggests that they are related through a particular kind of community attachment where members of the community feel the need to protect it by strongly policing its boundaries. At a psychological level, this community attachment, expressed through territoriality, can be identified as a toxic mix of pride and possessiveness towards their shared habitus: pride for what they regard as its quality, and possessiveness giving rise to jealousy and consequent hostility towards those whom they regard as threatening or violating that habitus. But where do these dispositions come from, who holds them, and are those who hold them in any way representative of their community? To answer these questions, it is necessary to look more closely at the numerous studies of communities that have been undertaken over the years, and in particular at how they police the activities of their members and how they behave towards outsiders.

Many of these studies have found communities that are strongly bounded as well as strongly bonded (see, for example, Crow and Allan, 1994; Somerville, 2000, pp 57–8). For example, Phillips (1986) points to the importance that communities attach to newcomers' 'fitting in' and participating in community activities. The strong connectedness within traditional place and ethnic communities make 'chains of interdependencies' (Elias, 1974), which are strong enough to discourage individual action that goes against local traditions (Anwar, 1985; Robinson, 1986). Some studies describe how bonding and bounding go together, for example those studies suggesting that gossip and mutual surveillance have been the primary means by which community boundaries are policed (Elias and Scotson, 1994; Roberts, 1995; Tebbutt, 1995).

In many strongly bounded communities the bar for membership can be set at a very high level indeed, such that one has to be *born* into the community in order to be accepted, and/or one has to be seen to meet very stringent moral standards. For example, Elias and Scotson's 1994 study of Winston Parva showed that newcomers who remained attached to patterns of behaviour that were regarded as normal and acceptable in their communities of origin (namely, noisy enjoyment and pub-going) but were disapproved of by the established residents were never accepted into the community; the status distinctions between the two groups were reproduced in succeeding generations (see Crow and Allan, 1994, p 72). In Bourdieusian terms, the two groups occupied different habitus (plural), related to social class. In contrast, Phillips' study of Muker in North Yorkshire shows how, where newcomers are prepared to 'muck in' (Phillips, 1986, p 151) – that is, they are willing to share the habitus of existing residents – they may become accepted into the community after a certain period of time (Somerville, 2000, pp 58–9). Is it Winston Parva, then, that is the stronger community because it can exclude groups of which it disapproves, or is it Muker that is stronger because it can assimilate newcomers without having to change very much? The question seems unanswerable. Yet Winston Parva appears to be more strongly bounded than Muker.

Where a community is relatively weak, particularly in terms of resources and organisation, it is possible for powerful newcomers to achieve a position of dominance in the community, for example, through processes of gentrification (see Chapter Two). The existing residents, perceiving this as a threat to the existence of their community, respond by attempting to strengthen the boundaries of their community. If this struggle is successful, it results in 'encapsulation' (Crow and Allan, 1994, p 81), whereby the existing residents come to form a 'community within a community' (Newby et al, 1978) – see *Box 1.3*.

> ## Box 1.3: Encapsulation
>
> An *encapsulated* (place) community is one that is entirely bounded by another community. This can happen in three main ways:
>
> - A more powerful group moves into an area, changing its character, and reducing the freedom of manoeuvre of the existing less powerful community – this is gentrification.
> - A less powerful group moves into an area, and maintains strong boundaries to protect itself against assimilation by the more powerful host community.
> - A less powerful community persists in a state of economic and social decline, disconnected from primary labour markets, with haemorrhaging of skilled workers to other areas.

Encapsulation is an important but neglected concept. It is the territorial expression of boundary strengthening by a community that is relatively small and weak, particularly in resources. An encapsulated community is one whose members live 'parallel lives' (Home Office, 2001a) to those of the community that surrounds it. This does not mean that territorial behaviour is necessarily characteristic of encapsulated communities but, as Kintrea et al (2008, p 19) state: 'Territoriality, especially when it has a clear ethnic underlying cause, can be viewed as a *possible manifestation* of "parallel lives"' (my italics). This was noted in the reports following the 2001 disturbances in Bradford, Oldham and Burnley, where the maintenance of boundaries of encapsulated communities took the form of open confrontation with the police and extensive damage to any property that was seen by the 'rioters' as 'legitimate' targets (Home Office, 2001a, 2001b, 2001c).[15] In Kintrea et al's (2008) research, encapsulation appears, if anything, to be even stronger. One interviewee in Glasgow, for example, reported:

> If your horizons are limited to three streets, what is the point of you working really hard at school? What is the point of passing subjects that will allow you to go to college or university if you cannot travel beyond these streets? What's the point of dreaming about being an artist, a doctor, etc, if you cannot get on a bus to get out of the area in which you live? (Kintrea et al, 2008, p 35)

Similarly, in Tower Hamlets, the researchers reported that young people 'seemed completely unaware of the rich possibilities of life in the capital beyond' (Kintrea et al, 2008, p 36).

An encapsulated community, like any other community, is characterised by meaningful connectedness within habitus. The process of encapsulation, however, with its strong emphasis on boundary maintenance and territorial defence, can have a corrosive effect on relationships within the community, making it both more intensely interconnected and yet more internally divided at the same time. This can be seen most clearly in the phenomenon of 'gangs'. A gang has been defined as:

> A relatively durable, predominantly street based, group of young people who see themselves (and are seen by others) as a discernible group for whom crime and violence is integral to the group's identity. (Hallsworth and Young, 2004, p 12)

This definition serves to make clear the nature of a gang as a community, namely, as a meaningfully interconnected group with a shared criminal identity, but it does not give a sense of what kind of community a gang is. This sense becomes clearer in Kintrea et al's study, where being a member of a gang is identified primarily with involvement in territoriality. Criminality is simply an unavoidable effect of such territoriality because defence of territory requires that gang members occasionally have to fight, which is illegal. Furthermore, the gang exists only in public space ('street based'), and the relationships among gang members can be extremely intense, with ties being in some cases as strong as those of family. As Kintrea et al conclude:

> Young people cohere around their neighbourhoods and seek to represent them whenever they are outside their own areas, and are prepared to defend them as required to gain or maintain respect. Territoriality emerges out of these emotions plus young people's routine use of the streets as a place of assembly and recreation. It is accentuated by inadequate home environments, so that the group they associate with on the streets becomes a kind of parallel to, or maybe in some cases a substitute for, household affiliations. At a time of adolescent uncertainty, there is a need for security in the form of a group to run with and to identify with. Young people then closely identify with their friends who inhabit the same spaces. (Kintrea et al, 2008, p 49)

This quote summarises the process whereby territoriality emerges from a certain kind of place attachment. It argues that territoriality is primarily an attribute of adolescents in the community (13- to 17-year-olds in the research), who see themselves as representing that community. However, it seems as if the young people are making their own community here, through membership of gangs and gang activity. It is not clear how they relate to the rest of their (encapsulated) community or whether they have developed a culture or habitus that is distinct from that community.

But why are so many young people in encapsulated communities so attached to them? Kintrea et al (2008, p 50) report that territoriality in their case study areas originally arose as a result of migration into the areas, resulting in competition for space (one thinks of the film *Gangs of New York*). In some of these areas, however, these original factors no longer existed:

> But territoriality remained in a new, more inward-looking and purer form. Here, an established tradition of territorial behaviour has been passed down the generations, in part through immediate siblings and 'olders and youngers', but it was also remarkable how ingrained territoriality was in many of the areas. Successive generations seemed to be involved in near-identical behaviour and today's adults often condone territoriality by regarding it as inevitable. (Kintrea et al, 2008, p 50)

Kintrea et al (2008) recognise that this does not satisfactorily explain the persistence of territoriality, although it is consistent with historical studies of poor neighbourhoods such as Meen et al (2005) and Robertson et al (2008). The latter study (of three neighbourhoods in Stirling) is particularly relevant for the evidence it provides of the long-term stability of neighbourhood habitus: 'while each of the neighbourhoods studied has undergone significant social changes, its relative social position has not altered greatly over the last 80 years' (Robertson et al, 2008, p 97). All of this suggests the importance of field characteristics, as yet not investigated or understood, whose interaction with habitus could produce such stable status distinctions.

A number of recent studies have thrown some light on the nature of working-class habitus, to the extent of suggesting how it might result in forms of territoriality in encapsulated communities. In their study of young people in 'Kelby' in Middlesbrough, for example, Robert MacDonald and his colleagues found that their respondents 'were united by a common experience of economic marginality' (MacDonald et al, 2005, p 876).[16] This experience continued into adulthood, where 'individuals remained tied to locally-rooted, social networks' (MacDonald et al, 2005, p 876). 'By their mid- to late-20s, virtually all interviewees remained living in the neighbourhoods in which they had been born and brought up' (MacDonald et al, 2005, p 877), and most of them 'did not seem short of strong, close, supportive relationships' (MacDonald et al, 2005, p 883). This study provided substantial evidence of meaningful connectedness (for an example of this, see ***Box 1.4***).[17]

Box 1.4: Meaningful connectedness in an encapsulated community

At the age of 20, Martin gave one of the most up-beat assessments of community life in Primrose Vale [one of the five most deprived wards in England]:

> **Martin:** Living here, it's brilliant. We have no problems with anyone. We know all the thugs and the thieves and whatever but everyone's okay ... It's a lot better if you know someone and something goes wrong. If you have problems, you can always call on people. They're always quite loyal in that sense.

> **JM:** Do you think there's a great community spirit?

> **Martin:** It depends on what you call community spirit. It's really an underground kind of thing. It's the backing ...//... everyone supports you. Neighbours come over and they wanna borrow money until they get paid, things like that. You know you'll get it back, so ... You can always rely on everyone else. If you're stuck, someone'll help you.

Source: MacDonald et al (2005, p 878)

This shows how a strongly connected but economically deprived[18] community continues to cope in the face of adversity and hardship. It appears, however, that this is an encapsulated community because most of its members:

> had very limited lived experience of places beyond Kelby ... They did not know how their contemporaries in more prosperous locales fared and without a more global vantage point it was difficult for them to perceive in full the spatial polarization of class inequality. Partly because they were so familiar with their own (geographic) place, they had strikingly little awareness of their subordinate place in wider class structures. (MacDonald et al, 2005, pp 879–80)

So the habitus of an encapsulated community is one in which the life-styles and dispositions of its members are such as to keep them ignorant of their position in the scheme of things. They live in ideology because they are interpellated as concrete subjects, through their connectedness with their family and friends. The 'police' who are responsible for this interpellation, therefore, are not so much the official authorities as the community itself, in a process of self-policing, particularly of its own boundaries. In this way, an encapsulated community is created by linking strong interconnectedness with strong boundedness. An encapsulated community is (largely) a *self-interpellating* community.

MacDonald et al (2005, pp 880–1) document how features of the 'field' (Bourdieu) or 'system' (Habermas) also serve to produce or reinforce marginality and encapsulation:

> [V]irtually all [of our interviewees] displayed work histories – into their mid- and late-20s – that consisted of various combinations of: government schemes that rarely led to lasting employment; unfinished and/or low-level educational courses; low/no skill, low paid, insecure employment; and recurrent periods of unemployment. Individuals transited between these labour market statuses with little sense of forward motion toward more secure, rewarding employment.

This shows how the labour market as a system is largely responsible for the community's lack of resources, which in turn makes it relatively weak, thus leading to its encapsulation. Specifically, MacDonald et al (2005, p 881) identify the existence of a *secondary* labour market as a key factor and conclude that 'unemployment, job insecurity and poor work have become common *working-class* experiences' (MacDonald et al, 2005, p 882). The interesting point here is that, in spite of divisions in the field (between primary and secondary labour markets), the habitus remains identifiably working class. MacDonald et al (2005, p 882) actually refer to 'a *hyper-conventional* attitude to work in which the getting of work, even "poor work", was the driving force behind most youth transitions'. Paradoxically, therefore, rather than weakening working-class habitus, the field of a secondary labour market is associated with a redoubling of efforts within the community to find work. Arguably, it is the same 'hyper-conventionalism' that leads to the increased attachment to the community that results in encapsulation. This happens for a number of reasons. First, most young adults get jobs through friends, neighbours and family members (MacDonald et al, 2005, p 882), so attachment to the community is seen as important for finding work. However:

Because those that helped in finding jobs were also typically confined to the same sectors of the labour market as them, our interviewees remained constrained to work at the bottom of the labour market that offered little chance of personal progression. Interviewees became trapped in insecure, 'poor work' with little or no training or prospect of internal promotion and few bridges to more permanent, rewarding employment and, thus, were unable to escape the churning of cyclical labour market careers. As the years passed, they became even less attractive to those with better employment to offer. (MacDonald et al, 2005, pp 884–5).

This describes vividly how the isolation of the community from the primary labour market is a key feature of its encapsulation. Working-class habitus and secondary labour market field become integrated so as to produce this result.

An important finding of the above analysis is that working-class habitus is not 'rooted within an earlier and now displaced industrial, Fordist political economy' (Watt, 2006, p 778) but remains alive and kicking within the so-called post-industrial, postfordist, 'flexible' society of today.[19] The change in the nature of the field from primary to secondary labour market does not necessarily result in an analogous change in the character of the habitus from working class to 'underclass' or 'sub-proletarian'. Working-class communities are not homogeneous, in that they have always been, and continue to be, characterised by status differences, for example, between skilled artisans and unskilled labourers. They have changed, as we have seen (for example, the spread and intensification of encapsulation), but this change cannot be 'read off' from changes in the labour market.

Much of the literature, however, seems to be less concerned about recognised status differences than about *claimed* status differences, expressed (for example) in terms of the distinction between 'rough' and 'respectable' people. Watt (2006, pp 778–9), for example, remarks: 'Intra-class status distinctions between the "rough" and "respectable" have a long historical pedigree in English working-class neighbourhoods and were prominent in both the pre- and post-war periods.' The distinction is related to recognised status differences but involves (alleged) behavioural differences as well:

Skill and income could play a part, with skilled manual workers and their families more likely to regard themselves, and be regarded by others, as respectable compared to the unskilled. Behavioural factors were also significant with the 'roughs' described by Roberts (1995, p 7) as those 'who can be characterized by violence, whether to people or to property, frequent drunkenness and petty criminality'. Respectability was signified by sobriety, respect for the law and hard work, while for women it was also associated with 'keeping up appearances' via the maintenance of a clean and tidy home. (Watt, 2006, p 779)

Problems arise with this distinction, however, when it comes to identifying who counts as 'rough' and who counts as 'respectable'. The main difficulty is that people are not always what they claim to be. In general, those of higher status are more likely to succeed in their claims than those of lower status, so someone from a skilled-worker family claiming to be respectable is more likely to have their claim accepted than someone from an unskilled-worker family – irrespective of any actual differences between the behaviour of the two individuals. Consequently, in the absence of a long-term mass observation project, it is practically impossible to sort the members of any working-class community into these two groups. The distinction is mythical in the sense that, even if it were possible to distinguish clearly between 'good' and 'bad' behaviour, one is always likely to find examples of both kinds of behaviour in all sections of the community, and even in the same individual. It is also insidious insofar as it feeds prejudice along lines of race as well as class, with whiteness tending to be identified with respectability and blackness with deviance. Finally, it seems almost irrelevant to understanding, let alone resolving, the problems identified in relation to territoriality (gang members have to be 'tough', rather than 'rough', to be respected and therefore presumably to be 'respectable'). This is not to deny, however, that anti-social behaviour can be a serious problem, particularly for people living in encapsulated communities where they lack resources and find it difficult to summon support and assistance from outside their community (this point will be considered further in Chapter Nine on community order).

A further study that helps to explain the attachment of young women in particular to encapsulated communities is that of Measor (2006). This was a study of young women living on two very deprived housing estates. On these estates, there was a high sense of risk and fear, especially of powerful families who had a 'reputation' in the area, and who could provide 'protection', particularly for young women. Measor shows how being 'hard', and coming from a criminal family who dominate the area, achieves relatively high status, which appears attractive to vulnerable young women. Her argument is that young women are helping themselves by 'building a tie of flesh, and sealing it permanently with a blood connection' (Measor, 2006, p 192). This seems to be a striking (and indeed 'hyper-conventional') example of the gendered character of the effects of encapsulation, whereby the male-dominated control of the boundaries of the community (which numerous writers have commented on – most notably, Campbell, 1993) is legitimated, reinforced and reproduced through the 'rational', self-interested choices of the female community members. Encapsulation is clearly revealed by the fact that in these communities no realistic alternative choices presented themselves.

In his study of the working-class residents of Kensington in Liverpool, Allen (2008) provides further important insight into the habitus of an encapsulated community. Allen's focus is on housing rather than employment, but it is clear that the habitus of Kensington is much the same as that of Kelby as reported by MacDonald et al (2005).

Although he does not explicitly consider territoriality (perhaps because he does not seem to have interviewed any teenagers), its existence seems to be implied by some of his interviewees. What Allen documents in no uncertain terms is the *symbolic violence* suffered by an encapsulated community. As working-class people, the residents of Kensington 'relate to their houses and neighbourhoods as "things" that are "ready to hand" rather than in terms of their symbolic or investment value within the space of positions in the market for houses' (Allen, 2008, p 126). In Marx's terms, houses for working-class people are of interest for their use value, not their exchange value – the residents are concerned with enjoying them for what they are, not with making money out of them (for what they could be). This general disposition of the working class, however, which is characteristic of working-class habitus, clashes with 'the dominant view of the market for houses as a space of positions' (Allen, 2008, p 89). When working-class people misrecognise this dominant view as legitimate (as Allen shows that they do), the result is a form of symbolic violence, which reveals itself in a number of ways: a 'general interest' in house prices (when they do not want to move and cannot afford to do so, anyway) (Allen, 2008, p 89), a perception of housing in terms of a housing ladder that they cannot get onto (Allen, 2008, pp 89–91) and a recognition of the dominant 'suburban ideal' (Silverstone, 1997, cited in Allen, 2008, p 91). Following Bourdieu and Passeron (1977), Allen argues that Kensington residents' recognition that they desired only what they could not possess served to reinforce their acceptance of their current circumstances as inevitable – that is, it strengthened their encapsulation. However, for some respondents, this acceptance did not occur without a certain amount of regret, for example, they saw themselves as having 'failed' (Allen, 2008, pp 97–8), even though they had not failed at all (because they lived in good-quality, comfortable housing), while other respondents openly rejected the dominant view as expressed in the media and in middle-class housing careers (Allen, 2008, pp 100–1). What this shows is that symbolic violence damages working-class communities although they are perfectly capable of resisting it: either way, however, encapsulation tends to be reinforced, not undermined.[20] Self-interpellation remains dominant in such communities, even though the 'self' in question is weak and is made even weaker by symbolic violence.

Conclusion

How are communities changing in Britain today? Watt (2006) has identified clear 'narratives of urban decline', which reproduce the myths of a lost golden age traditionally found in rural communities (Williams, 1985, p 35). Decline has related to the disappearance of many traditional working-class and rural occupations and industries, to the exodus of young and skilled people from such communities, and the decline and loss of many community services, such as shops, pubs, primary schools, cottage hospitals, general practitioners, post offices, open spaces and so on (Hopper, 2003; Lupton, 2004; Day, 2006). At the same time, however, many working-class and rural communities show *resilience* in the face of such decline, for example, with evidence of continuing strong attachment to place (Robson et al, 1994; and references above), the survival of strong local networks (Page, 2000; Lupton, 2004; Day, 2006; CIC, 2007) and long-term path dependence focused on neighbourhood identity (Prior et al, 2007; Robertson et al, 2008).

Scholars differ on the question of whether community (as meaningful connectedness) is really declining or not. Arguably, however, the question is virtually impossible to answer and advocates on both sides of the debate can point to ample evidence in favour of their view. Those who believe that community is not declining can point to the evidence of resilience as discussed in this chapter, and those who think that it is declining can point to the dislocations produced by diasporic forms of identity, global flows and movements, and new modes of communication, all of which tend to 'free' individuals from the ties of community (Savage, 2005). What many commentators seem to fail to appreciate, however, is the sheer complexity of community. Any single community can be growing stronger and weaker at the same time, and in very different ways, so it is far from clear how such changes are to be aggregated across the totality of communities – even supposing it were possible to aggregate across communities, anyway.

This chapter has attempted to throw light on such questions by clarifying the meaning of community as meaningful connectedness and locating it within habitus of different kinds, understood as relatively stable everyday ways of going on in the world. Particular attention has been paid to the question of what counts as a *strong* community, and it has been argued that this involves a combination of strong and weak ties that enable effective deployment of resources. This concept of a strong community contrasts with the governmental concept of an integrated and cohesive community, which is silent on the crucial issue of community resources and unreasonable in expecting culturally diverse communities to have a 'shared vision'. The chapter makes an important distinction between the related concepts of bondedness and boundedness: bondedness is to do with the nature of community itself as meaningful connectedness, while boundedness refers specifically to how strongly its boundaries are policed (in particular, in terms of who is or is not allowed to join the community). This distinction led to a discussion of territoriality, as a particular expression of strong boundedness in relation to communities of place and ethnic communities. Strong boundedness, including territoriality, appears to be a common characteristic of poorer, less resourceful communities, where it tends to lead to encapsulation, understood as the formation of a community within (that is, entirely bounded by) another community.

The chapter has focused on working-class habitus but without offering a precise definition – though fundamentally it involves a disposition to waged labour as the means of survival. It was noted how changes in the field of the labour market since the 1960s have been associated with the encapsulation of poorer working-class communities in many areas – a complex process whereby these communities strengthen their boundaries in order to maintain their habitus. The evidence discussed here suggests that the nature of working-class habitus has not changed, but nevertheless it is possible that encapsulation is symptomatic of a general fragmentation of the working class. For example, it could be that working-class communities vary in terms of how well their habitus is integrated with a corresponding field. Habitus of the type found in the encapsulated communities discussed in this chapter appear to be only weakly integrated with the field of the labour market (territoriality, for example, works against such integration) and hardly at all with the field of the housing market (as a space of housing positions). Other working-class communities that are not encapsulated, however, may be more strongly integrated with markets of both kinds. Allen (2008, p 197), for example, refers to the 'relatively mobile fragment of the working class' that has moved to the suburbs and seeks 'respectability', by which is meant adopting, to some extent, middle-class dispositions and therefore acquiring a middle-class habitus and distancing itself from the working class. This process, which used to be known as *embourgeoisement*, has long been associated with skilled manual-worker groups. For just as long a time, however, study after study has found little evidence that such 'social mobility' actually occurs, at least not to any great extent (from Goldthorpe et al, 1969, to HMG, 2009b).[21] Rather, the symbolic violence that continues to be inflicted, particularly on less resourceful communities, tends to trigger a range of responses, many of which, such as territoriality, largely exacerbate the symbolic violence to which they are already subject.

Notes

[1] They could simply be *invited* to act or participate, on the assumption that they have, or should have, a disposition to do so – that is, by virtue of their presumed membership of a particular community.

[2] Bourdieu (1998) describes this as a form of *enchantment* ('*illusio*') – 'community' acts as a kind of spell, which holds us all in thrall. Brent (2004) refers to community as 'continually elusive' (p 213) or an 'illusion' (pp 214–16) or 'unattainable' (p 221). But again, following Althusser, community is an illusion that alludes to the possibility of actual community (Brent, 2004, pp 215–16), it has real effects, emerging from an imagined past into an indefinable presence (p 220) and moving towards an unknowable future.

[3] Connectedness should be distinguished from belonging (Savage et al, 2005). Belonging is more contentious because it suggests ownership or property. The problem with this is that: 'Property appropriates its owner, embodying itself in the form of a structure generating practices perfectly conforming with its logic and its demands' (Bourdieu, 1990, p 57). One can be strongly connected, for example, to a group or place, without belonging to it. Arguably, it is not even healthy to feel that one is owned by a group or a place. After all, the corollary would be that the group or place belongs to oneself, which could result in exclusive and oppressive forms of territoriality (see Kintrea et al, 2008; Clarke, 2009, p 90; and further below). These problems with the idea of belonging are not widely recognised in the literature – see, for example, Buonfino (2007).

[4] Bourdieu talks of having a 'feel for the game' (Crossley, 2002, p 182).

[5] This theory of ideology is similar to that found in Althusser (1970), where ideology is seen as illusion that alludes to its material underpinning. Bourdieu, however, sees habitus as more than ideology, more than a system of communication.

[6] In Durkheim's terms, the '*conscience collective*' under organic solidarity has low volume, low intensity and low determinateness.

[7] Communication means giving and receiving, not just of information but of value of different kinds (for example, meaningful objects, free labour, recognition).

[8] By the same token, following Habermas' idea of colonisation, connectedness among persons can be rendered *less* meaningful by the encroachments of state and market power – consider, for example, Marx's (1970) analysis of the fetishism of commodities. When labour power itself becomes a commodity (to be bought and sold in labour markets), the labour process becomes depersonalised, that is, expressed in the abstract terms of capital.

[9] Conversely, unlike the lifeworld, habitus (plural) vary according to the nature of fields.

[10] A good example here is Gilchrist's (2004) concept of the 'well connected' community. This could mean either that members of the community are well connected with one another or that the community as a whole is well connected with powerful agencies outside the community.

[11] In Northern Ireland, of course, the cultural similarities are greater, the main difference being that of religion, but the political divide between the two communities cuts very deep and is centuries old.

[12] Indeed, such a condition seems objectionable, as it privileges a certain uniformity of perspective and it devalues dissent and diversity of vision.

[13] On the other hand, a well-bonded community is in a better position to cope with the challenges posed by having less well-defined boundaries. A more weakly bonded community might feel the need for stronger boundaries in order to protect itself.

[14] Ordsall estate is bounded by three main roads: Trafford Road, Ordsall Lane and Regent Road. Trafford Road separates the estate from the prestigious redevelopment of Salford Quays.

[15] The encapsulated communities were those of Manningham in Bradford, Werneth in Oldham, and Daneshouse and Stoneyholme in Burnley. Evidence of territoriality has been found in many other studies, for example, Clarke et al (2007, pp 92–4) – in Bristol and Plymouth.

[16] Such marginality suggests encapsulation, but this is not clearly stated by the researchers.

[17] Another example is that provided by Connelly and Healy (2004) in their study of working-class and middle-class boys in Belfast. They found that the habitus of the working-class boys was clearly linked to manifestations of territoriality.

[18] Two of the seven wards that comprise Kelby were in the five most deprived wards in England (MacDonald et al, 2005, p 875).

[19] Indeed, habitus cannot be said to be 'rooted' in economy at all, as economy has to do with field rather than with habitus.

[20] Strictly speaking, the 'space of positions' here is the *field* of a housing market. One of the characteristics of an encapsulated community is that its habitus is not integrated with the field that encapsulates it. Agents in this field, or representing the positions in this field, simply do not recognise the boundaries that are so important for an encapsulated community.

[21] Saunders (1990) is one of many who has argued that sections of the working class have been 'captured' for capital. His argument is that home ownership enables capital accumulation and this puts the owner in a different class position, oriented towards investment rather than consumption. Such an argument is problematic on two grounds. First, it takes no account of the fact that markets fall as well as rise. Second, even where owner-occupation does enable working-class households to live off unearned income generated through property exchanges, they do not

necessarily become middle class because they may still lack the 'bundles of capitals' (cultural, organisational) associated with middle-class habitus.

Summary

Notions of community are highly contested. This chapter has analysed the meaning of community, identifying key possible elements such as network, sociability, connectedness and cooperation. It has been argued that community is experienced, felt and imagined as a collective entity or project. As such, it is distinct from system or field, and cannot be reduced to idealised or imaginary constructions. Community is, above all, rooted in our everyday ways of going on in the world – that is, in habitus. This point is illustrated in particular in relation to studies of working-class habitus.

The chapter has further explored possible conceptions of 'strong', 'integrated' and 'cohesive' communities, and criticised current governmental versions of these conceptions as ideological, in the sense that they systematically misrecognise the nature of social divisions within communities, ignoring key issues of poverty and inequality. An important distinction has also been made between the 'bondedness' and 'boundedness' of a community, and this distinction has then been used to explain the bases of territoriality and encapsulation.

Questions for discussion

- What would be an example of an imagined community?

- What does a strong, integrated, cohesive community look like?

- How and why might a community become encapsulated?

- Is there really such a thing as working-class habitus?

Further reading

Allen, C. (2008) *Housing market renewal and social class*, London: Routledge.
Brent, J. (2004) 'The desire for community: illusion, confusion and paradox', *Community Development Journal*, vol 39, no 3, pp 213-23.
MacDonald, R. and Marsh, J. (2005) *Disconnected youth? Growing up in Britain's poor neighbourhoods*, Basingstoke: Palgrave Macmillan.
Mooney, G. and Neal, S. (2009) 'Community: themes and debates', in G. Mooney and S. Neal (eds) *Community: Welfare, crime and society*, Maidenhead: Open University Press, pp 1-33.

two

Making sense of community development

Overview

This chapter considers what it might mean to develop a community. It is argued that:

- *'community development'* is an ambiguous and highly contested term;
- the concept of a *'beloved community'* has potential to act as a shared normative ideal;
- the main approaches to community development are neo-colonial (development done *to* the community), welfarist (development *for* the community), collaborative (development *with* the community) and self-organisation (development *by* the community);
- although all current approaches to community development are flawed, there are, nevertheless, ways in which communities can organise and work with others to achieve social justice objectives.

The chapter also examines the concept of social capital, arguing that it is of some use in making sense of community development, but the extent of its contribution remains unclear.

The contested character of a 'developed' community

We saw in Chapter One that part of what it might mean for a community to develop is to become stronger. Recalling the two senses of 'strong' here (namely, strongly interconnected and empowered), this could mean that a community develops when the network of ties among its members becomes denser and the ties themselves become stronger, or when the community becomes more powerful – that is, more resourceful, more organised, more capable of concerted action. These two interpretations of community development overlap to a large extent (for example, stronger and denser ties are related to greater degrees of organisation and capacity for collective action) but their focus is subtly different (for example, a more strongly interconnected community is not necessarily one that is rich in resources).

Apart from these two senses, however, a 'developed community' can have many other meanings, for example, healthy, wise or fair – a community that enjoys 'wellbeing' (Hothi, 2007; Vaitilingam, 2009). Again, a developed community might be regarded as one that is sustainable, vibrant, and in balance with the rest of the world. However, a community that is inclusive, open and forward looking may have difficulty in developing because these attributes may place it in a vulnerable position, creating instability, fragmentation and destructive conflict. A developed community seems to be a desired end state, therefore, but is there any real consensus about what that end state should look like and what characteristics communities need to have in order to attain that state?

Contrast, at one end of the spectrum, communism or 'deep cooperativism' (Ratner, 2007), where individual interests are progressively subordinated to the common good, with, at the other end, forms of libertarianism such as Nozick (1980), where the common good is firmly subordinated to the interests of individuals. In the former case, the desired end state is one in which all resources are held in common by the members of the community and decisions are taken democratically on how those resources are to be distributed. In the latter case, resources are held as much as possible by individuals, who decide for themselves how they should use them, and the role of community organisations is to facilitate these choices and arbitrate in the event of disputes and conflicts. These two extremes represent radically different visions of how a community should be. Falling between them lie a wide range of possible ideal communities, all of which can be claimed to be strong, just and so on, and to represent the epitome of sustainable well-being.[1]

Clarke (2009, pp 67–71) suggests that, in practice, four popular desired end states can be identified:

- *Restoration* of a real or imagined past community. This desire is largely a response to a sense of loss arising from unsettling social change. It emphasises the need to remake social order and envisions a community in which people 'know their place'.

- *Security*, with regard to employment, family, housing, health, income support and so on. Here the desired end state is a community that does not have to worry about the future, so can look forward with confidence.
- *Sociality*, which seems to mean a combination of civility and sociability (Misztal, 2000) – that is, the desired end state is a community whose members get on well with one another, on the basis of mutual respect.
- *Solidarity* is about 'the construction of a common purpose despite differences' (Clarke, 2009, p 70). I shall have more to say about this in Chapter Three.

Clarke provides no evidence for the existence of any of these popular desires except the desire for restoration (this is well established in the literature – see, for example, Williams, 1985). Nevertheless, probably everyone does want to live in a community where they feel secure and where they get on with their neighbours. Whether they seek to live in a community that constructs commonality across difference, however, is a different matter entirely. Indeed, as we have seen in Chapter One, solidaristic action across differences seems to be the exception rather than the rule. Even so, it might be argued by some that having a sense of common purpose is desirable for a community, though this would be as a means to an end rather than an end in itself (Clarke, 2009, p 70, cites the example of defending a local hospital against threatened closure).

So there is no agreement on what a developed community might look like. It seems unlikely that it would resemble some past idyll, but it would appear to be one in which people feel secure and get on well with one another, and that requires a certain level of resources, sufficient for it to hold its own in relation to the rest of the world. Beyond all this, though, it seems that what might count as a developed community is a matter of contention. A clearer perspective is required, therefore, in order to make sense of community development.

At this point, I would like to suggest that Martin Luther King's concept of a 'beloved community' offers such a clearer perspective (see King, 1986). According to this idea, each individual must be free to fulfil his or her highest potential, but this can happen only through membership of a community of a certain kind. This 'beloved' community is a *just* community in which resources and power are distributed in such a way as to enable every individual to actualise their potential, and in which every member respects and values every other member equally. In this book, it will be argued that this beloved community is one that everyone can recognise as a developed community.

Neo-colonialism and gentrification

When one considers the nature of community development in practice, one finds a great variety of approaches. Historically, community development arose as a colonial project. As Clarke (2009, p 82) points out, it emerged out of the need to 'divide and rule', to control colonised populations in India, Africa and other parts of the world (see also Robson, 2000). In this approach:

> Government stands *outside and above* the field of communities, providing the framework to enable communities to reconcile their differences. So, colonial governments simultaneously invented and enforced these categories of community and claimed to stand outside intercommunal tensions. As the representatives of 'civilisation', colonial governors administered and adjudicated between the different 'native communities'. (Clarke, 2009, pp 82–3)

From this perspective, community development involved preparing 'native' populations for independence and helping to ensure their continued cooperation with their former colonisers in what was to be the post-colonial era. Echoes of this approach can still be heard today in some of the thinking that permeates so-called 'development studies', where development is understood in terms of 'strengthening voice and strengthening responsiveness to voice' (Gaventa, 2004). According to this thinking, which I call 'neo-colonial', the primary purpose of community development is to *build good relations between communities and governments*. This is to be achieved in two ways: on the one hand, by strengthening the interconnectedness of communities, thereby enabling effective representation ('voice') (compare the coloniser's preparation of its colony for independence by establishing the civic infrastructure necessary for democratic government); and on the other hand, by strengthening the capacity of government to manage the demands voiced by communities (obviously, it will not be able to meet all these demands) – compare the role of, for example, the Department for International Development in responding to the needs of post-colonial populations.

From the coloniser's point of view, neo-colonialism has been extremely successful. For example, nearly all ex-colonies of Britain have become members of the British Commonwealth (the most notable exception being Eire), and relations between the mother country and the other members have generally been good (the most notable exception in recent years being Zimbabwe). The situation looks very different, however, from the viewpoint of the colonised. In what is known as the global South, community development has often been seen as a creature of governmental elites in both the mother country and the newly independent country and, to a lesser extent, of powerful non-governmental organisations (NGOs) (see, for example, Hall and Midgley, 2004). The former colonies have largely been left to their own devices,[2] with substantial well-intentioned intervention being only a very rare occurrence (for example, in the case of the civil war in Sierra Leone).[3]

What has perhaps been less recognised is the extent of neo-colonialism *within* the UK. Northern Ireland, as Clarke (2009, p 82) recognises, has long been regarded by the British government in a colonial light, as divided between 'the two communities'. Mainland Britain too, however, has long been divided, but along lines of social class. The neo-colonial approach to community development within Britain is clearly revealed in its governmental claim to stand outside class divisions as well as racial and ethnic divisions, and in its various attempts over the years to achieve harmony and cohesion between all these different 'communities'.[4] Some scholars even go so far as to argue that the processes involved in this community development amount to a new form of colonisation. For example, in commenting on the most recent developments in inner-city areas, Rowland Atkinson asserts:

> The colonisation of many areas within towns and cities that were previously considered too 'dangerous', either as areas for financial investment or personal safety, has been a defining feature of the current urban renaissance. A socially selective embracing of the central city by empty-nesters, gay households and young professionals has spread well beyond London's centripetal forces. (Atkinson, 2006, p 821)

Here Atkinson is talking specifically about *gentrification* as a process that is not so much neo-colonial as *neo-colonising*. Gentrification is a term that was originally coined by Glass (1964) and has been defined as 'a process whereby a residential area which is predominantly occupied by relatively low-income households ... switches into occupation by relatively high-income households' (Merrett, 1976, p 44). Gentrification is commonly regarded as a market-led process, whether this be motivated primarily by profit (for example, Smith, 1979) or by culture (Ley, 1996). It has attracted a considerable amount of research (see, for example, Butler, 1997; Savage et al, 2005; Allen, 2008), which has shown that gentrifiers are largely newer middle-class households who are rich in cultural capital (through higher education and so on). This capital enables them to acquire an 'aesthetic sensibility' (Ley, 1996, p 310), which disposes them to wish to live in the inner city because of its features such as 'heritage' (Butler, 1997) and centres of cultural activity (theatres, concert halls, prestigious restaurants, exclusive clubs and so on). As a form of capital, cultural capital is self-expanding, meaning here that gentrifiers are oriented towards remaking the landscape of the inner city according to their own image – what Allen (2008, p 50) has called 'the valorisation of ugly landscapes'. So gentrification is simultaneously economic and cultural, in that the value it adds is both monetary and aesthetic. Gentrification, therefore, is an example of what Bourdieu (1984) called social distinction, as it is a process whereby a section of the middle class establishes its distinctiveness in the hierarchy of social classes. It does this by creating, to some extent, its own habitus, but this creation is achieved by invading and colonising a space that was previously home to a working-class community (see, for example, Smith, 1996; Allen, 2008).

Atkinson (2006) interestingly describes the process of gentrification in terms that echo the encapsulation of working-class communities described in Chapter One. He claims to detect practices of 'insulation', 'incubation' and 'incarceration' that correspond to gentrifiers' activities of pioneering, home building and defending, respectively (Atkinson, 2006, p 825). The term 'defending' here has clear echoes of the territoriality discussed in the previous chapter. The way in which middle-class gentrifiers 'defend' their territory, however, is altogether different from that of the working class. In the case of the latter, as we saw, the defence was focused on a public space, whereas for the gentrifiers the emphasis is on the defence of private property. As colonists, the gentrifiers are 'attackers' rather than 'defenders', and they attack more as individual households than as a group; in contrast, the encapsulated working class are fighting to defend their community from an external threat (which may, in some cases, come from these same gentrifiers), and they defend more as a group than as individuals.

Recently, it has been recognised that analysing gentrification as a market-led process has tended to neglect the major role that the state plays in gentrification (see, for example, Uitermark et al, 2007). This point is well expressed by Wacquant (2008, p 202):

> The ritualised opposition between Neil Smith's economic explanation and David Ley's culturalist take … is problematic for what it leaves out: politics, policy and the state. The 'rent-gap thesis' favoured by neo-Marxist analysis, the 'cultural distinction' approach adopted by neo-Weberian or postmodernist scholars …, and the globalization thesis inspired by Saskia Sassen all leave out the crucial role of the state in producing not only

space but the space of consumers and producers of housing ...
Pierre Bourdieu ([2000] 2005, pp 30–1) has shown in *The Social
Structures of the Economy* that housing is 'the product of a double
social construction, to which the state contributes crucially', by
shaping the universe of builders and sellers via fiscal, banking
and regulatory policies, on the economic side, and by moulding
the dispositions and capabilities of house buyers (including the
propensity to rent or buy), on the social side.

Wacquant goes on to document the further ways in which the state affects
the housing market through urban and regional planning, infrastructure
maintenance, schooling, transportation, provision of cultural amenities
and policing. The point to note here, however, is that the state, at both
national and local levels, acts in such a way as to prepare the ground for the
gentrifying colonisers, both materially (for example, through infrastructure
provision) and symbolically, for example, through an:

> alliterative garble of revitalization, renaissance, regeneration,
> renewal, redevelopment, rejuvenation, restructuring,
> reurbanization and residentialisation – terms that bolster a
> neoliberal narrative of competitive progress (Tickell and Peck,
> 2003) that carves the path for stealth gentrification (Wyly and
> Hammel, 2001). (Slater, 2008, p 219)

The neo-colonial approach to community development, therefore, involves
a conception of a developed community as one that has achieved certain
standards of '*civilisation*' (see later discussion in Chapter Nine). These
standards are never precisely specified but would appear to include a
reasonable standard of living, democratic government and fair treatment
of community members. Behind this conception, however, lies a set of
practices in which middle-class 'colonisers' are favoured over working-class
'natives', where professional 'experts' exercise power over lay people, where
market forces are allowed to reinforce and exacerbate divisions within
the community, where property is given priority over people and where
governments put themselves outside and above their citizens. As a result,
sections of the community continue to find that their standard of living is
under threat, weaker members of the community are denied justice and
democratic government remains an unfulfilled aspiration. In spite of the
government's avowed aim to build good relations among communities
and between communities and government, therefore, the effect of neo-
colonisation is often precisely the opposite.

Working with communities

The neo-colonial approach is an example of community development that is done *to* the community. Other approaches commonly work *for* or *with* communities, or else they involve self-development *by* the community. The sheer variety of approaches is confusing, and indeed bewildering, but what they generally have in common is an emphasis on participation and social justice. Their notion of a developed community is one in which its members participate actively on a long-term basis and no one is placed at a significant disadvantage in relation to anyone else. Where the approaches differ is in relation to the nature of the participation they believe to be necessary and in their interpretation of what social justice involves.

Take, for example, the most widely accepted definition formulated by the Community Development Exchange (2001):

> Community development is about building active and sustainable communities based on social justice and mutual respect. It is about changing power structures to remove the barriers that prevent people from participating in the issues that affect their lives.

One problem with this definition, apart from its highly abstract character, is that it is only partly definition, the other part being aim or aspiration. Yet it has no clear vision of what a developed community might look like, so it is not clear what it is aiming for or aspiring to. A developed community is assumed to be an active community, but it is by no means clear why a community has to be 'active' in order to count as 'developed'. No rationale is offered for the over-riding importance that the definition appears to attach to participation. Arguably, for example (as shown below), an injection of relevant resources into a community, or a fairer distribution of resources within the community, could assist in its development without very much (more) activity being required from its members.

In practice, the following broad types of community development tradition emphasising participation can be identified:

- Development *for* the community, that is, philanthropy, charitable contributions, voluntary service, for example, the settlement movement (Fisher, 1994). This tradition tends to suffer from what Gilchrist (2004, p 14) calls an 'underlying patronising ethos', that is, intended beneficiaries have to be seen as 'deserving' of assistance. Participation is emphasised primarily in the sense that the participants are expected to demonstrate evidence of moral improvement. For this tradition, therefore, a developed community is primarily a morally improved community. There are echoes of this tradition in government policy today relating to social inclusion and the increasing emphasis on making welfare conditional upon the 'right' sort of conduct.

- Development *with* the community, that is, partnerships between paid community workers or community organisers and 'the community', typically conceived as the residents of a particular neighbourhood or housing estate. The role of the community worker/organiser is pivotal in this tradition, while the role of the community and the purpose of community participation tend to be less clear. What counts as a developed community in this tradition therefore tends to be whatever the community worker/organiser thinks is such. In the UK, this tradition is now dominated by government, and much will be said about this in later chapters.
- Development *by* the community, that is, self-help, mutual aid, community self-organisation. This tradition encompasses a wide range of possibilities, including the Co-operative movement, identity-based social action, and grassroots social movements generally. A high degree of participation is regarded as essential within this tradition.

Those coming from the second of these three traditions tend to emphasise the distinctiveness of community work as an occupation, to the extent of placing it within a 'third sector', separate from the public and private sectors. For example:

> Community development supports networks that foster mutual learning and shared commitments so that people can work and live together in relatively coherent and equitable communities. The purpose of community development is to maintain and renew 'community' as a foundation for the emergence of diverse initiatives that are independent of both the public and private sectors. (Gilchrist, 2009, p 21)

Here community development is seen in terms of supporting networks (which constitute a way of organising social relations that is different from hierarchies and markets), and this leads to a belief that community work is outside the public and private sectors, because the former sector is ruled by the principle of hierarchy while the latter is governed by market forces. Further, since social capital can be defined as networks sustained by norms and sanctions (Halpern, 2005), it follows that community development can be understood in terms of the construction and activation of social capital. It is not at all clear, however, why community development should be restricted to activities in a third sector or why it should be conceived only in terms of social capital (as we saw in Chapter One, community is not to be identified with networks).

Reading Gilchrist (2009), it is difficult to identify any conception of what might count as a developed community, an ideal community or a desired end state for a community. In the end, the concept of community itself seems to lose all meaning:

> Community is the 'emergent property' of a complex social system operating at the 'edge of chaos', ensuring co-operation and cohesion without imposing formal or centralised control. In this respect, 'community' is not simply equivalent to a 'social system', but is rather the outcome of continuous interactions within networks. 'Community' represents both the context and the process through which collective problem-solving emerges, in much the same way as life forms evolved from the 'primordial soup' of previous aeons ... (Gilchrist, 2009, p 130)

One idea that emerges very clearly from the book is the claim that community workers do a very important job, and it is not my purpose to question this. As Gilchrist (2009, p 38) herself says:

> the community development worker is concerned not with their own interests and needs, but instead supports community members and activists to organise activities, take up issues and challenge unjust discrimination.... the role is fundamentally about working with people in communities so that they have more influence over decisions that affect them, whether this is about their own lives or about what happens in the world around them.

The problem, however, is that this tells us nothing about what kinds of support community members need, what sorts of activities should be supported, what issues are worth taking up and so on. Above all, again, it seems to assume that active participation by community members is unquestionably the key to development, without discussing the desired nature of the participation, the character of the participants or what else, apart from participation, might be required to achieve development. It seems particularly naïve to argue that, whatever skills they may have, community development workers working with people in communities are single-handedly going to achieve any major change in power relations in our society.

Perhaps conscious of these drawbacks, which seem typical of a professionalisation project (that is, a project that arrogates to an occupation more expertise, authority, legitimacy, autonomy, political influence and so on than is justified by its performance or demonstrated effectiveness), Butcher et al (2007) advocate what they call '*critical community practice*' (see also Ledwith, 2005). By this they mean working with and alongside disadvantaged, excluded and oppressed communities, challenging established power, acting reflexively and aiming for transformational change (Butcher, 2007a, p 34). Critical community practice has a number of advantages:

- As just stated, it specifies the kinds of communities that are to be the focus of community work.
- It provides a justification for community participation as involving a widening and deepening of local democracy (Butcher, 2007a, p 45).
- Rather than placing community workers in the lead, it recognises that leadership can be distributed and shared among a number of parties (Butcher, 2007a, p 46; Banks, 2007, pp 103–4).
- It emphasises the importance of structures for (democratic) governance and support (that is, not just community workers on the ground) to sustain community development.
- It can point to successful initiatives such as youth councils, community enterprise and participatory budgeting, which have followed a critical community practice approach.

Critical community practice, however, also has certain weaknesses, particularly on the issue of community participation or 'active community'. This becomes clear in Banks (2007, p 78), where 'active' is taken to mean being involved in activities of mutual interest or for the collective good. This is problematic because what counts as the collective good is usually a contentious issue, so it may not always be possible to distinguish clearly between actions that contribute to the common good and those that do not. In some cases, however, the identification of a common good can result from a process of community organisation (see, for example, *Box 2.3*).

Banks (2007, p 78) goes on to say: 'If "community" implies a sense of belonging, solidarity and significance among its members (which might be described as latent "social capital"), then "active community" is about mobilising this social capital.' Translated into the terminology used in this book, this statement says that, if community is interpreted as meaningful interconnectedness, then the latter can be regarded as a resource that can be mobilised. The question is, however: mobilised for what purpose? Banks (2007, pp 78–9) lists five possible reasons for desiring 'active communities':

- as a good in themselves, that is, community participation is desirable for its own sake
- as a means to desirable ends, for example, for community members, others, society, the planet
- to improve governance – by voicing specific groups or sectional interests
- to renew civil society
- to improve service delivery – by increasing responsiveness and effectiveness.

Banks also recognises that government plays a key role in mobilising active communities but is less clear about other ways in which communities can be mobilised. Nor does she critically evaluate any of the five reasons for community participation. Nor is it clear how some of these reasons relate to a conception of a developed community or a desired end state for a critical community practice.

First, whether or not community participation is desirable for its own sake is a different question from whether it is necessary or desirable for community development. Second, if community participation is a means to desirable ends, we need to be told what these ends might be and why they cannot be achieved without community participation. Third, if community participation can improve governance, we need to know how it can do this and why it cannot be improved otherwise, for example, through improved systems of representation.[5] Fourth, civil society depends crucially on participation by citizens in public life but, in order to determine whether this is desirable, we need to know about the nature of this participation and of the participants – for example, does renewing civil society involve strengthening or challenging the vested interests of the powerful? Fifth, a developed community can clearly be interpreted as one that enjoys services of a high standard, but the nature and extent of community participation required to achieve that standard is not so clear.

All of this suggests that 'critical community practice' may not be critical enough. Contrary to what Henderson (2007, p 156) suggests, the problem does not lie with its emphasis on values, but with the indeterminate nature of those values, such as participation, social justice and sustainability, which can be made to mean all things to all people. Even if we agree, for argument's sake, that community development involves broadening and deepening community influence over decision making, and so improving the quality of life and well-being (Banks, 2007, p 92), it does not follow from this that community participation (still less professional networking) is the only, or even the best, way to achieve such change (for example, certain forms of devolution of democratic government might be more effective). To be fair to Butcher et al (2007), critical community practice is not actually a professionalising project but it has the potential to be one, with its emphasis on 'critical reflection' (Butcher, 2007b, p 72) and disembodied 'theory', both of which can be interpreted as claims to professional expertise. The problem is that, with Butcher et al (2007), as with Ledwith (2005), critical thought and action appears to be something that is imported into communities from outside, rather than something that communities develop for themselves. And the critical thought itself does not seem to be based on a clear understanding of the communities it aims to help – their resources, their problems or their needs.

Putting professionalising projects and 'critical community practice' on one side, there are many other ways in which workers and volunteers have worked successfully with communities to achieve development of a kind desired by the communities themselves. It is notable, however, that all of these involve combinations, of different kinds, of organisers working with communities and communities acting for themselves. For example:

- the '*radical action*' of Saul Alinsky and his colleagues in the US in the 1930s, revived in the Civil Rights movement of the 1960s, subsequently emulated in many other countries, particularly in Latin America, India and South Africa, and continuing to this day in the work of organisations such as ACORN (see www.acorn.org). This approach is based on the struggle of 'have-nots' against 'haves' and uses tactics of confronting established power (see **Box 2.1** and Dreier, 2005);
- the *critical pedagogy* movement of popular education associated with Paolo Freire in Brazil (see Freire, 1996). This approach uses learning groups/ sets of community members and community theatre to develop their critical understanding of community issues and develop their organising and leadership skills:

  > Rather than having a pre-set curriculum, the educator listens to what people in the community say they want and need, and organizes those people into a learning group where they bring their skills and knowledge into the learning process. They begin to teach one another, developing relationships and leadership skills in the process. They also begin to develop a broader understanding of their community's issues through this process, and of their place in the broader political economic system. Out of this process, then, people organize for social change. (Stoecker, 2001, p 7)

- small or 'light-touch' projects. For example, the Joseph Rowntree Foundation Neighbourhood Programme (see **Box 2.2**).

Box 2.1: How ACORN works

ACORN (Association of Community Organizations for Reform Now) is the largest national network in the US devoted to organising poor communities. It campaigns for a living wage for all workers and for justice for those on 'workfare'. It emphasises building organisations from scratch controlled by community leadership, and collecting dues from members to make the organisations as self-sustaining as possible. In Alinsky style, the organiser's role is to build local leadership, and to remain in the background as support when it comes time for public actions and negotiations.

ACORN follows four main steps in its campaigns:

Step 1 – Organise

ACORN employs its own organisers across the US, recruited largely from their own communities. Organisers start by knocking on every door in the community, learning what issues are of concern to people, and signing people up as members. Then they organise small block meetings, then multi-block meetings, then neighbourhood-wide meetings. Members gradually move into positions of recruiting other members to join, go to meetings, and do the work of the organisation.

Step 2 – Get the message out

ACORN has a reputation for holding large rallies and public meetings and other confrontational actions when needed, along with employing a sophisticated negotiation model whenever possible. Use of the mass media figures very strongly in disseminating the message to as many people as possible as powerfully as possible.

Step 3 – Political pressure

Public and private sector organisations that have the power to do something about the problem are approached directly with clear practical demands. For example:

Los Angeles County Department of Health Services. This organisation relied heavily on employing people on 'workfare' (so-called 'general relief' workers).

ACORN demanded:

- jobs at the hospital doing building and grounds maintenance
- jobs in building a new hospital
- negotiations with the hospital within two weeks

- negotiations with the County Department of Human Resources within two weeks.

Step 4 – Arrest retrenchment

ACORN has found that, unless punitive policies against the poor are vigorously and persistently opposed, then even more punitive policies tend to follow further down the line. Therefore it is essential to keep up the pressure – sometimes, a case of running to stand still.

Sources: ACORN video (2000); Dreier (2005)

Box 2.2: The JRF Neighbourhood Programme

This programme involved five independent 'facilitators' working with 20 community-based organisations for up to 10 days per year over a period of three years, with a budget of between £5,000 and £10,000 for each group to spend at its own discretion. The facilitators 'variously operated as mentor, a critical friend, a mediator and an independent broker as required' (JRF, 2007, p 10). According to an independent evaluation (Taylor et al, 2007), the programme was successful in developing the community in a number of respects:

- cleaner, safer open spaces, for example, local park reclaimed from the drugs trade;
- improved community facilities, for example, community shop/cafe;
- volunteer street representatives, providing a link between the organisation and local residents;
- improved communications, for example, through community newsletters;
- youth forums, to give young people a voice in matters affecting their community;
- increased capacity of community organisations to act strategically, through learning to 'reflect on what they were really about, to understand the context in which they were working and to determine short (one year) and longer-term (three years) priorities' (JRF, 2007, pp 5–6);
- creation of partnerships that built bridges across different groups and communities, for example, across ethnic and generational divides, and integrating new migrant communities.

All these ways require a certain degree of participation by community members, according to the needs of the community at the time and the purposes of the action involved. For example, in the case of the JRF Neighbourhood Programme, a larger pool of active residents:

> increases the energies and resources available to an organisation; it ensures that the organisation is responding to local needs and aspirations; it gives the organisation legitimacy when it is dealing with outsiders; and it ensures that engagement is not dominated by one or two individuals, however well-intentioned. (JRF, 2007, p 6)

This is helpful because it provides a rough guide as to the extent of participation that might be deemed to be desirable in relation to the community organisations that feature in this programme.[6]

It is important to note, however, that 'many community organisations still feel marginalized in partnerships with statutory authorities and agencies' (JRF, 2007, p 8) – so the success of this programme should not be overstated. In particular, many of the achievements of the programme may be sustainable only with continuing support from public authorities, so if this support is not forthcoming and in the right form, then these achievements may not last. It is also recognised that more intensive support is needed 'where there is a long history of disadvantage, where there is a fragmented community and where there is a major change at community level, e.g. as a result of regeneration programmes' and 'where there are pockets of disadvantage in more affluent areas' (JRF, 2007, p 2). The possible nature of this more intensive support, however, is not explored. One thinks, for example, of the encapsulated communities discussed in Chapter One. What community organisations are to be found in such communities, and what forms of intensive support do they need?

To conclude this section, working with communities is a theme that will recur throughout this book. So far, however, as will become increasingly clear as we proceed, such working remains more of an aspiration than a reality of everyday practice. Three reasons for this will become apparent: first, gross and unrecognised inequalities between the two 'partners' (the community on one side, the professionals and politicians on the other);[7] second, lack of understanding of the nature and dynamics of the communities concerned; and third, unreasonable, unrealistic and/or unclear expectations about how such partnerships should work, for example, in terms of the commitment and participation required. It seems clear that, although there are examples of working with communities that are moving in the right direction, the achievement of the beloved community has a long way to go.

Community self-development

Development by the community itself for itself has the longest historical pedigree, being as old as the human species. Perhaps the oldest type of such development is self-help or mutual aid, where communities sustain themselves largely through informal networks of material and emotional support. In a comprehensive review of the literature in this area, Burns and Taylor (1998) suggested that there were three possible contributions that such activity made: first, it seemed to be a more 'natural' way of meeting needs that were not met by formal organisations; second, it was a route into individual empowerment or engagement; and third, it was an alternative and preferred way of meeting needs. Research suggested, however, that the volatility and transience of informal networks limited their capacity to act as a dependable solution to social exclusion (Taylor, 2003, p 61). What this means, therefore, is that this method is important, possibly even crucial, for community self-development, because it builds sociability (the strengthening of weak ties) and can link individual community members to resources that are valuable for the community. On its own, however, it is unable to achieve stable and durable community development.[8]

So what is needed for community self-development apart from a certain level of sociability and access to valuable resources? The answer seems to lie in a sustained willingness or commitment to act together in pursuit of certain objectives that go beyond everyday norms and practices of mutual aid (see, for example, Putnam, 1993). This happens, for example, when people have a strong attachment to their community as a place or as a group identity (see, for example, Livingston et al, 2008) – the common aim is then to be loyal to that place or identity. What is perhaps required for successful long-term community self-development, therefore, is a strong community as described in Chapter One, namely a community that is both strongly and weakly interconnected, resourceful, and capable of united action, with the addition of common attachments that motivate that united action (for an example of such united action, see **Box 2.3**). Furthermore, for a beloved community, such action must be based on principles of substantive equality and justice, involving mutual and equal respect among the members and measures to reduce discrimination, exploitation and gross economic and social inequalities.

It is salutary to be reminded here that community self-development does not necessarily lead to a beloved community. Bauman (2001, p 17), for example, argues that 'attempts to reconstruct community will produce the very opposite of people's imagined idea of community. The really existing community will be unlike their dreams – more like the opposite – it will add to their fears and insecurity instead of quashing them or putting them to rest.' This happens because, as we saw in Chapter One, a stronger community can be more strongly bounded, in the sense that out-groups are more strongly defined, and these out-groups may then be represented as undesirable and even demonised (for more discussion of this point, see Chapter Nine). It is also important to note, however, that community self-development does not have to be like this.

Box 2.3: London Citizens

London Citizens does not fit easily into any of the familiar political models. 'It is not a political party, not an advocacy organisation, not a social provider, not a single issue campaign group, not a social movement, not even a community group in the conventional sense' (Jane Wills, spokesperson for London Citizens). Instead London Citizens describes itself as a broad-based alliance, made up of diverse, grassroots community organisations, working together for the common good (compare ACORN in *Box 2.1*).

London Citizens' philosophy begins from the premise that citizen self-organisation, civil society, 'the third sector' has been undervalued in favour of the market and the state. London Citizens builds relationships, both between individuals and among institutions. It believes that, by investing energy in getting to know one another, trust and solidarity is developed between disparate communities. Relationships within the organisation are built in regular two- and five-day training sessions at which leaders from member organisations are taken through the basics of community organising (compare Freire's popular education discussed above). The most important lesson is always the one that teaches participants how to do one-to-one meetings. This is the core of relational organising. The aim of such a meeting is not to 'sell' London Citizens, nor to recruit someone to a campaign, but to find out who they are and what moves them. London Citizens organisers are appointed by trustees from member organisations as part of a process of finding and developing community leaders.

The leadership attributes that organisers are looking for are not always the obvious ones. Leaders are people with passion and anger, who can see the world 'as it should be'. They have a 'following' not necessarily because they hold any official position but because their neighbours, colleagues or workmates listen to them and respect their views. And they are prepared to act to bring about change. Leadership for London Citizens is a collective process, not reliant on charismatic individuals.

London Citizens is bold, whereas many other organisations are timid. Member organisations are expected to take action on the issues that concern them. If a local group identifies a campaign it wants to pursue, it will set up an action team to drive the strategy through.

London Citizens has campaigned on issues that range from local problems like the lack of bins in Southwark and street lighting on Whitechapel Road to larger-scale issues such as the living wage for London or the treatment of migrants coming into the UK. These campaigns are not discrete. One segues into another, as campaigners discover that low-paid workers need affordable housing and that irregular migrant workers struggle to earn a living wage. So taking part in action teaches both political skills and a wider social analysis. London Citizens has had some spectacular policy victories. Its living wage campaign has changed the industrial relations climate among private contractors and their clients. Once large employers washed their hands of employment matters; once they contracted out their cleaning and catering. But London Citizens has insisted that employers take responsibility for ensuring that all staff, whether employed directly or through private contractors, are paid a wage adequate to live on. Major firms in the City and Canary Wharf, as well as health trusts and universities, now require their contractors to pay a living wage.

Perhaps most surprising has been the success of Strangers Into Citizens, a campaign to establish a route into citizenship for irregular migrant workers, which was launched in 2006 and endorsed by all four mayoral candidates in 2008. A more timid organisation would not have taken on something so controversial, but London Citizens has proved that it is worth pushing boundaries to bring about social change.

London Citizens is an example of a combination of community self-development and working with communities. It operates on different scales: neighbourhood, district (London borough) and city (London as a whole). From its roots in community unionism in the East End (TELCO) [The East London Community Organisation], it has grown to speak and act for Londoners generally. Its organisers are products of community self-development and they also work with communities of different kinds, in different areas and on different scales.

Source: Adapted from Littman (2008)

The shibboleths of 'participation', 'engagement', 'involvement' and 'empowerment'[9]

In Chapter One, I argued that communities are groups of people who are connected with one another in different ways, not only through networks but also through attachments, obligations, shared identities, habitus and so on. I shall now argue that the concepts of participation, engagement and involvement, as they appear in much of the literature, cannot easily be reconciled with this conceptualisation and are in fact shibboleths because they function to reveal the true character of people pretending to be what they are not.

The first point in the argument is that communities are always already active and engaged on or involved in their own affairs, so to regard them as needing to be activated or mobilised or engaged or involved is in itself to misunderstand and patronise them. Basically, communities have been constructed by 'community developers' as initially inactive or non-engaged, consisting of non-participants. What is at issue here, however, is the nature of the activities in which community members are engaged or involved and whether those activities are such as to move the community towards the ends that it desires.[10]

Second, the emphasis on participation mistakes means for ends. What matters for community development is not so much the extent or even the character of community participation as extending the range and depth of meaningful interconnectedness.[11] Developing communities is, after all, primarily about developing *community*. Widening one's sphere of obligations to others, deepening one's sense of common identity with others, strengthening one's habitus, all involve certain actions by a community member, but these actions do not seem to equate with what the literature calls 'participation' – they do not necessarily involve joining an organisation or network, for example, they do not necessarily involve going to meetings, sitting on committees and so on, although all of these activities clearly *can* contribute to community development. Participation is emphatically *not* something to be pursued for its own sake, as any 'burned-out' participant will testify. On the contrary, participation must have a clear purpose, of which community development can be one. Where participation does not have a clear purpose, the chances are that it is primarily serving the purposes of powerful organisations.[12]

Box 2.4 gives an example of this. Here the researchers appear to assume that it is desirable for communities to 'engage' with statutory organisations. From the point of view of the South Asian LGTB community in Bradford, however, it seems clear that it is not desirable for them to engage at all. Indeed, it appears that it may be quite dangerous for them to do so. It is generally implied in the research report that such 'minorities within minorities' need to engage so that their voices can be heard. There is no indication here, however, that if they do voice their needs and concerns they will be listened to, let alone responded to, nor is there any sense of what might count as an appropriate forum in which such voices can be raised. For the South Asian LGTB community in particular, who are clearly an 'active community' in their own right, no reason is given for why they should 'participate' in the affairs of statutory organisations in Bradford or 'engage' with such organisations. Indeed, as a 'community within a community', it is likely that they share some characteristics of the encapsulated communities discussed in Chapter One, which would make it unreasonable and unrealistic to expect such participation or engagement. Because of its emphasis on the overriding need for 'participation' and 'engagement', however, the report does not consider such possibilities. The interesting point about this research is how it shows that, even when the researchers are keen to improve their understanding of how communities work, their adoption of the perspective of the statutory agencies (with the latter's emphasis on getting communities to 'participate' and 'engage') actually prevents them from understanding how those communities work and from identifying the needs of those communities as recognised by the communities themselves.

Box 2.4: The South Asian LGTB community in Bradford

The South Asian LGTB community in Bradford faces religious and cultural intolerance, which is expressed as religious and family disapproval, social isolation, stigma and even violence. This has a major impact on the ability of people from this community to get involved in local consultation and decision making.

The centrality of the mosque to community activities and participation is problematic for this group, in the context of religious condemnation. In addition, the close nature of Bradford's South Asian communities can be experienced as a form of surveillance, limiting people's freedom to act as they wish. These dense social relations, alongside religious and cultural judgements about sexuality, often discourage people from the South Asian LGTB community from getting involved in wider community activities.

As a result, organised participation by this community tends to take the form of mutual solidarity and support, rather than engaging with statutory organisations. The Asian and Black Communities (ABC) LGBT group in Bradford provides a much-needed and valued space for this community, drawing participants from South Asian communities beyond Bradford. However, a particular concern was that lesbian and bisexual women are reluctant to attend even this group. In terms of more formal forums for participation, the interviewees shared a general sense that there was institutional indifference to the needs of this community.

Sources: JRF (2006, p 3); Blakey et al (2006)

The argument in this section has strong resonances with that of Davies (2007). In a nutshell, Davies' argument is that, rather than participating in state-led 'partnerships' (that is, engaging with local authorities and other statutory authorities in formal governance structures), communities would in some cases (specifically, Dundee and Hull) be better off organising themselves outside of such partnerships. He cites the successful examples of the anti-poll tax movement of 1989–92 and what is now London Citizens (see ***Box 2.3***), both of which created autonomous forms of action not tied in to governmental networks. This is not to deny that participation may occasionally be beneficial (for example, to gain funding) but: 'Ultimately, the choice between participation and exit is tactical and context-specific' (Davies, 2007, p 796). The problem is that: 'Where incompatible common-sense understandings of purpose combine with both blatant and subtle inequalities in political power the prospects for an equitable consensus seem poor' (Davies, 2007, p 793). The consequence of this is that 'disempowered actors who carve out autonomous spaces and act coercively against dominant interests can influence governing outcomes better than those collaborating with governing elites' (Davies, 2007, p 780). This appears to be at least partly because such community organisations can act 'as a bulwark against colonisation [in Habermas' sense] and as part of a public sphere where "citizens can debate the ends and means of governance" (Edwards, 2004, pp 14–15; Wills, 2004)' (Davies, 2007, p 795). This point will be discussed further in Chapter Three.

Of course the focus in the above examples tends to be on less powerful communities, that is, communities that have fewer resources or less capital generally. For better resourced, not to say richer, communities, the risks of partnership may be lower although, by the same token, the potential benefits of partnership may be smaller. In all cases, however, the crucial issue of how a community is to be developed is reduced to a question of how that community is to participate in certain governmentally prescribed structures or networks, and evidence suggests that this approach fails to do justice to the needs, sensibilities and aspirations of the community concerned (see, in particular, Taylor, 2003, pp 123–39).

The concept of (social) capital

Community as meaningful interconnectedness represents a resource that can be used to increase value. That is, it can function as capital. Community development can then be understood in one sense as involving the mobilisation of such capital and a developed community can be regarded as one that is rich in capital.[13] Such mobilisation can be achieved by the community entirely through its own efforts or with help from others. As Bourdieu (1986) noted, capital can be economic, social, cultural or symbolic. Is it possible that community change, including community development, can be explained by reference to how bundles of capital of these different forms are mobilised?

Take economic capital first. For Bourdieu, as for Marx, this is a type of value that is expressed through a process that moves in an expanding cycle. This cycle passes through stages such as investment, production and realisation of value. Each stage involves a different form of capital, such as money (for investment), labour and commodities (whose sale generates more money). Each of these different forms of (economic) capital is itself expressed through a self-expanding cycle, commonly known, for example, as the money market, the labour market and commodities markets. These cycles and sub-cycles do not continue expanding indefinitely; rather, capital is continually destroyed (or devalued) as well as created (or revalued) through these processes. At the same time, capital itself acts as creator and destroyer – in particular as creator and destroyer of fields (new versus old enterprises, new versus old structures) and destroyer of habitus (as noted earlier with respect to gentrification).

Cultural capital was mentioned in Chapter One. It can be understood as the forms of knowledge (not just what you know but also who you know), skills and educational qualifications that produce value in terms of higher social status, distinction and influence. In relation to community, its significance lies in helping to make sense of gentrification and of the drive towards middle-class 'respectability' in matters of taste and fashion. The concept of cultural capital warns us, for instance, that 'development' itself is a loaded term, in the sense that it carries a huge cultural baggage – what counts as 'developed' is likely to reflect the views and interests of the wealthy and privileged. Cultural capital seems to be of key importance in devaluing and revaluing habitus itself.

Symbolic capital is to be understood as the value produced by the investment of symbolic power, which Bourdieu (1990, p 131) defines as 'the power to secure recognition of power'. This is achieved through processes of institutionalisation, which:

> sets up strictly established, legally guaranteed relations between recognised positions, defined by their rank in a relatively autonomous space, distinct from and independent of their actual and potential occupants, themselves defined by entitlements which, like titles of nobility, property titles or educational qualifications, authorise them to occupy these positions. (Bourdieu, 1990, p 131)

So symbolic capital enables the accumulation of economic capital by, for example, providing a durable framework of property law, and it enables the free circulation of cultural capital through a system of universal education (Bourdieu, 1990, p 132). Symbolic capital seems to be of key importance in the devaluing and revaluing of fields.

All capital, including economic capital, involves a social relation. As a resource deployed to increase value, capital implies a relationship between the possessors or users of the resource (for economic capital, these are typically known as 'employers') and those who are used as the means for its deployment (typically known as 'employees'). Such a relationship, however, presupposes a certain level of social organisation, and it is this social organisation that gives rise to social capital. Basically, social capital is self-expanding social organisation: value (including economic value) is added through durable social relations that facilitate the expansion of value (see ***Box 2.5***).

> ## Box 2.5: Definitions of social capital
>
> ... the aggregate of the actual or potential resources which are linked to possession of a durable network of more or less institutionalised relationships of mutual acquaintance and recognition ... (Bourdieu, 1986, p 248)
>
> ... a variety of entities, with two elements in common: they all consist of some aspect of social structure, and they facilitate certain actions of actors ... within that structure ... (Coleman, 1988, p 96)
>
> Features of social life – networks, norms, and trust – that enable participants to act together more effectively to pursue shared objectives ... Social capital, in short, refers to social connections and the attendant norms and trust (Putnam, 1993, pp 664–5)

The definitions in ***Box 2.5*** all agree that social capital has to do with networks of social relations that enable or facilitate action of some kind. If capital is understood to mean self-expanding value, this suggests that social capital can be identified with the value or benefits (and also loss or disadvantages) contributed by sociability (see Halpern, 2005, for a comprehensive account of what this value involves; see also Putnam, 2000; Aldridge and Halpern, 2002; Johnston and Percy-Smith, 2003; Kearns, 2004; Taylor, 2007, p 9).

The significance of the concept of social capital for this book arises from its alleged potential to explain how community development occurs (see, for example, Halpern, 2005). What is particularly interesting here is the distinction made between different functions of social capital, namely bonding, bridging and linking (Putnam, 2000; Woolcock, 1998). This is illustrated in *Table 2.1*.

Table 2.1: *Functions of social capital*

Function	Type of social tie	Effect	Metaphor
Bonding	Strong, horizontal	'Getting by' (survival)	Social glue
Bridging	Weak, horizontal	'Getting on' (cohesion)	Social oil
Linking	On-off, vertical	'Getting up' (empowerment)	Social grease

As can be seen from *Table 2.1*, the distinction between bonding and bridging social capital closely parallels that between strong and weak ties discussed in Chapter One. These are network ties between people within a 'close' community (strong ties) or between acquaintances in different groups or communities (weak ties). Putnam (2000) referred to bonding social capital as the 'glue' that binds people together and bridging social capital as the 'oil' that makes for smooth relations among groups. What is new here, however, is the concept of linking social capital. This was originally suggested by Woolcock (1998) and refers to the 'synergy' that can exist between civil society, such as particular communities, and the state. In *Table 2.1* I suggest that the ties involved in linking social capital cannot be characterised as strong or weak because they are predominantly tactical and instrumental, and not durable. However, they are an important means for strengthening communities and for raising them up, so an appropriate metaphor to describe their function might be 'grease'.

Using this distinction between three functions of social capital, community development can be understood in three ways:

- the development of bonding social capital within the community, for example, increasing the number, size and activity of community groups, and deepening mutual trust and commitment among community members;
- the development of bridging social capital across communities or across different groups within a community, for example, bringing people together from different backgrounds or with different connections, for mutual benefit and to develop mutual trust;
- the development of linking social capital, for example, growing trust between communities or community groups and public authorities.

There now exists a considerable literature on social capital (see, for example, Halpern, 2005), focused on measuring it, establishing whether or not it is declining, how it contributes to economic development, how it aids community learning, improves community health and community safety and, not least, its importance for a healthy democratic system (Putnam, 2000). One problem with the concept, however, is that it provides no clear way of characterising the value that social capital can produce (and so serves to highlight the problematic character of value generally). Take, for example, Halpern's (2005) claim that trust in strangers (an ingredient of bridging social capital) is the key factor for economic development. On the one hand, this must be true: in a world of increasing interdependence, most of those on whom we depend are not known to us and we therefore have to trust them to do the right thing by us if we are to survive. On the other hand, it conveys no substantial information because it says nothing either about which strangers we can trust or about the value of the development produced by that trust (for example, is it development that enhances community or undermines community?).[14]

This example reflects a more general problem with the concept: it does not tell us which social capital is 'good' for community and which is 'bad' or why it works in the way that its advocates state. Putnam (2000), for example, argues that *civil* engagement (voluntary participation in formal organisations) leads to *civic* engagement (participation in the political system). Not only is this not necessarily the case, as trust between members of networks or organisations does not necessarily spill over into trust of those outside those networks/organisations (Stolle, 2003), but also it makes no distinction between different types of formal organisation (those that might have some relationship with political activity and those that would probably not), and does not envisage the possibility that some voluntary organisations and networks might be highly mistrustful of government and politicians or that this distrust might motivate them to participate more rather than less in the political system (though not perhaps in the ways that Putnam deems to be appropriate) (see also POWER, 2005). In short, the concept simply does not connect with the complexities and ambiguities of everyday life.

More recently, some scholars, critical of the way the concept of social capital has been used by Putnam, Halpern and others, have attempted to develop a more nuanced concept, in which all functions of social capital are seen as simultaneously inclusive and exclusive, creative and destructive (Leonard, 2004; Bruegel, 2005; Skidmore et al, 2006; Franklin, 2007). Linking social capital, in particular, has been criticised as leading only to increased social inequality (Skidmore et al, 2006) and reinforcement of the status quo (see, for example, Davies' (2007) analysis of how communities lose out in 'partnerships' with public authorities). Through her research on West Belfast, Leonard (2004) was able to show that, unlike some other poor encapsulated communities, Catholic West Belfast showed evidence of strong bonding social capital. She explained this as follows:

> In politically sensitive societies, negative images of particular areas can be challenged rather than accepted by residents. In this respect, the 'troubles' which erupted in Northern Ireland in the late 1960s had certain beneficial consequences for marginalized areas. This was particularly the case for working-class Catholic localities that had experienced high levels of long-term unemployment and other social ills. Blame for the apathy, deprivation and destruction that existed on these estates could be transferred from the shoulders of the residents to the Protestant controlled Stormont government and then later to the British State. Social support networks emerged as ways of challenging the State's inability to provide employment for its citizens. Because of the political situation, residents were less willing to accept blanket statements by governments concerning individual deficiencies and were able to lay the blame for their situation on inappropriate, misguided and sectarian government policies. As part of this, bonding social capital came to be seen as a political strategy rather than simply a solution to individual or community disadvantage. (Leonard, 2004, pp 932–3)

This echoes some of the comments made in Chapter One about encapsulation involving collective action in response to a perceived threat to a community. There, however, the response was mainly in terms of strengthening the boundaries of the community. Here, the emphasis is more on strengthening the bonds that tie the community together. As mentioned in Chapter One, however, it is not unusual for boundedness and bondedness to be mutually reinforcing.

In West Belfast, bridging social capital was particularly important for accessing informal employment, although this had its disadvantages:

> Recruitment was mainly by word-of-mouth and access to such opportunities depended on the strength of the individual's links to these information channels, which operated through kinship, friendship and neighbourhood networks. In the process this ensured continuous recruitment into highly disadvantageous forms of employment where participants earned wages which were only viable when combined with welfare benefits. Yet these

exploitative features were often unacknowledged by participants who viewed their involvement as a way of 'hitting back' at the State. (Leonard, 2004, p 936)

In such circumstances, it is far from clear what might be involved in developing bridging social capital. For example, the entrepreneurs who provide goods and services to such a community, and who might act as employers of those working informally, may themselves be locked into these informal networks. It may be beneficial for them to develop bridging social capital to other, more prosperous communities, but such development may involve acting more within the formal economy and so loosening the ties with their original informal networks, resulting in a loss of social capital for that community. In the case of West Belfast:

This can be illustrated by looking at how some entrepreneurs in Belfast tried to establish bridging social capital through formalizing their local skills. Individuals who were involved in the informal production of goods and services within the area were encouraged by policy-makers to combine their efforts in more structured formal environments. Some of these projects were initially successful. However, their initial clientele came mostly from the surrounding area and emanated from the exploitation of social networks. Building up friendships and relationships with others in the area was often a cultural device, strategically used to make money. On the other hand, community members often used kinship and friendship ties to obtain special terms on the goods and services offered. Those who provided goods and services within the estate charged money well below the market value of the work. These goods did not command fixed prices. Rather payment was constantly negotiated and re-negotiated depending on the relationship between seller and buyer. The closer the relationship between the two, regardless of whether this was based on friendship or kinship, the more flexible the pricing became. Hence, social and, in a sense, non-economic factors profoundly characterized economic transactions. However, in order to develop outwardly, these new enterprises had to start charging higher prices to cover overheads and additional expenses. Once personal networks had been exhausted, some of these enterprises found it difficult to sustain their existence and went out of business. Those that remained in business ended up supplying outside customers and to maintain their economic viability they had to price their products out of reach of the local community. (Leonard, 2004, pp 936–7)

This quote clearly shows how the building of bridging social capital can work *against* community development, rather than in favour of it. It may be important to note, however, that the stimulus for this bridging social capital appears to be coming from 'policy-makers', so there may also be an element of linking social capital here.

How, then, can a community that lacks resources develop its bridging and linking social capital? Skidmore et al (2006) have pointed out that 'those already well-connected tend to get better connected'; by the same token, *communities* that are already well connected will tend to get better connected. So, other things being equal, developing linking social capital will tend to increase inequalities within communities and across communities. Similarly, Stone (2002) has argued that linking social capital is divisive because it requires communities to contribute resources in order to be effective, so if they lack resources they lose out. Again, Bruegel (2005, p 12) has pointed out that linking social capital actually requires that the capital be scarce in order for it to produce value: 'If every young black in Brixton can call on a mentor in the City, the value of that tie in getting a job is much more limited than where such links are rare.' So the answer to the question at the beginning of this paragraph seems to be that social capital is yet another shibboleth: a community without resources cannot satisfactorily develop its bridging and linking social capital unless it is given resources, distributed on the basis of need – or, to put it more simply, a community without resources needs resources other than those of bridging and linking social capital.

What sorts of resources are at stake here? Leonard (2004) is clear that these resources consist primarily of economic and cultural capital and that West Belfast can access them only through the political process. For this to happen:

> the norms around which bonding social capital took root need to be diluted. Notions of community trust and bonding social capital that fed on internal opposition to outside institutions needs [*sic*] to be replaced with more open social networks. This entails community leaders establishing new norms involving collaboration and cooperation with bigger players. (Leonard, 2004, p 939)

In other words, community development in West Belfast requires a certain weakening of the existing bonding social capital and new ways of engaging with forces outside the community – a clear move away from encapsulation.[15] In making this change, however, it is important not to disrupt, weaken or undermine existing networks of mutual support.

In all, therefore, the contribution made by the concept of social capital to understanding community development remains unclear. It appears that economic and cultural capital play a more important role and that social capital is effective primarily as a mediator of these more important resources. This mediation, however, can itself be an important function. Thomson and Caulier-Grice (2007, p 6), for example, draw evidence from studies in a number of countries (not only the UK but also Denmark, Australia, Canada and France) that suggests that small community organisations can generate and mobilise different types of social capital, break down divisions in communities and empower individuals (see also Richardson, 2008). Economic capital in the form of funding for such community groups can be very helpful in enabling them to build trust within and between groups, which leads to a range of other benefits (see also Taylor et al, 2007, discussed above). Many other studies have shown that the development of community networks increases the choices and information available to communities, as well as their capacity for collective action (see, for example, Jochum, 2003; Johnson, 2004; Kapasi, 2006; and the studies in Rogers and Robinson, 2004) – in other words, building social capital is important for community development.

It is possible, however, to detect a certain circularity in some of these arguments, in that lack of social capital signifies a need for community development while community development is taken to mean the building of social capital. Starting from the assumption that, broadly speaking, community groups are doing good work, it is inferred that developing such groups, encouraging them to work with other, similar groups and getting them to work together with public authorities, will be in the interests of the communities concerned. Community development is then simply equated with bonding, bridging and linking social capital, respectively, and the importance of economic and cultural capital disappears from the scene. Social capital becomes an end in itself, rather than a means to an end, and the political and societal context in which social capital development takes place is thereby ignored or treated as being of secondary importance. Worst of all, the goals of community development other than that of building and mobilising social capital get lost.

Social capital theorists generally recognise that social capital has a 'dark side' (starkly revealed, for example, in the discussion of territoriality in Chapter One, where the 'community group' is a 'gang'). Following Putnam (2000), however, they tend to interpret this in terms of excessive bonding social capital, which can be corrected through building bridging social capital. This interpretation fails to recognise that all functions of social capital can be exclusionary and divisive, so does not resolve the problem of the 'dark side' of social capital. As a consequence, the concept of social capital provides no way of distinguishing between desirable and undesirable community development, that is, between development that does and development that does not move a community towards a desired end state of whatever kind. It loses all capacity that it might have had to explain what community development is or why it takes place.

Conclusion

To conclude this chapter, I would like to suggest that community development can be explained, not in terms of social capital (or any other kind of capital) alone, but in terms of specific combinations of economic, cultural, symbolic and social capital, generated by communities located within specific habitus (plural) interacting with specific fields. This is difficult to prove but Putnam's (1993) study of northern Italy actually provides, to some extent, a model of how such development comes about. Over a long period of historical development, opportunities for making money combine with a supportive culture of 'co-opetition', which creates competitive advantage. This advantage becomes institutionalised in legal and political structures, which in turn facilitate further community development. Economic capital, therefore, in combination with cultural and social capital, and all regulated and legitimated by symbolic capital, produces the development of a community. Increasing meaningful interconnectedness, which is at the heart of community development, depends on this dynamic of legitimated resourcefulness.

This is by no means the whole story, however, because we also know that the 'bundles of capital' model of development involves losers as well as winners, excluded as well as included and so on. Development for the few is not development for the many, but it is the narrative of the successful few that tends to dominate such historical accounts. Consequently, the development that is explained by this theory is not the development of a beloved community. In order for a community to develop as a whole, together and fairly, the community must be well connected internally and externally, and the connections must be not only in terms of networks but also in terms of shared attachments, identities, obligations, sympathies, affinities and so on. How this can begin to happen is explored in later chapters of this book.

Notes

[1] 'Sustainable communities are settlements which meet diverse needs of all existing and future residents; contribute to a high quality of life; and offer appropriate ladders of opportunity for household advancement, either locally or through external connections. They also limit the adverse external effects on the environment, society and economy' (Kearns and Turok, 2003).

[2] Even existing colonies have been neglected – hence the Argentinian invasion of the Falklands in 1982, although this invasion then triggered a massive response from the British government.

[3] Ill-intentioned interventions, however, such as the expulsion of the Chagossians from their homeland and the invasion of Grenada, have probably been more common than we realise. If we include countries that have not exactly been colonies but have been under the British yoke, many more such neo-colonial adventures could be mentioned, for example, Suez in 1956, Afghanistan in 2001 and Iraq in 2003. Huge military support of course continues for Israeli colonisers, in spite of their illegal seizures of land and uncompromising anti-Arab racism. And this is not even to mention the enormous economic effects on ex-colonies, for better or worse, arising from their generally weaker trading positions – for example, brain drain, anti-competitive pricing, national debt and so on.

[4] Some of these attempts will be considered further in Chapter Four.

[5] It cannot be assumed a priori, for example, that greater participation must lead to more democratic decision-making – it all depends on who participates and how they participate.

[6] The guide can only be rough because the community organisations differ considerably in their nature, size and functions.

[7] Understandably, where the balance between the two parties is unequal, there is a risk of neo-colonialism.

[8] Although radical in their inspiration, autonomous social centres are also an example of such mutual aid and informality of networking – see www.socialcentrestories.org.uk.

[9] Empowerment is tackled more explicitly in Chapter Four. Suffice it to say here that empowerment is typically defined as 'the process of increasing the capacity of individuals or groups to make choices and to transform those choices into desired actions and outcomes' (World Bank, 2009). This definition glosses over crucial issues of power such as control over resources and the ability to make decisions on the direction of one's life (De Vos et al, 2009, p 25).

[10] Countless publications on community development outline roles and levels of participation without ever pointing out that this approach is not centred on the community at all but on the delivery of some project, initiative or programme in the community. The top-down character of this perspective is revealed in the fact that 'participation' is understood entirely in terms of participation in the project.

Even at the top level of participation, where communities are fully in control, what they are in control of is still only a project.

[11] This also requires the community to be relatively strong in the double sense described in Chapter One, that is, as strongly connected and resourceful. Strong communities are therefore a means to the end of community development as understood here.

[12] Participation should perhaps be distinguished from *volunteering*, which has no necessary connection with community development. Begum (2003), for example, found that voluntary organisations provided stepping-stones for individuals to become involved in voluntary action, as well as a route into decision-making structures. Such organisations include those involved in community self-development such as London Citizens. Again, however, it seems important that such organisations should have clear purposes, to which the volunteers can be committed.

[13] This does not mean that the capital is *owned* by the community. Recall the argument in Chapter One that a community does not *belong* to its members and its members do not *belong* to a community. Meaningful interconnectedness as capital is characteristic of habitus and does not lead to capitalism as a system.

[14] Interestingly, Casey (2004, p 113) argues that 'the validity of social capital as an explanation for economic performance must stand as "not proven"'.

[15] Arguably, it is the *boundedness* of the community that needs to be weakened (particularly in relation to issues of crime and policing – 'community justice' in the form of punishment beatings continues, mainly for crimes committed against the community such as drug offences and joy-riding – Leonard, 2004, p 940), but not necessarily its *bondedness* (see Chapter One).

Summary

In evaluating community development, this chapter is critical of all current approaches, but devotes particular attention to those that emphasise the role of 'participation' in achieving community development. It is argued that participation, however it is defined, is only a means to an end, and both ends and means need to be specified more clearly. This in turn requires that the value and desirability of participation be considered more carefully.

The chapter is also critical of the concept of social capital, arguing that it leads to circularity and emptiness of both explanatory and evaluative force, over-emphasis on self-organisation, and glossing over problems of social inequality, division, conflict and exclusion.

Questions for discussion

- What is meant by 'community development'?

- What is wrong with gentrification?

- How critical is 'critical community practice'?

- Does 'community organising' work? If so, why?

- What is the point of participation/involvement/engagement, and so on?

- How helpful is the concept of social capital for explaining how communities work?

- Can communities really develop themselves?

Further reading

Butcher, H., Banks, S., Henderson, P. with Robertson, J. (2007) *Critical community practice*, Bristol: The Policy Press.

Leonard, M. (2004) 'Bonding and bridging capital: reflections from Belfast', *Sociology,* vol 38, no 5, pp 927–44.

Taylor, M. (2003) *Public policy in the community*, Basingstoke: Palgrave Macmillan.

three

The politics of community

Overview

A political community is a community of a special kind, namely, one whose members recognise a common authority, exercised over a common territory. This chapter is critical of nationalism (understood as an ideology of the nation as an imagined ideal political community). It also distinguishes different ideologies of political community:

- *communitarianism* - emphasising the strong ties of bonding social capital
- *cosmopolitanism* – emphasising the weak ties of bridging social capital
- *participationism* – emphasising the on-off ties of linking social capital.

Historical and existing embodiments of these ideologies are criticised but it is also suggested that they can allude, in their characteristic ways, to the possibility of a beloved community. Indeed, they also echo the three ideals of the French Revolution, namely, liberty (cosmopolitan outlook), equality (rights of citizens to participate) and fraternity (communitarian solidarity).

The concept of political community or polity

In Chapter One, a community was argued to be an embodied or imagined group of persons who are meaningfully interconnected within habitus (understood as relatively stable everyday ways of going on in the world). Numerous studies (particularly in Britain) have revealed that habitus (plural) are often characterised in terms of the social class of their inhabitants, although type of location (for example, urban or rural) and ethnicity can also be important. The nature of meaningful interconnectedness was explored further in Chapter Two, in terms of functions of social capital – bonding, bridging and linking. Doubts were raised, however, about the adequacy of the concept of social capital for explaining community change.

This chapter starts with an analysis of political community or polity and goes on to show how this specific category of community extends our understanding of meaningful interconnectedness to include the wider context of social and political relations. Community action comes to include forms of social and political action based on a political community, and community change comes to be understood in terms of the effects of social and political movements.

A political community or polity can be defined as an embodied or imagined group of persons who recognise a shared authority (typically a public decision-making forum or assembly) within or pertaining to a shared territory. A polity is therefore a special kind of community in at least two senses: first, its members (typically known as citizens) are bonded together by their recognition of a common authority; and second, they are bounded together by their attachment to a common locality (which can vary in size from a small neighbourhood to a country – and potentially to the world as a whole).

In classical Greece, political communities were largely the citizen bodies of city-states, in which the citizens were free men (not women or slaves), the territory was the city and the authoritative body took the form of a citizens' assembly (democracy), a council of elite citizens (aristocracy) or a single citizen (tyranny). Today, polities are mainly (but by no means entirely) the citizen populations of nation-states, in which the territory is that which is occupied by a nation and the authority typically takes the form of a body that is elected by the citizens, who are, by and large, adult members of the nation. These polities are commonly called democratic but they differ from ancient Greek democracies in that the citizens do not decide for themselves but only through their elected representatives.

How are citizens meaningfully interconnected in a modern democratic polity? What is the nature of the habitus involved? How is this habitus related to the field of state action? Habermas (1974) attempted to answer questions of this kind through his concept of a *public sphere*, created in the coffee houses of 18th-century cities in countries such as England and France. This 'sphere' was originally the habitus of a bourgeois community, whose members consisted of merchants, businessmen, professionals and other individuals who could qualify as 'burghers' (men of wealth and influence in the city or town). Bourgeois communities around the country developed their own organisations to represent their interests at national level, including political parties, and the restriction of the franchise to men of property enabled the creation of a bourgeois polity, that is, a political community whose citizens consisted entirely of rich men.

A nation, however, is much more than a single class or gender, so it was possible to argue that the bourgeois polity unjustifiably excluded people within the same territory who recognised a common authority and held to the same nationality. Over the course of the 19th and early 20th centuries, then, the franchise in bourgeois polities was extended to include all adult males and females. The political community became more closely identified with the national community. This process continued after the Second World War, with the enhancement of citizenship rights for nationals, and increasing restrictions on non-nationals (so-called immigration control) from the 1960s right up to the present day.

As Anderson (1983) said, nations are imagined communities, but how does this imagining come to pass? Gellner (2006) argued that modern nations were formed by industrialisation, as a way to restore the sense of community undermined by economic and social change. A nation was identified primarily with a shared culture, with a particular emphasis on a common language. In contrast, Conversi (2007, 2008b) emphasises the importance of wars and the military in shaping modern nations, and argues more generally that modern nations have been created by modern states, with the French Revolution playing a particularly important role (Connor, 2004). These states have attempted to mould their citizens into a single, culturally uniform body, so that they can be easier to govern. Techniques such as mass conscription and compulsory education have been key to achieving this effect. In general, it could be said that the state works by interpellating its citizens as subjects of its authority, as noted in Chapter One. It actively encourages the building of a nation as an imagined community. In Bourdieusian terms, therefore, we could say that the habitus of a nation and the field of the state[1] are strongly integrated in modern nation-states: vast economic, social, cultural and military resources have been invested in the development of nations, and this investment has been deployed largely through the structures of capitalism and state power, involving what Pandey (2006) has tellingly called 'routine violence'.

For these reasons, it is necessary to be sceptical about the concept of a nation as a basis for a free and open political community, that is, one that is not oppressively conformist, homogenising, militaristic, or exclusive of difference of any kind (see Conversi, 2008a).[2] Given the historical problems associated with nationalism, it seems important to find an alternative to the nation as the basis for modern political community. This is easier said than done, however, particularly when what might be called 'small nation' nationalism (for example, Scotland, Wales) can continue to seem progressive and attractive, and when supra-national alternatives such as the European Union may not look any more preferable.

The remainder of this chapter considers alternative ways of thinking about political community that attempt to avoid the pitfalls of nationalism. For convenience, these are grouped under approaches that emphasise bonding social capital, bridging social capital and linking social capital. The communities imagined by each approach have their own particular forms of meaningful interconnectedness, related to the membership criteria commonly recognised by their members.

The politics of bonding social capital – communitarianism

Nationalism emphasises bonding social capital because it is a belief that citizens are bonded together in nations. The political community is characterised by strong ties forged by a shared historical experience (or, at least partly, state-constructed historical experience) of war and culture as mentioned above. Members of the same nation are seen as tied together most strongly by blood and sacrifice, as well as by attachment to the same homeland (which also can be imagined rather than, or as well as, experienced).

Nationalism, however, is not the only belief that involves a bonded political community. Alternative beliefs include those of *communalism* and *socialism*, and the generic term to describe all beliefs that emphasise bonding social capital as the foundation for political community is *communitarian*. Nationalists and socialists are all communitarians to the extent that they believe that strong ties of nation or class can provide a foundation for political community.

Communalist communities have been defined as 'voluntary, small-scale communities in which co-operation is all-encompassing and in which egalitarian values and practices, group ownership and control are supreme' (Melnyk, 1985, p 79).[3] Apart from the small size and egalitarian character of such communities, Melnyk also notes their isolationist and separatist tendencies and the charismatic nature of their leadership. Such communities have existed since time immemorial, frequently motivated by strong religious beliefs and commitments. Most such communities do not outlast their founding members but some, such as the Hutterites and Amish communities in North America, have survived for hundreds of years. A good historical example of a communalist political community is that established by the Jesuits in Paraguay from 1607 to 1767 (see ***Box 3.1***).

Box 3.1: The Jesuits in Paraguay

[The villages were] ruled, or rather guided, by a handful of priests, whose instruments of government seem to have been almost exclusively the sacraments of penance and communion ... The Jesuits did not establish their villages as communes deliberately. They simply adapted the social organization of the Indians. The little societies were rather highly structured. Status derived both from offices in the community government and from eagerly sought-after roles in the various ceremonials ... In Paraguay a few villages founded by the Jesuits survive to this day. The social and economic relationships are those of free enterprise, but the memory of the communities of three hundred years ago lingers on. In many ways the Jesuit 'reductions', as they were called in Paraguay, are one of the best organizations of society ever to exist, either in theory or actuality. The Indians were certainly happier than anyone would be in Plato's Republic, or St. Thomas More's Utopia. Life was an almost uninterrupted ritual, a kind of group contemplation suffused with joy. The extraordinary thing is that nothing like it has ever happened at any other time in history, certainly not since the Neolithic village.

Source: Adapted from Rexroth (1974)

As Rexroth (1974) points out, there is general agreement about the factors that make for a successful communalist community (or commune). These include: a powerful ideology shared by all members of the community, which includes the belief that other forms of community fail to provide sufficient value for a life worth living; a strong, well-balanced, multi-talented leadership who are able to create a sustainable economy and to persuade others of the 'truth' of their cause; and an accepted method of assigning and rotating tasks. A successful commune is therefore one that is strongly bounded as well as strongly bonded: the criteria for membership can be very strict indeed, as is the case, for example, with monastic communities (for example, poverty, chastity and obedience).

Paradoxically, however (with the possible exception of the Jesuits in Paraguay), the exclusivity that makes a communalist community successful and long lasting is also what ensures that its effects on other communities remain limited. In the case of religious communes, Melnyk (1985, p 101) reports that: 'The most successful communes are those that rejected the concept of their commune as a heaven on earth, and insisted it was only a waystation to something higher.' In other words, the most successful religious communes are those that are fixed more on the next world than on this one. Far from wanting to change this world, they want to prepare themselves for life in the hereafter. In the case of secular communes, their task is far more difficult: 'the contradiction of secular communalism [is that] it seeks to escape society and simultaneously transform it' (Melnyk, 1985, p 90). The problem is that, in order to survive, communes have to build strong boundaries against the ways of life that they reject, but the very institution of these boundaries helps to ensure that those ways of life continue. As Melnyk (1985, p 101) says: 'Communalism needs an inward–looking and self-contained reality to maintain its practice', but this militates against achieving any significant durable social change. Moreover, Melnyk (1985, p 100) points out that: 'Communalism survives only when it is tolerated by the state or has sufficient backing in the wider society.' In other words, even if a commune is self-sufficient economically, it is still vulnerable to pressure from wider social forces, particularly the state, and depends on at least the goodwill of the wider political community in which it operates.

It appears, then, that communalism is not a viable alternative to nationalism for building or transforming political community. This is because it sidesteps the problem of how to create bonding social capital across people of different groups, different ideologies and different ways of life.[4] Ultimately, it assumes a degree of common purpose and values that seems very far from the reality of modern society, and it serves to increase rather than reduce the risk of fragmenting existing polities. This is not to say that communal communities could not play a significant role within a wider non–nationalist movement for social transformation (for example, Christian millenarianism or Salafism or global socialism of some kind) but currently such a role seems relatively undeveloped.

A very different variant of *communitarianism* is that of Amitai Etzioni (1995). In this variant, the bonding social capital required for political community is understood in terms of shared values, political community itself is represented as a community of communities and one of the key shared values seems to be that the rights of individual members of the political community are conditional upon the discharge of obligations to that community.

The problems with Etzioni's vision, however, are fairly obvious. First, the principle of shared values asks too much of any polity: it seeks an unachievable and possibly undesirable conformity of culture and behaviour (which, as noted above, usually forms part of a nationalist project). As Elizabeth Frazer points out, it misses 'the freeing effects of simple relationships and loose networks' (Frazer, 1999, p 244). Second, Etzioni identifies his 'community of communities' with the American nation and is therefore committed to a project of (re)building that particular nation – that is, a nationalist project. Arguably, however, this is too crude a representation of the composition of a modern nation, which cannot be adequately understood as an aggregate of different communities. Third, the priority of obligations over rights runs the risk of violating basic personal freedoms in pursuit of some unattainable social cohesion or harmony. It is at least arguable that the needs of the individual should take priority over their obligations to others.

Socialist communitarianism is different again, and itself takes different forms (see, for example, Delanty, 2003). Some forms of socialist communitarianism are linked to nation-building or nationalist projects such as Zionism (mentioned above) or Ujamaa socialism in Tanzania (for an evaluation, see Melnyk, 1985, pp 64–7). Others are state initiated, promoted and maintained and form part of a centrally planned, government-controlled economic system – for example, Kolkhoz in the former USSR, communes in the People's Republic of China, or workers' self-management in the former Yugoslavia. What the different forms have (or had) in common is an opposition to capitalism and private property and a commitment to cooperative production and common ownership. Arguably, the differences between the different forms are not that great, as they all involved the creation of communes or collectives that were harnessed to a nationalist project – they are all forms of national socialism.[5]

The problems with socialist communitarianism are also fairly clear. Although in principle it is based on mass recognition of working-class solidarity, in practice its aspirations for global emancipation have been subordinated to the requirements of the modern nation-state. For much, if not most, of the 20th century and beyond, working-class communities have been sacrificed to the cause of building militarised, culturally uniform states that cannot seriously be regarded as communities of communities. This is not to say, however, that it might not be possible to develop new forms of socialism that are not exclusively focused on developing a bonded political community. There is a sense in which the beloved community could be said to be a socialist one, if socialism is taken to involve the maximisation of individual freedom through forms of cooperation with others on an equal basis.

The politics of bridging social capital – cosmopolitanism

A political community does not have to be one whose members are tied together by shared experiences of war and culture, by shared living, by shared values or by shared political or religious ideology. In short, the members of a political community do not have to share the same habitus. Instead, they could be held together by weak ties, that is, embodied or imagined relationships with others that involve forms of solidarity, mutual cooperation, mutual accommodation, mutual obligations and constitutionality that cut across different groups and communities.

The belief that a polity can be constructed on the basis of such weak ties is associated with two traditions of thought: civic republicanism and cosmopolitanism. The former places more stress on political liberty and independence, and the latter on political obligation and interdependence.

The central idea of *civic republicanism* is that citizens, acting freely in the sense of not being subject to any arbitrary power (whether this be an employer, a parent, a prince, a government official, a landlord or a gang leader), can nevertheless be tied together by respect for the same political institutions, the same legal and constitutional framework, and so on. Republicans see a commonly agreed system of rules as essential for the peaceful government of relationships among the citizens of a political community (Pettit, 1997). The only shared value required is civic virtue, understood as valuing the public good over and above personal or sectional interests, and such virtue can itself be encouraged by appropriate laws and regulations.

Civic republicanism is useful for drawing attention to the *possibility* of a political community that endures without apparently having to invoke the strong ties of kinship, friendship, shared culture, shared values and shared living generally. Problems arise, however, when it comes to asking how such a community is to be actualised. It is all very well, for example, to talk about the 'public good' and how best to realise that good (for example, forms of deliberative democracy, involving accountable representatives and drawing upon appropriate 'expert' advice and so on), but this assumes a prior agreement about who constitutes the 'public' whose good is to be realised, and such agreement may not be forthcoming. Yet without such agreement, a political community cannot exist.

The problem of knowing the nature of the 'public' is the problem of identifying the *boundaries* of the political community. The strength of nationalism lies in its ability to provide a neat solution to this problem, namely by identifying the public with the nation. As members of the same nation, we know who 'we' all are, even though we may not know one another very well at all. 'Belonging' to a nation seems to be a purely imagined form of recognition of oneself and of others. But can the boundaries of a political community be anything other than national boundaries?

This is where *cosmopolitanism* comes in. Both as a world-view or outlook and as a condition of being (Fine, 2007, p 134), it involves a movement towards a global political community. The central idea of cosmopolitanism is that, as members of a common humanity, we have inalienable obligations to one another based on mutual recognition of our equal value. The precise nature of these obligations, however, is very difficult to specify, and global recognition of the equal value of all human beings seems very far from current realities. Dobson (2006) suggests the adoption of what he calls a 'thick' cosmopolitanism, according to which we recognise the 'causal responsibility' (Dobson, 2006, p 172) we have for one another, that is, we recognise the obligations we have to one another as a consequence of the foreseeable effects of our actions upon one another. The case for a global political community, therefore, is based on the argument that we have to find a way of living together fairly on the same planet, sharing the earth's resources more equitably, if we are to survive at all.

Saying something must happen, however, does not mean that it will happen. Consequently, a number of writers have attempted to address the question of how political community might be developed so that it becomes more cosmopolitan in outlook and condition (or in its consciousness and its existence). One idea is that of 'cosmopolitan patriotism' (Appiah, 1996), whereby membership of a polity on one scale provides a basis for membership of polities on 'higher' scales (see also Habermas, 2000). A local polity, for example, could be part of a national polity, which could be the basis for a continental polity (for example, a European political community), which could form part of a global polity. This idea of what might be called 'nested' polities actually serves to highlight the complexity of the problem that faces cosmopolitans: it reminds us that existing polities are already multiscalar and characterised by different combinations of strong and weak ties on different scales.[6]

The advantage of the idea of nested polities lies in its implication that polities on different scales do not have to be incompatible with one another: strong nations, for example, can decide to pool their sovereignty in larger groupings, as in the European Union. The disadvantage, however, is that the relations between scales are relatively ill defined and, in general, political decision making becomes far more complicated. It is important to note, following Conversi (2007), that the principle of self-determination cannot help here because there is no clear way of deciding what the 'self' is that can determine itself. In other words, if it is left up to everyone to determine the boundaries of their political community as they wish, then different people will choose different boundaries (typically based on national, regional and local identities and allegiances), making it impossible for them to agree where the boundaries should lie.

These arguments suggest that cosmopolitan patriotism is not a convincing solution to the problem of identifying a common understanding of the boundaries of political community. Rather, it is an attempt to construct those boundaries in a new way, which retains a form of nationalism (or 'patriotism') on one scale, but sets this within a more cosmopolitan context. This is formally similar to Etzioni's communitarianism, in that each nation functions as a community within a group of nations, with a group of nations being imagined (perhaps more loosely) as a 'community of communities'. The model for this is the European Union (EU), but the fact is that the EU is very far from being a community in the sense used in this book. And if it were a community, this would raise issues about European supranationalism that would be formally similar to those raised above in relation to nationalism (for example, homogenisation, militarisation, eurocentrism) (for further discussion, see Fine, 2007, pp 44ff).

The truly worrying thing in our era is that there is no clear form or ethic of global solidarity that transcends nationalism or supranationalism. Global civil society has been seen as a foundation for such solidarity but civil society associations lack the authority required for political community (Fine, 2007, p 62). Legal or constitutional approaches are also criticised because, in order to work, cosmopolitan law has to be grounded in a cosmopolitan politics, and such a politics does not exist (Fine, 2007, p 77). Rather, what exists is national and international politics, based on nation-states and their relations with one another. Nevertheless, cosmopolitans such as Fine (2007, p 136) believe that they can detect an evolving set of social forms, which Fine identifies with what he calls 'the cosmopolitan condition'. These forms include new practices, institutions and laws in interstate relations, changing the global field of right and law (for example, by incorporating human rights, international criminal courts, forms of universal citizenship), and leading to a recalibration of the 'system of right' as a whole.

Some thinkers on the political left either do not accept that recognition of a common authority is necessary for political community or else they reject those authorities that currently exist and do not propose any to take their place. *Autonomists*, for example, participate in a global network of alliances organised through People's Global Action, committed to the principle and practice of autonomy from all forms of capitalist authority. Could this be the missing element of community in Fine's evolving set of social forms? Cunninghame (2008) argues that autonomism is a new type of global social movement, which does not rely on shared habitus, shared ideology/values, shared position in a political field or centralised coordination, so it appears to avoid the pitfalls both of communitarianism and of previous social movements (for example, labour movement, women's movement, green movement and so on). Hardt and Negri (2000) talk of the '*Multitude*' as the collective actor in this movement. This concept of multitude, however, is problematic precisely because those who are opposed to global capitalism do not constitute a coherently recognisable group, let alone a potential future political community. The multitude is, at most, only 'a collective actor in formation' (Cunninghame, 2008, p 15), and the evidence for the existence of this formation is very patchy. Time will tell.

The Citizens Organising Foundation (COF), of which London Citizens forms a part (see **Box 2.3** in Chapter Two), is another example of an autonomous organisation. As Skidmore (no date, p 5) notes: 'There is nothing particularly revolutionary about COF's techniques: the emphasis on campaigning; the slow, painstaking construction of a coalition of progressive organisations in particular areas; careful, inclusive negotiations to establish shared priorities; realistic goals for change; judicious selection of targets, most famously the Canary Wharf financial institutions; a willingness to embrace creative, eye-catching ways to get their message across.' The COF succeeds because it secures direct, tangible improvements in people's lives.

There is a sense in which the beloved community could be said to be cosmopolitan, if cosmopolitanism is taken to involve mutual recognition of their equal value by free individuals seeking to fulfil their highest potentials. So the beloved community can be, and maybe has to be, a cosmopolitan socialist one.

The politics of linking social capital – participationism

The third possibility for political community, apart from communitarianism and cosmopolitanism, is that a political authority such as a state works together with citizens in making and implementing decisions. Citizens and state occupy the same field but do not necessarily share the same habitus. The ties between them cannot usually be described as consistently strong or weak but are turned on and off, according to circumstances. Such ties can be patrimonial (where citizens enjoy favours from politicians in return for supporting them[7]) or electoral (where citizens elect representatives to the decision-making assembly) or more broadly interactive (where state officials meet with citizens in decision-making forums of various kinds).

I shall say no more here about patrimonial ties, though their continuing importance should not be underestimated (they can be relatively durable weak ties). My concern is rather with electoral and interactive ties. In a political election, citizens participate as voters and the tie between voters and their elected representatives exists only through the election itself. The relations between citizens and their representatives can be very indirect, mediated in particular by political parties and the media. This indirectness can lead to a sense of political alienation among citizens, who feel that politicians are insufficiently responsive to their needs and concerns between elections or cannot be held to account except perhaps at election time. Consequently, there has been increasing emphasis on new methods of political participation to remedy what is sometimes seen as a 'democratic deficit' (see, for example, Somerville, 2005). These new methods mostly involve more interactive relationships between politicians and public, in an attempt to make the ties between them more durable (see, for example, POWER, 2005).

There is now a huge literature on state–citizen interaction. As mentioned in Chapter Two, much of this literature sees nothing problematic about seeking to build good relations between government and people, with particular emphasis on trust and mutual benefit. As also mentioned in Chapter Two, public participation/involvement/engagement has come to be a shibboleth, whose value is not to be questioned. In recent years, this approach has crystallised into the doctrine of '*active citizenship*', which some commentators believe lay at the heart of New Labour's project (see, for example, Marinetto, 2003; McInroy and MacDonald, 2005; Ministry of Justice, 2008). Active citizenship has been described as:

> a process in which a new culture of participation in civic life (including politics and work) is being developed, indicative of a new era in relations between the citizen, services and the local and central state ... active citizenship is about developing a sense of belonging in which people are interested and able to play a role in public affairs and the delivery of public goods (McInroy and MacDonald, 2005, p 6)

What this really means is that, as the state is becoming more active and interventionist, it is expecting its citizens to become more active in return. It is not enough merely for them to vote in elections, they must also involve themselves in community associations, school governing bodies, primary care trusts, housing association boards, neighbourhood watch committees, neighbourhood policing panels, increasing numbers of partnership bodies, consultative forums of various kinds, and so on. And these involvements are not occasional one-offs but typically require regular, lengthy meetings over periods of years. As can be seen from the quote too, participation in political life is not enough either – citizens are also expected to be active in workplaces (volunteering, perhaps?) and in public service delivery (as social entrepreneurs? or active consumers?).[8]

The evidence on public participation tells a different story to the glowing one painted by McInroy and MacDonald. The Commission on Poverty, Participation and Power (CPPP, 2000), for example, found what it described as an overwhelming level of anger, distrust and cynicism among grassroots activists (an alternative term for 'active citizens'). It found meetings conducted in jargon, in surroundings in which people did not feel comfortable; endless paper-based questionnaires from a myriad of initiatives and organisations; plans and reports that did not highlight people's real concerns in plain language; and monitoring and evaluation arrangements – nearly always conducted by independent experts – which did not get to the nub of problems. The Commission concluded that the main problem was that too often people experiencing poverty did not feel respected and too often they were not respected.

It does not seem that the situation has improved much since the CPPP's research. Marilyn Taylor pointed out that communities or members of the public still:

> do not decide the game that is being played; they do not determine the rules of play, the system of refereeing or, indeed, who plays; and the cards are stacked in favour of the more powerful players. In fact, many find they are in the wrong game altogether. (Taylor, 2003, p 123)

Taylor (2003, pp 125–30) goes on to describe the rules of the game in terms of structures and systems of decision making, codes of behaviour and the system of refereeing. Public sector cultures assume that the public will not understand the complexity of the decisions that have to be made, will not be willing to make the sacrifices dictated by limited budgets and by the need for fairness, and will be ruled by self-interest. State–citizen partnerships are overwhelmed by a culture of consensus, which implies that the most powerful view wins out. And state agendas are swamped by monitoring and accountability mechanisms, with the concern being to spend the money 'properly'. The dominance of the audit culture diverts community energies or professionalises how they work, placing power in the hands of those who can interpret the rules – what Bauman has called the 'command economy of thought'. Consequently, government is forcing communities to restructure, centrally reshaping them to become part of the 'solution' instead of articulating the problem. But it is doing this in such a way that the communities cannot win because those who control the resources and possess strategic knowledge have privileged pathways, from which organised community groups are excluded.

Many studies since then have confirmed the stark inequality of power between professionals and public in these interaction processes (see, for example, Shiner et al, 2004; Maguire and Truscott, 2006; Barnes et al, 2007). Non-professional opinion is either dismissed as 'uninformed' or, when clearly informed, it is portrayed as the concoction of undemocratic 'usual suspects' promoting their particular hobby horses (Maguire and Truscott, 2006; Taylor, 2006, p 274). Some studies have also highlighted the inequalities *within* communities that can be exacerbated by public participation: 'those already well connected tend to get better connected' and 'community participation tends to be dominated by a small group of insiders who are disproportionately involved in a large number of governance activities' (Skidmore et al, 2006).

Arguably, the New Labour government's position, at least up to 2007, was one of active disrespect towards communities, and particularly their poorer citizens. For example, its Respect Action Plan stated that: 'Respect cannot be learned, purchased or acquired, it can only be earned' (Respect Task Force, 2006, p 30). It would appear to follow from this that all those who have not managed, for whatever reason, to 'earn' the respect of others, are not entitled to be respected by them. It is also notable that the Plan had nothing to say about the government's own responsibility to 'earn' the respect of others, including its citizens, and particularly those citizens whom it is precisely disrespecting by its policy approach (for further discussion of this issue, see Bannister and Kearns, 2009, Somerville, 2009a, and Chapter Nine of this book).

Given the strength of all these criticisms, it is difficult to understand, first, why citizens (at any rate, less powerful, less 'respectable' ones) would want to work together with government officials of any kind, and second, what kind of political community might be created or developed by such interaction. Indeed, some critics argue that community participation is inevitably limited, relatively ineffective in solving community problems, under-focused on structural issues of poverty and redistribution and over-focused on local-issue or single-issue problems (DeFilippis et al, 2006, pp 683–4). Worse still, participation can actually damage communities, as activists become recruited to local leadership coalitions that do not work in the interests of poorer communities (Purdue, 2005, p 260). Davies (2007) argues further that the inequality of power between state and citizens in many of these interactive arrangements ('partnerships') is so great that the citizens would be more politically effective if they withdrew from such arrangements and organised and acted separately and coercively against governing institutions and elites.

Davies' argument is so important that it is worth examining in detail. He is not denying, of course, that powerful citizens, rich in economic and social capital, can and do work well with governments. The reality, however, is that citizens are unequal in terms of capital of all kinds, and this is what makes political participation problematic. It is necessary, therefore, for disadvantaged groups to organise themselves *outside* of governmental institutions, to build their own forms of bonding and bridging social capital, or they will simply be co-opted to the agendas of the powerful. Also, in order to be effective, disadvantaged groups must act *coercively* against the state, using tactics such as strikes, demonstrations, pickets, blockades and other forms of civil disobedience (Davies, 2007, p 785).

But why might coercion stand a greater chance of success than participation? Davies' research on Hull and Dundee suggests a significant lack of mutual understanding between public managers and community activists. Whereas the former were committed to a neoliberal agenda, concerned with developing an efficient market economy, the latter wanted to see the community developing itself as it saw fit. Basically, managers and activists had different kinds of habitus and therefore had different understandings of what was meant by community empowerment, different interpretations of political community and of the politics of community. For managers, it was all about coordination, 'joining up', achieving consensus and reconciling people to the global neoliberal status quo, whereas for activists it was about democratic community control, eliminating disadvantage and achieving economic and social justice. In these circumstances, it is argued, participation is likely to achieve very little. Certainly, Davies (2007, p 794) reports that in Dundee and Hull the habitus of community activists was maladjusted to the field in which participation occurred, with the result that the activists were very critical of partnership practice. As Davies (2007, p 795) recognises, however, whether a strategy of separation and coercion (which he calls an 'exit-action' strategy) would be any more successful is by no means certain.[9] Much, if not everything, depends upon the context in which participation takes place, particularly the dispositions of state managers and the power they hold relative to that of communities.

At the heart of the problem of participation, therefore, lies a basic inequality between different groups of citizens in the polity. These groups occupy habitus of different kinds and are not meaningfully interconnected. This does not mean, however, that meaningful interconnection is impossible. One can envisage, for example, forms of participation that involve the construction of strong and weak ties across the class divide, and that lead to more authentic forms of political community. Envisaging, however, is not the same as accomplishing. What evidence actually exists of participation that is more productive of political community?

First, there are reasons for thinking that Hull, in particular, may be (or may have been) a special case. Lowndes et al (2002, cited in Barnes et al, 2004, p 5), for example, contrast Hull with Middlesbrough:

> Middlesbrough appears to be part of that gang of North East local authorities (Gateshead, Hartlepool would be others) that although along [*sic*] standing Labour strongholds appear to have embraced both political and managerial modernisation. Hull until recently could be seen as a classic example of a council that

has remained a focus for narrow political control through the Labour party operating through a management system in which officials were cowed by political fear and intrigue. Add to that the relatively well organised and effective civic arrangements of Middlesbrough and the dynamic but divisive arrangements of Hull and the explanation of the difference between the two localities begins to become crystal clear.

Barnes et al (2004) highlight two major factors for explaining productive (rather than destructive) state–citizen interaction: the strategy and culture of the ruling political party; and the supportiveness of the arrangements in place to enable participation to flourish (what they call 'civic infrastructure'). It is notable, however, that, although they discuss in some detail whether the nature of a community affects the amount and kind of participation within it, they do not address the question of the effectiveness of this participation for any particular community.[10]

Barnes et al (2004) believe that, although political participation might not have been worthwhile for disadvantaged groups and communities in Hull, the prospects for such participation may be more promising in other areas. Evidence to support this, however, is lacking. Rather, it would appear that, although some public authorities are more responsive to, and more encouraging, of participation than others, in no case has it been shown that any disadvantaged group or community has, by virtue of its participation in decision-making processes, made a real difference to local policy formation. More recent studies (for example, Barnes et al, 2007, 2008; Ray et al, 2008) have focused on the civic infrastructure for community or citizen participation but have tended to neglect the role of political parties and have not explicitly addressed the question of the circumstances in which it is worthwhile for disadvantaged groups to participate in these structures.[11] The result is a certain depoliticisation of the issues concerned – the concept of a political community, in which each citizen has an equal voice, is peculiarly lacking in these studies.

Of their 17 case studies of public participation, Barnes et al (2007, p 184) acknowledge that many 'seemed to have achieved little in terms of challenging professional expertise or bringing about changes in the ways in which services were delivered'. They mention only two that have produced successful outcomes: a campaign to keep a health centre open and a campaign on fuel poverty. They provide no details on the former case, and it is all too clear in the latter case why the participation succeeded: 'The fuel poverty group was addressing an issue on which battles had been fought and won in securing legislation and the issue at stake was how to develop an implementation strategy' (Barnes et al, 2007, p 181). In other words, this was an issue only of ensuring that already agreed policy was effectively put into practice, not one of initiating a new policy, or abolishing or transforming an existing one.

Given their general lack of effectiveness, one might conclude (following Davies, 2007) that the participating groups in these case studies could have spent their time more fruitfully on other activities, or at least the possibility of such alternative activities might have been considered. This is not the position taken by Barnes et al (2007), however. They recognise that community groups need to operate autonomously, in their own forums, and they are also clearly aware (*pace* Taylor, 2003) that public bodies hold all the cards:

> Despite the 'official' discourses of empowerment or partnership, of consumerism or stakeholding, which pervaded the language of policy documents and, in many cases, of the 'strategic' managers we interviewed at the outset of the project, it seemed that public bodies managed to retain and even enlarge their power. This was evident in the power of public officials to constitute their public in a way that best fitted their needs (rather than to engage with pre-existing and more potentially troublesome groups); the power to set the rules and norms of engagement; and in many cases to set the agenda of what issues were, and were not, to be opened up to public deliberation. They also had the power to decide what legitimacy to afford to different voices and different modes of expression; and ultimately, of course, the power to decide whether or not to take account of the views expressed. (Barnes et al, 2007, pp 190–1)

Above all, on the issue of material and/or institutional change, they recognise that: 'The evidence across our case studies suggests that such change is not much in evidence as an outcome of new deliberative practices' (Barnes et al, 2007, pp 201–2). In spite of all this, they insist that it is possible in some cases for officials and publics to move closer together over time (they cite the example of a lesbian and gay forum), though they do not discuss the possible advantages and disadvantages of this (for the lesbian and gay community in particular – see ***Box 2.4*** in Chapter Two). They report that 'we can see officials becoming more closely aligned with "lay" perspectives, perhaps because of closer contact with the public through the process of deliberation, or perhaps because of their own experience or political allegiances' (Barnes et al, 2007, p 194). The officials involved in participation processes often share some form of identification with those they are seeking to engage with, for example, as women, gay or lesbian, or as members of the same community. Barnes et al (2007, p 195) recognise that this means that they are more likely to come into conflict with their employer, but they do not point out that the likely winner in such a conflict will be the employer, and therefore fail to draw the conclusion that the involvement of such sympathetic officials is not likely to make much difference in most cases.

Barnes et al (2007, p 202) also suggest that political participation is more likely to be successful where the participants are members of organised social groups,

> mobilised by shared frameworks of meaning and action, developed in alternative public spaces. It is notable that where groups with a prior existence (formed around community activism, social movement politics or in other alternative public spaces) were invited to participate as stakeholders in a particular policy or service area, deliberation was more likely to produce challenges to the status quo and some element of transformation – if not in terms of quantifiable outcomes, then at least in terms of attitudes and orientations of public officials.

Here it is not mentioned that the public officials concerned are likely to be those in the front line ('street-level bureaucrats'), not the senior managers who wield the most power, and therefore the institutional transformation may be only superficial. It is also important to note the fact that these groups participate by *invitation*, which suggests that they are seen to be important enough to be singled out for consideration. One could add that the most important such groups are political parties, because they are organised specifically to win elections to public decision-making assemblies, but political parties are rarely asked to participate in joint state–citizen decision-making forums and may even be explicitly excluded from such forums.

The silence of much of the public participation literature on political parties is deafening (but for a notable exception, see the work of Copus, particularly Copus, 2001). It is as if someone has decided in advance that such participation should be kept strictly separate from the core business of politics. In reality, however, political parties are the main type of organised social group that participate in politics, and they participate directly and profoundly in key citizen assemblies. In contrast, the multitude of forums in the participation literature are strictly peripheral to the concerns of these assemblies. The public officials who serve these forums may see themselves as accountable to their communities but their more powerful accountability is to their political masters in local or national government. It is no wonder, then, that participation in such forums should prove so ineffective for communities. A more attractive way forward, in addition to the forms of direct action mentioned above by Davies (2007), would be for disadvantaged communities to lobby leading politicians and political parties more directly, and possibly, in time, to form their own political parties. This possibility, however, has to be weighed against the arguments that lobbying by disadvantaged communities has traditionally had little effect and that rank-and-file members of political parties these days have little influence over government policy (hence the decline in party membership). In these circumstances, it seems that such communities have no alternative but to resort to forms of direct action.

This problem could, of course, be a consequence of UK-centredness. In spite of a certain devolution of power to Scotland and Wales, the UK (or, at any rate, Britain) remains a highly centralised state, with a hugely dominant position in its political community. Although British citizens generally like to believe that their national assembly, the House of Commons, has supreme authority, the reality is that, over the years, the power of the people's representatives has gradually seeped away and become concentrated in the hands of the executive, that is, the Cabinet and, ultimately, the Prime Minister. The power of political parties has declined correspondingly, as governments feel free to ignore party policy as they wish. Consequently, the membership of political parties falls, along with the turnout of voters on election day.

In other parts of the world, however, things can look very different. In Kerala and West Bengal (in India) and in Porto Alegre (in Brazil), for example, it has been argued that the political participation of disadvantaged groups has been 'directly linked to the pursuit of redistributive policies that have had pro-poor outcomes' (Hickey and Mohan, 2004, p 162). Because these groups have worked through their own political parties, such as the Communist Party of India (CPI) and the Workers Party in Brazil (PT), they have increased the 'political space' outside state institutions within which poor groups can mobilise. In the absence of such a party with its own programme for social justice, participation inevitably risks becoming routinised, captured and co-opted, reproducing the power of existing local and national elites. With the existence of such a party, however, collective action can be effective *both* in cooperation with the state (as in participatory budgeting in Brazil – see Gret and Sintomer, 2005) *and* in opposition to the state, as recommended by Davies (2007).[12]

The argument in this section suggests, therefore, that building linking social capital is an effective way to develop a fair and open political community only if and when the citizens themselves are well organised in their own political parties on an equal footing with the state and its representatives. The problem here is that, in many countries, including the UK, the politics of participation is dominated by the state, which interpellates participants as 'active citizens', in much the same way as, more generally, it fashions the imagined community of a nation out of those over whom it has authority. Also, participation seems in practice to be overwhelmingly local and subject to the dictates of national policy. Consequently, the politics of community in these countries tends to focus not on the nature and (re)production of political community as such, but rather on how local communities can or cannot be recruited to serve the ends of government. The literature on political participation then has value insofar as it shows the lack of meaningful interconnectedness in modern political society – in other words, the political community imagined by both communitarians and cosmopolitans, by both nationalists and governmentalists, stands revealed as seriously divided, if indeed it exists at all.

There is a sense, nevertheless, in which the beloved community could be said to be participationist, if participationism is taken to involve every community member taking part freely, on an equal basis, in the affairs of the community, either on their own account or through their representatives, as a necessary means to fulfil their highest potential. The beloved community can be, and maybe has to be, cosmopolitan, socialist and democratic.

Conclusion

This chapter has considered the idea of political community, originally defined as a group of persons who recognise a shared authority within a shared territory. The chapter has gone on to question whether in fact this authority needs to be a state. In Bourdieusian terms, political community is a feature of habitus, related to class and culture, while the state has the characteristics of a field. In principle, therefore, a political community could exist in the absence of a state. It could be defined more precisely as an embodied or imagined group of persons (or community) who recognise one another as members of the same group for the purposes of making decisions for the group as a whole. Clearly, there has to be a decision-making body of some kind, but this body does not have to be a state.

Given the problems with nationalism, the chapter examined alternative ways of realising political community in the modern world. These ways were classified according to whether they emphasised bonding social capital, bridging social capital or linking social capital – that is, depending upon whether they saw political community as held together primarily by strong ties, weak ties, or on-off ties between citizens and state. These three approaches were identified with communitarianism, cosmopolitanism and participationism, respectively. It was argued that there were problems with each approach but it was suggested that these problems might be resolvable by finding the right balance between them.

In the case of communitarianism, the main problem is that it has not succeeded in transcending a nationalist position, and it is difficult to see how it can do so unless it begins to take on board arguments emerging from the other approaches. The basic point is that, if the existence of a political community requires only strong ties, then it is practically inevitable that the boundaries of each such community will be limited in size – the imagining of a global community of communities (nations) of communities looks far-fetched, to say the least. In the case of cosmopolitanism, the problem is that weak ties are simply not strong enough to hold a political community together, so, as people connect with different people in different ways, political communities will lack generally agreed boundaries, and this will result in conflicting allegiances and fragmentation of decision making. As with communitarianism, the prospect of a global political community, held together by general recognition of our obligations to one another as equal citizens of the world, seems a long way off, even though some believe they can detect the emergence of social forms and collective actors that will eventually bring about the existence of such a community.

The case of participationism is rather different. Here political community is accepted for what it is, namely an unfinished project to reform or transform a deeply divided and problematic society in such a way as to achieve a more meaningful interconnectedness of citizens. There are many obstacles, however, that have to be overcome in the realisation of this project. First, the institutionalised nature of social inequality in many countries (Wilkinson and Pickett, 2009) results in the institutionalisation (or possibly exit or burn-out) of the participants themselves. Second, the participants typically have no clear, stable role in the participation process – for example, it is not clear whether the purpose of the participation is to develop strong ties or weak ties or something else. Third, participationists encounter a dilemma concerning whether to take part *within* state structures ('partnership') or to take direct action *outside* such structures. Evidence suggests, at least in the UK, that participation in partnerships is rarely worthwhile for poorer citizens, and does little to develop a fair and open political community. On the other hand, there is also little evidence that forms of direct action have been very effective either. Outside the UK, however, it is notable that disadvantaged citizens organised in their own political parties have won important victories, at least at local level (or state level within a federal system).

Overall, then, the search for political community requires striving for a balance in at least two different ways: between participation inside and outside state structures; and between the forging of strong and weak ties.

In the first case, the point at which the balance is drawn depends entirely on the context within which the participation takes place (specifically, the habitus of the participants and their relationship to the political field) – different strategies and tactics will be required in different contexts. In the second case, what seems to be required above all is a worldwide expansion in the numbers of both strong and weak ties, not necessarily material (as this would be limited by practical considerations) but imagined or virtual, as made possible, for example, by the internet. We already speak of a global community, but currently this is no more than an aspiration. New weak ties are needed in terms of law and regulation, and new strong ties in terms of a sense of our common humanity, particularly in the face of global threats such as climate change. Participation is required to abolish the social inequality that fractures political community, while new strong and weak ties are required to achieve meaningful global interconnectedness. We must therefore be, at one and the same time, communitarians, cosmopolitans and participationists.

Notes

[1] Strictly speaking, perhaps, we should say 'fields' of the state. Jessop (2002, p 145), for example, defines the state as: 'an ensemble of socially embedded, socially regularised, and strategically selective institutions, organisations, social forces and activities organised around (or at least actively involved in) making collectively binding decisions for an imagined political community'.

[2] It goes without saying that nationalism is incompatible with the beloved community because it assigns priority to those of one's own nation above all others.

[3] This is obviously to be distinguished from communalism in the Indian subcontinent, which is a form of sectarianism based on religion or ethnicity.

[4] Actually, some types of commune have been strongly associated with nationalism – for example, kibbutzim with Zionism, Mondragon cooperatives with Basque nationalism and so on (Melnyk, 1985, pp 53, 101).

[5] Nazism itself was a national socialist project, in that it attempted to build a homogeneous Aryan nation (*ein Volk*), free from racial or other contamination, and involved a system in which capital was firmly subordinated to the interests of the *Volk*, embodied in the person of the *Führer*.

[6] This point will be taken up later.

[7] Patrimonial ties are not necessarily corrupt – for example, the politician may be convinced of the justice of the citizen's cause, or may be sponsored by a particular interest group (on interest groups, see Jordan and Maloney, 2007).

[8] It is already becoming apparent that the coalition's concept of the 'Big Society' is an extension of this governmental approach.

[9] Davies cites only one successful example, namely that of the anti-poll tax movement of 1989–92, where coercive tactics included non-payment, courtroom

disruption, physical defence of property against bailiffs, mass demonstrations and a riot against police and property in Trafalgar Square.

[10] Effectiveness is measured only in terms of outcomes such as percentage of council tax collected and percentage of pupils achieving five or more A to C grade GCSEs – and for the local authority as a whole, not for particular communities.

[11] The term 'citizen-centred governance' (Barnes et al, 2008) is particularly ambiguous and misleading, on a number of grounds: first, the governance of a community is confused with the governance of an organisation, so that the specifically political meaning of governance is lost; second, the term 'citizen-centred' suggests that the governance is working in the interests of the citizens concerned, but this is not necessarily the case, particularly where poorer citizens are concerned; and third, the structures of participation discussed are not necessarily involving people as citizens but rather as service users and consumers.

[12] Such opposition is practised, for example, by the MKSS (Mazdoor Kisan Shakti Sangathan – Organisation for the Emporwerment of Workers and Farmers) based in Rajasthan – confronting corruption, using public hearings to locally verify official accounts, and large-scale protests to get rights of access to government information (Williams, 2004, p 99).

Summary

The politics of community is a complex and vexed issue, involving much confusion and misunderstanding. This chapter attempts to clarify the issue by analysing the main ideological perspectives involved and by relating this analysis to distinctions made in the previous chapter between different functions of social capital. Because of its topical nature, much of the chapter is devoted to criticising participationism, as expressed in the doctrine of '*active citizenship*'. This argument can be extended to include the current (2010) coalition government's concept of the 'Big Society', where citizens are increasingly expected to assume responsibility for their own lives. The Big Society is, in effect, nothing less than the political community of the nation as a whole, which the government is now interpellating to take over responsibility for public services and public affairs. Since this is clearly impracticable, it follows that the beloved community must remain as far away as ever.

Questions for discussion

- What is wrong with nationalism?

- Why did socialism fail? Or has it not been given a fair chance?

- Is cosmopolitanism realistic? If so, how far can it be developed?

- What is wrong with active citizenship? Why doesn't it work?

- Can a balance be struck between the three main approaches to political community (between strong and weak ties, and between participating and not participating)? If so, where does the balance lie?

Further reading

Barnes, M., Newman, J. and Sullivan, H. (2007) *Power, participation and political renewal: Case studies in public participation*, Bristol: The Policy Press.

Davies, J. (2007) 'The limits of partnership: an exit-action strategy for local democratic inclusion', *Political Studies,* vol 55, pp 779-800.

Fine, R. (2007) *Cosmopolitanism*, London: Routledge.

Frazer, E. (1999) *The problem of communitarian politics: Unity and conflict*, Oxford: Oxford University Press.

Melnyk, G. (1985) *In search of community: From Utopia to co-operative society*, Montreal-Buffalo: Black Rose Books.

Governmental approaches to community

Overview

UK governmental approaches to community since the Second World War can be described as mainly neo-colonial and increasingly neoliberal. This involves:

- seeing communities as needing improvement, modernisation, regeneration, renewal, and so on – basically to be remade or remoulded in the image of the (neo-)colonisers; and:
- interpellating community members as responsible for their own futures, ensuring that communities are better equipped to prosper in the global market place.

The problems with 'active citizenship' identified in Chapter Three are explored in detail in relation to governmental approaches to community engagement/involvement/participation/empowerment. It is argued that shifts have occurred on three fronts:

- in the recognition and understanding of communities and their needs;
- in the nature and extent of state intervention deemed to be necessary and desirable; and
- in government perceptions of its relationship with communities, particularly in ensuring that communities' needs are met and in involving communities in their own development.

The core argument in the chapter is that governmental agendas increasingly offer a vision of empowerment to communities that is largely illusory. This flaw continues with the coalition government's vision of the 'Big Society'.

Historical background

In the aftermath of the Second World War, the emphasis was on rebuilding the nation after the wholesale destruction of the economy and built environment by the ravages of warfare. Mass house building was the order of the day, along with mass health provision and mass education, reflecting the mass manufacturing industry that underpinned Britain's status as a global imperial power. The needs of individual communities were subsumed under this national agenda. The government did have a concept of a 'balanced community' (in the New Towns Act 1946), but this was understood simply as a neighbourhood in which every family (households were understood entirely in terms of families) had access to employment, housing, schools and health services.

This neglect of local community began to change in the 1960s. Poverty was rediscovered in the 1950s (see Townsend, 1979), and it was noticed that it appeared to be more prevalent in certain areas, such as inner cities. Consequently, from the 1950s onwards, governments promoted 'special initiatives' to deal with this problem, although these initiatives were largely disconnected from mainstream government policy (Hastings, 2003, pp 87–8). The assumption behind these initiatives was that both the causes and the solutions of the problem lay in the neighbourhood itself, and were primarily physical and cultural.[1] Basically, the local environment was of poor quality, and the residents were believed to lack a work ethic or to lack appropriate skills. The possibility that there might be causes external to the neighbourhood, such as long-term industrial decline, rogue absentee landlords, housing-market collapse and even harmful government policies, was not entertained.

Probably the most well-known examples of such initiatives were the Urban Aid Programme and Community Development Projects (CDPs) launched in 1968. Like the other initiatives, these assumed that the 'deprived' were responsible for their own deprivation and therefore needed only 'capacity building' in order to be rescued. The CDPs were unique, however, in embedding university researchers within the projects themselves, and their research soon showed that capacity building on its own would not be enough to turn these areas around and that more 'structural' changes were required, such as the creation of well-paid jobs in new types of industry, substantial investment in housing and environmental improvements and, above all, more political clout for the communities living in these inner-urban areas. Since the governments of the time were unwilling to adopt such recommendations, because of the costs and political risks involved, the funding for CDPs was stopped in 1976 (for more information, see Loney, 1979).

The election in 1979 of a more self-consciously neoliberal government under Margaret Thatcher led to a more explicit emphasis on the role of market forces in developing communities.[2] There was a continuing emphasis on the role of government in the development of appropriate physical infrastructure – for example, through urban development corporations (especially the London Docklands Development Corporation) and the Community Programme. However, there was now a recognition of certain *external* causes of underdevelopment, namely:

- *Public sector monopolies*. It was argued that lack of competition led to inefficient, unresponsive and insensitive public services. Basically, the less powerful the service users, the worse the service was likely to be.
- *Local authorities*. These were particularly blamed, perhaps not entirely fairly, for the failures of previous area-based initiatives and for generally poor performance. They were regarded by Conservative ministers as excessively bureaucratic, mostly incompetent and often corrupt.[3]
- *Deindustrialisation*. The Conservatives recognised that long-term industrial restructuring in Britain's older cities was a key cause of the problems of urban communities.

In the light of this diagnosis, the Thatcher government attached particular importance to economic initiatives that would encourage employers to invest in inner-city areas (for example, Enterprise Zones) and would open up labour markets generally. It also encouraged competition within the public services (for example, through compulsory competitive tendering), as well as the transfer of publicly owned assets to the private sector (privatisation).

Later in the 1980s, and even more so under John Major, the Conservative government began to emphasise the social market as well as the private market. This showed itself in a range of partnerships with local authorities and with communities. These largely involved so-called 'challenge funding' initiatives (such as City Challenge), where local authorities competed with one another for substantial pots of government funding to address urban problems, and Estates Renewal Challenge Fund and Single Regeneration Budget, where local communities were engaged directly in planning and implementing the regeneration of their areas.

As these policies developed, it can be seen that increasing emphasis was placed on involving communities. Although they continued to be directed at making the community fit into the wider economy and society (for example, in terms of employability and acceptance of market rule), the initiatives also began to recognise that community members are themselves actors in the market and have important roles, for example, in holding public authorities to account and in helping to improve public services.

By 1997, then, government was beginning to see the potential of community for revitalising public services and regenerating poorer urban areas. However, the role of community in public policy had not yet been explicitly recognised – it remained essentially undeveloped.[4] Evaluations of urban policy up to 1997 suggested that little improvement had occurred in the most deprived areas and that there had been little change in the focus of mainstream budgets (ODPM, 2002a).[5] Lupton (2004) suggested that areas had been improved but not regenerated – that is, their underlying ('structural'?) problems remained. Other commentators noted that major divisions within communities had not yet been addressed – for example, on race and gender (Brownill and Darke, 1998), on social class (Page, 2000) and on disability (Edwards, 2003).

New Labour's approach

This situation was to change significantly with the advent of the New Labour government in 1997. Suddenly, community was placed at the heart of public policy.[6] This can be seen as a natural progression from the approach of the previous government, in three ways. First, New Labour, like its predecessor, saw communities as actors in the market, helping to shape that market in their own interest, through the choices they make as individual and collective consumers. To that extent, New Labour continued the neoliberal project that it inherited. Second, New Labour followed the Major government in recognising that community involvement can add value or legitimacy to government action, because communities may know better what needs to be done or what is most likely to work in their communities, and because community involvement can facilitate the formation and shaping of public opinion and of collective action to the benefit of government itself. Third, New Labour recognised that communities should be seen as partners in governance, alongside the public and private sectors, working to improve public services and rebuild local politics. This is shown in its support for the development of, and working in partnership with, the voluntary and community sector (Lehning, 1998; Hall, 1999; Mohan and Mohan, 2002; Page, 2006, cited in Thomson and Caulier-Grice, 2007, p 16). Although characterised by some commentators (for example, Giddens, 1998) as a new 'Third Way' (based on the 'third' sector – the voluntary and community sector), this is in fact quite traditional and perfectly compatible with a neoliberal approach.[7]

There are other respects, however, in which New Labour differed from previous governments. These can be broadly identified as its communitarianism, its neo-colonialism and its strategic interventionism. The communitarianism manifested itself in a number of ways. Essentially, it followed Etzioni, as discussed in Chapter Three, by seeing Britain as a 'community of communities', so making it a form of nationalism. The envisaged constituent communities of Britain, however, were essentially vague: they could be nations in themselves (such as England, Scotland and Wales), they could be regions (mainly of England), they could be counties (for example, Cornwall and the shires), they could be cities, boroughs or districts, they could be parishes or towns, they could be ethnic groups (typically minorities, but possibly also local white working-class groups), they could be interest groups (for example, the 'business community'), they could be faith based (for example, Christian or Muslim) or identity based (for example, lesbian or gay) – or anything else that the government deemed to recognise as a community. New Labour emphasised above all the *inclusion* of all these communities within the overall national community and their *cohesion* with one another. Cohesion requires active communities and active citizens, while inclusion requires a correspondingly active, interventionist state (see discussion of integrated cohesive communities in Chapter One). Essentially, New Labour's communitarianism involved the *self-help of social groups*, and the role of government was seen as one of removing the barriers to such self-help (identified variously as lack of skills or fear of crime) and giving communities a leg up – or rather a hand up. As with Etzioni, therefore, this amounted to a liberal and nationalist communitarianism.

New Labour's second innovation, namely its neo-colonialism, followed straightforwardly from this. It aimed to strengthen community voice and strengthen government responsiveness to voice, to build 'consensus' and 'trust' between government and communities. It had a 'civilising mission' (McLaughlin, 2002), in which the disciplinary powers of the state (the so-called 'nanny' or *dirigiste* state) were to be used firmly to ensure that people behaved in the 'right' way. Indeed, behaving in the right way was seen as a condition for being eligible for a hand up, that is, for social inclusion. Finally, the discipline itself is of course that of the labour market and of the rule of law that supports that market. New Labour went further, however, in expecting that citizens should be actively seeking not only work but also opportunities for volunteering, 'taking responsibility' and other forms of 'participation' and so-called 'active citizenship'.

Thirdly, New Labour's approach to community involved a new strategic application of the concept of social capital (see, for example, Halpern, 2005). It saw the government's role as one of providing infrastructure that would facilitate the growth of social capital, and such infrastructure could be physical and institutional, involving, in particular, civic and political opportunity structures – in short, the conditions in which social capital can thrive (Maloney et al, 2000; Lowndes et al, 2006). What this all means is explained further below.

A key publication for understanding New Labour's approach to community is *Firm Foundations* (CLG, 2004). Here the government saw the role of citizens and community groups as one of influencing their quality of life, shaping the services that affect them, and contributing to sustainable development in the wider world. The process of 'government through community' (Rose, 1996) was seen as one of strategic targeting of communities for government interventions (for example, through the National Strategy for Neighbourhood Renewal – SEU, 2001) and making them responsible for implementing government policies. *Firm Foundations* represented the first clear statement of government commitment to community development. It recognised a number of community needs, such as for meeting spaces, seedcorn funding, access to development and learning support (from community anchor organisations), and a forum or network. It further recognised that community forums/networks needed to be open to all community members, inclusive of all sections of the community and encouraging of participation by as many community members as possible. Learning and development support was seen as necessary to equip people for active citizenship and engagement – that is, to build their capacity to engage with government policy: 'Activities, resources and support that strengthen the skills, abilities and confidence of people and community groups to take effective action and leading roles in the development of their communities' (CLG, 2004, p 7), for example, through community empowerment networks (CENs).[8] The emphasis on community anchor organisations was particularly important. These were multi-purpose, resident-controlled organisations, involving all sections of the community and facilitating its development (CLG, 2004, p 19). They included broad-based community associations, well-established residents' associations, development trusts, tenant management organisations, neighbourhood partnerships/networks/federations, village halls, faith-based organisations, schools, New Deal for Communities partnerships, Single Regeneration Budget successor bodies, neighbourhood watch groups and possibly organisations with a cultural or sports focus (CLG, 2004, p 20).

Firm Foundations was followed by *The Community Development Challenge* (CLG, 2006a). This publication developed the argument in the earlier paper so as to take more account of the role of the community development worker. It suggested that building social capital could not be led by the community directly: 'community-led *as mediated by the community development worker*' (CLG, 2006a, p 23). It argued that such mediation was necessary because 'what the community wants or needs' is complex. The role of the community development worker was then characterised as one of developing and supporting community organisations, developing and improving community services and facilitating community access to resources and influence on policy makers (CLG, 2006a, p 15). Above all, the paper emphasised the need to adopt a *strategic long-term approach* to community development: 'it is not clear either in government policy or in community development theory what the specific role of community development as an occupation or a set of methods needs to be in order to achieve the social vision currently shared by government policy and community development values' (CLG, 2006a, p 29). This approach involved coordination and long-term investment by all agencies concerned and an arena where this coordination could be accomplished (CLG, 2006a, p 22), using local action planning (CLG, 2004).

These ideas were taken further in subsequent government publications. The Cabinet Office (2007), for example, allocated £515 million for the purposes of supporting community organisations to build their capacity, to become more effective, to help them transform public services and to give them, and those they work for, a greater voice. Following the government's belated discovery of '*community empowerment*'[9] (CLG, 2006b, 2007a – but see Blears, 2003, as a trail-blazer for this discovery), a major White Paper (CLG, 2008b) proposed a range of measures to serve these purposes. These included special funding for community enterprises,[10] better funding for small community groups, a way for local communities to hold neighbourhood policing teams to account, forms of support for involving young people (for example, youth councils, young mayors) and community contracts (between communities and service providers – see, for example, CLG, 2008c, on local charters). The overriding image conveyed by this White Paper is one of the active citizen, who acts as a volunteer in the community, who seeks better information with a view to action, who has a real influence over policy decisions, who holds public officials and elected representatives to account for what they do, who seeks swift and fair redress when things go wrong, who is willing to stand for public office (elected or appointed) and who is prepared (in cooperation with fellow citizens) to take on responsibility for running local services. This set of ideas very much prefigured the 'Big Society' idea of the current government (Conservative Party, 2010).

Critique of New Labour (and the Big Society)

There are good reasons, however, for being sceptical about the practicability of the proposals in these government papers (and therefore of the Big Society now). As mentioned in Chapter Three, research to date does not tend to support the optimism of the main political parties on the question of active citizenship. CLG (2008b), for example, shows detailed awareness of the nature and extent of public disengagement with politics but little understanding of the reasons for this disengagement. All the Labour government papers seemed to confuse three different types of involvement (as service users, as community members and as citizens), or at least to assume that there are correlations between these different types. This is not helpful if one wants to understand why people get involved or what they are likely to get involved in. Further, the measures proposed seem far from sufficient to bring about the active citizens that the government said it wanted to create – or at least there is nothing to show what effect the measures were likely to have (Taylor and Wilson, 2006, politely referred to this as 'the implementation gap'). What small community groups need most, and what they have pressed for most strongly for years (see, for example, Thomson and Caulier-Grice, 2007), is long-term core funding, but this need was only just beginning to be recognised by the Labour government at the time of its demise. Before that, radical proposals for reform, such as massive transfer of assets to communities, double devolution (Mulgan and Bury, 2006) or right to recall elected representatives, were repeatedly watered down when processed through the machinery of government.

These criticisms can be taken much further (see also Chapter Three). For example, although politicians on the right as well as the left now claim that they want to involve as many people as possible, they must be aware that it is likely that only a small minority will ever do so. In reality, governments generally are primarily interested in involving people who can play a 'constructive' role within the established system, for example, by assuming responsibility for governance tasks and representing their communities effectively on decision-making and consultative bodies. Labour's emphasis on community anchors and strategic partners both implied and reinforced this. To develop communities, however, community *action* is required more than community representation – action by the community on its own or in concert with other parties. Rather than promoting such action, however, the Labour government seemed more inclined to control it and to channel the energy involved into its own projects, programmes and so on. It is not yet clear, at the time of writing, whether the Conservative/Liberal Democrat coalition government will be able to resist such temptations. Meanwhile, evaluations of government participation programmes continue to find little evidence that community involvement in them makes any significant difference. For example, an evaluation of Community Participation Programmes in England found that 'there was little evidence as yet of them [through Community Empowerment Networks] influencing the "mainstream"' (Taylor, 2006, p 272; see also Taylor et al, 2005); an evaluation of the government's support for the voluntary and community sector found that its primary focus was on support for service providers rather than on community development or civil renewal (Macmillan et al, 2007, p 4); and an evaluation of the Communities First programme in Wales reported that 'there is little evidence of community influence over budgets and service delivery, and no evidence of bending mainstream services to reflect the partnership process' (Adamson and Bromiley, 2008, p xv).

It seems clear from these evaluations that, throughout its rule, the Labour government's main purpose for community involvement was that of improving public services (as set out most clearly in ODPM, 2005), and community development came a poor second to this. This could explain why there was no long-term investment in community development as such, no specified arenas in which such development was to take place, little evidence of any effective local action planning, no evidence of attempting to reach a shared vision with communities (except perhaps a vision of quality public services!) and no encouragement of wider community action that might challenge governmental policy or practice. The government professed to want active citizens, but the actions it wanted those citizens to take were primarily those that produced what it regarded as more efficient and effective services. Arguably, however, this reveals a narrow, consumerist understanding of citizenship, in which political decisions are reduced to the governance of the relationship between producers and consumers. Fundamental political issues such as climate change, redistribution through tax and spend, membership of the European Union, waging war, migration, greenhouse gas emissions, industrial relations and the rule of law are all thereby excluded from the active citizenship agenda. It is little wonder, then, that citizens are increasingly disengaged from this depoliticised politics.[11] It remains to be seen whether the Conservatives' idea of a 'Big Society' will be any different (see concluding chapter).

Even in its own terms, however, New Labour's approach to community never seemed likely to succeed – that is, it was not clear that services would actually improve in the ways it suggested. For example, community involvement itself might not turn out to be cost effective, in many cases local people might not be any better at running local services, or local communities might decide to run their services in ways of which the government did not approve. Beyond that, the 'hand up' that the government offered to communities typically did not look attractive enough to make it worth their while to respond. There remained a huge gap between the lived experience of poorer communities and the government's understanding of that experience. It seems unlikely that the new coalition government will do any better. Arguably, its leaders are less in touch with poorer communities than Labour was. They may be inclined to be less controlling and more keen on providing incentives to participate, but there is little evidence that they have the understanding of how to work constructively with communities.

Managerial and social coordination – 'joining up' and community cohesion

Finally, the Labour government's approach to improving services was incoherent. It confused two different kinds of 'joining up' or coordination, which I shall call managerial and social coordination. Managerial coordination is to do with the 'joining up' of services delivered to communities, while social coordination refers to building the social capital of communities. To complicate the issue, both kinds of coordination occur across different scales (local, regional and national). For Labour, managerial coordination was to be achieved through a wide variety of 'partnerships' and was focused particularly at local level, through local strategic and other partnerships and neighbourhood management. Over the years, however, research has shown that such coordination has had little success (Bogdanor, 2005). Partners may sometimes appear to work well together but there is little evidence of positive outcomes from the partnership itself (Percy-Smith, 2006). According to Davies (2009, p 80), this is because 'joining-up efforts disproportionately emphasise technical, managerial and cultural problems, ignoring the fragmentary effects of persistent value conflict'. As a result, there exists only what he calls a 'shallow consensus', and so-called 'silo' practices remain unchallenged within the partnerships. The value conflicts that Davies describes are not only between community activists and public managers (discussed in Chapter Three) but also between professionals of different kinds, such as between health service managers and those emphasising economic and physical regeneration, and between competing priorities (related to different services) of income redistribution, physical development or human capital. In evaluating crime and disorder reduction partnerships (CDRPs) in particular, Loveday (2006, p 120) was even more critical, arguing that the separate performance management regimes for public service providers that Labour introduced could actually 'undermine the partnership approach it wishes to establish at CDRP level' because they dictated conflicting priorities for local partnership members, for example, on education, health and crime reduction. In a detailed study of public officials and community involvement in local services in Haringey, Ray et al (2008, p 54) concluded that: 'While officials valued a diversity of engagement structures to suit different purposes and to engage different communities, there was also a pervasive feeling that there were too many structures with no overall local co-ordination.'[12]

To be fair to government, it is necessary to be careful not to over-generalise about management coordination initiatives. Evaluation of Labour's neighbourhood management pathfinders, for example, consistently found modest improvements in services, in involving communities and in resident satisfaction, with positive effects on wider mainstream services and on neighbouring areas (SQW, 2008a). Similarly, evaluation of the New Deal for Communities (NDC), which aimed to join up services in housing, environment, crime, health, education and employment, found improvements in the first three of these, though slower progress on the latter three (Lawless, 2008; see also CLES, 2008). In the case of the NDC, however, it is not clear to what extent the improvements were due to community involvement, or even to what extent they were due to improved management coordination itself – they could, for example, have been simply the consequence of increased investment and expenditure in the NDC areas. This is not to say that there are not some NDCs in which communities have been involved in a positive way, contributing to their own development – for example, Marsh Farm in Luton (Wainwright, 2003) – but it seems that such community self-development is atypical.

If the achievements of managerial coordination are so meagre, one may question why it should be regarded as so important by government. Davies (2009) suggests that it can be explained as a historical response to the political defeat of the Left in the 1980s:

> Defeated in struggle, organized labour, the Left in the Labour
> Party and Left-leaning local authorities abandoned confrontation
> and their belief in state-led economic development and made
> their peace with capital. After the late 1980s, they accepted that
> growth should be market-led and later that social inclusion
> should be pursued through a mixture of supply-side enticements
> to investors, investment in human capital, means-tested benefits
> and community mobilization (Bevir, 2005, ch 2). (Davies, 2009,
> p 92)

For those so defeated, partnerships between public, private and third sectors seemed preferable to being left out in the cold. Modest improvements were regarded as better than nothing at all. This does not really explain, however, why such partnerships should prove attractive to governments generally, and this point is explored further below.

Social coordination, as mentioned above, is about building the social capital of communities. This was a key aim of Labour's community participation programmes: 'these policies sought to build bonding social capital within communities, bridging social capital across communities and linking social capital between communities and decision-makers/ service providers' (Taylor, 2006, p 271). The distinction between the three functions of social capital was expressed here in Labour's concept of a strong, cohesive, active community: a strong community is one with strong bonds, a cohesive community is one that has built bridges across its different groups and sections, and an active community is one that helps itself and/or participates in governmental arenas. In practice, Labour policy on communities focused almost exclusively on bridging social capital through its policies on community cohesion and on linking social capital through its policies on active citizenship and democratic renewal.

The term 'community cohesion' originally appeared in response to the 2001 disturbances in Bradford, Oldham and Burnley mentioned in Chapter One, and referred to the need to resolve alleged 'cultural' differences between communities in these areas. After that, however, the concept was extended to include differences of any kind within a community, not just those of race or ethnicity. SQW (2008b, p 5), for example, in a study of five neighbourhood management pathfinders (NMPs), found that most of them have 'taken the view that the more important cohesion issues relate to age, gender and territory rather than to race and ethnicity'. However, SQW felt that some of the NMPs were not taking race equality seriously enough:

> Part of the core definition of community cohesion calls for those from different backgrounds to 'have similar life opportunities' and be able to 'trust local institutions to act fairly' [see CLG, 2008a]. This relates directly to the work of neighbourhood managers in improving services in their areas for all. Yet our research suggests that the extent of information about both the quality of services at a local level, and who is accessing them, is highly variable and many cohesion projects do not directly address this.[13] (SQW, 2008b, pp 5–6, 31)

Broadly speaking, Labour's approach to community cohesion was to leave it to local authorities to set local strategic frameworks for promoting such cohesion, following central government guidance (LGA, 2004; LGA and IDeA, 2006). A study of six local authority districts by Ipsos MORI (2007) found a wide variety of activities, including supporting new arrivals, developing English-language skills, creating neighbourhood forums and local associations to facilitate interaction between groups from different backgrounds, and strengthening organisations that could act as community anchors (that is, those seen as best placed to understand local issues, most likely to be trusted by community members and most likely to engage with so-called 'hard-to-reach' groups). Many of these activities are no doubt useful in their way (for example, English-language classes), but it is not yet clear how effective they have been in achieving government objectives. SQW (2008b, p 25) noted that there was a fall in the proportion of people in all five of its case study areas who believed racial harassment to be a problem, but it was not possible to say whether or not this was due to the work of the Pathfinder in the area. It appears, however, that actions to defuse situations that might increase tension between communities (such as British National Party (BNP) marches in Bermondsey and mosque-related issues in Westminster and Stockton) were effective.

There are serious problems with the community cohesion agenda, which, if not addressed, are more or less guaranteed to ensure its long-term failure. The first is its notion of a strong, cohesive, active community that was criticised in Chapter One. This notion assumes the absence of an analysis of the problems and value conflicts that beset communities in Britain today: it alludes to those problems, but in such a way as to depoliticise them and turn them into problems of municipal management. It's a *'why can't we all just get on?'* approach, which attempts to divert attention from deep divisions of social class, political belief, gender, generation and territory, and from fundamental disagreements on foreign policy, immigration, religion, taxation and so on. Second, the agenda has no clearly defined purpose. What exactly are the different groups, sections, identities or communities that the government wants to bring together and what is to count as brought together? Given the origins of the agenda, it seems reasonable to argue that its purpose is one of public order or the avoidance of disorder, but this purpose is not explicitly stated in government publications. If this is indeed the purpose, then it is to be expected that community cohesion activities would address causes of disorder, not just symptoms, but it is by no means certain that they do this.[14] Third, community cohesion requires that all community members have similar life opportunities (otherwise, as discussed in Chapter One, there cannot be the meaningful cross-cultural contact that leads to community cohesion). This cannot be achieved, however, through local means alone – it requires effective government action at a national level to achieve greater social equality. Yet evidence suggests that inequality of income, in particular (which is as good an indicator as any of life opportunities), has actually increased since New Labour came to power (National Statistics Online, 2009). Fourth, the agenda seems to assume that British society is becoming increasingly segregated (see, for example, Cantle, 2008; Lownsbrough and Beunderman, 2007), while more in-depth analysis suggests that it is becoming increasingly integrated (see, for example, Phillips, 2006). Fifth, community cohesion requires that communities trust local institutions to act fairly (otherwise, presumably, communities will become antagonistic to those institutions, resulting in conflict and disorder). This approach, however, says nothing about trusting national institutions, in particular Parliament and government itself, and the community cohesion agenda proposes nothing in this regard. Thus, by localising the 'problem' of community cohesion, the agenda sidelines the question of the government's responsibilities and forgets its own vision of Britain as a 'community of communities'.

More recently, perhaps in anticipation of some of the criticisms voiced above and moving towards what would become the Conservatives' 'Big Society' idea, the Labour government focused more explicit attention on the conditions for what it called 'positive' and 'meaningful' interaction across communities, which it regarded as crucial for community cohesion (see CLG, 2008d; Orton, 2009). Much of this seemed to be about encouraging sociability (see Chapter One), which is all well and good, but it is far from clear what expertise government has in this area. The government itself recognised that: 'It may seem strange that government should be suggesting that local areas get involved in what comes naturally to people and where the outcomes seem quite fluffy or woolly' (CLG, 2008d, p 14). And yes, it does seem strange, to put it mildly, particularly when the government has no clear idea of what might count as a 'positive' action. There is no understanding here that, for example, some kinds of conflict, though apparently 'negative', might be healthy for the community as a whole. It is, in short, just another example of the *'why can't we all get on?'* approach criticised above. The 'Big Society' sounds very similar to this.

An excellent illustration of the ignorance embodied in this approach is the quote from the founder of the Living Library: 'We work on the principle that extreme violence and aggression happens between people who don't know each other' (CLG, 2008d, p 31). The statement is revealing because it expresses the belief, clearly supported by government, that familiarity with one another produces social order (rather than, say, contempt). In fact, however, on an individual level, most murders and extremely violent acts are committed against people who are well known to the perpetrator. And on a community level, serious conflicts typically arise not from ignorance (fortunately, as otherwise none of us would be alive today) but from recognition of opposing interests and from deep and long-standing grievances. There is a circularity of argument here, anyway, which parallels that regarding social capital generally as pointed out in Chapter Two: it is argued that community cohesion is produced by 'positive' interaction, but 'positive' interaction seems to be equated with whatever produces community cohesion. The government's approach here is therefore shallow, simplistic and superficial in the extreme, resting on a severely impoverished and vague notion of human sociability, which fails even to distinguish between strong and weak ties. There is a particularly patronising section of the guidance (section 12), entitled 'helping to give people a voice' (CLG, 2008d, pp 40–1), which appears to assume that people do not have a voice and are unable to develop one themselves without help from government. Yet the government's own evidence from the National Community Forum report (Orton, 2009) showed that people or communities have a voice already but the government listens only to what it wants to. One can only hope that the new government will be more open to what communities have to say.

If we want to know what really promotes community cohesion, we have to go back to initiatives such as the JRF Neighbourhood Programme (see **Box 2.2**) or Labour's Community Chest programme (see the positive comment on the latter in Orton, 2009, p 41).[15] Even a cursory examination of such programmes is enough to show that they are not just about 'positive' interaction (although this is important) but about community development more generally. This involves, in particular, processes of community learning whereby community members improve their understanding of different communities, how they work, their dependence on one another, their varied experiences, hopes, dreams, anxieties and so on. Even such programmes, however, commendable though they may be, are not sufficient to deal with the elephant in the room, which is structural inequality between different groups or different communities. For example, some of the encapsulated and/or deprived communities discussed in Chapter One and elsewhere (for example, by Page, 2000; MacDonald et al, 2005; Allen, 2008; Kintrea et al, 2008) need far more substantial development if bridges are to be built between them and their neighbouring communities.

Labour's approach to building bridging social capital was therefore seriously flawed, based on systematic confusion between strong ties and weak ties, lack of understanding why different groups or communities would or would not want to get on with one another, and wilful ignorance of the multiple dimensions of social inequality that can make building bridging social capital virtually impossible, or even inappropriate in certain circumstances. Social coordination, however, also involves building *linking* social capital between communities and government itself. Here Labour's efforts were of three kinds: first, 'choice', in which community members as service *users* 'are able to engage directly with providers to tailor the service to fit their circumstances, for example, through direct payment schemes in social care, choice-based lettings or personalisation via Connexions advisers' (Blake et al, 2008, p 10); second, 'partnership', in which *communities* are invited to engage with government officials in decision-making forums and processes, for example (as discussed earlier), local strategic partnerships; and third, 'voice', in which the government makes legislative and institutional reforms that give *citizens* more influence over local (but not necessarily national) decision making, for example, stronger petitioning powers, participatory budgeting, youth parliaments and so on (CLG, 2008b; HMG, 2009a, pp 59–61).

The issue of community members acting as service users will be discussed in detail in later chapters, so will not be considered here. On the issue of partnership, the key question concerns Labour's purposes. Ostensibly, its main purpose was to improve the efficiency and effectiveness of service delivery, particularly in poorer areas, but we have now seen that the improvements achieved were not so remarkable. A second purpose was that of empowering communities through building their linking social capital, but again the achievements of any significance in this respect seem relatively few so far (see Somerville and Haines, 2008, for some examples[16]). To be charitable, this could be because Labour was still developing this particular agenda up to when it lost the election; for example, it was only just beginning to understand how best to use community anchor organisations. On the other hand, however, it could be argued that this lack of progress occurred because Labour's real, underlying purpose was to achieve a form of social inclusion in which the process of developing and empowering communities was subordinated to the requirements of social order. Essentially, it sought to engage with communities as 'partners' in order primarily to discipline them and control them, to ensure that they did not pose a threat to its rule. Part of this discipline involved the interpellation of certain individuals as 'representative' of their communities (in an attempt to ensure that the community as a whole was signed up to the partnership), while at other times dismissing the same individuals as the 'usual suspects' when they were perceived to be too vocal, too powerful, too oppositional, obstructive, disruptive or simply too time consuming.[17]

Representation and power – how governments rule communities

The question of representation lies at the heart of the legitimacy of these new 'invited spaces' (Cornwall and Coelho, 2006) of decision making.[18] Barnes et al (2007) show how such legitimacy can be conferred on the participants in three kinds of ways: first, through a process of democratic selection or election by their respective 'publics' or constituencies (for example, service users, neighbourhood residents, local electors, demographic categories based on age, gender, ethnicity and so on); second, through nomination by organisations that have a key stake in the decision-making process (for example, residents' groups, social movement organisations, trade unions or the organisation issuing the invitation); and third, through possessing experience or expertise that is particularly pertinent to the issue to be decided (for example, parents in the case of a Sure Start partnership) or through having some other status that is valued by fellow participants (such as an impartial observer or an 'ordinary' resident). The more representative the participants in any of these three senses, the more legitimate the decision-making body will (be seen to) be, and this increased legitimacy strengthens government and increases its capacity to shape the agendas of its non-governmental partners.[19] It is important to note here that this agenda shaping can be beneficial as well as harmful for all participants (an example of what Foucault called 'pastoral power').

Through an evaluation of Local Strategic Partnerships (LSPs) and New Deal for Communities (NDCs), Fuller and Geddes (2008) argued that New Labour was a variant of a neoliberal project, known as extended reproduction (or 'roll-out' – Peck and Tickell, 2002) neoliberalism. Fuller and Geddes (2008, p 262) echo many of the criticisms of New Labour made above:

> While the participation of residents in NDC partnerships (where they are often in a majority on partnership boards) gives them more access to state decision-making than before, ... it is becoming clear that this may not give them much real power, since they have to understand and overcome the institutional parameters and behaviours of public sector bodies that possess the decision-making powers and resources to enact change. While New Labour emphasises development of the capacities and skills of citizens to lead bodies such as NDCs, in reality these bodies have been given little time to train local people, thereby further reducing their scope to play an active role in such bodies and challenge established interests. These processes may well add to the multiple deprivation from which they suffer that of 'burnout' as a result of long and unsocial hours spent as largely unpaid volunteers within the state apparatus.

Fuller and Geddes (2008, p 262) also comment on how New Labour used the discourse of 'community' to discipline residents:

> For New Labour, 'community' is a foundation of social organisation and interaction. There is a need for citizens to belong to communities, since citizens are interdependent and have shared responsibilities and rights. The importance of 'community' is most noticeable in policy initiatives at neighbourhood level, where key institutional innovations such as NDC partnerships are permeated from top to bottom by

rhetorics of community – whether used to imply a veneer of common interest among residents in localities which in reality are inhabited by shifting and multiply fractured populations, or to suggest a particular priority for certain groups – 'the black and minority ethnic (BME) community' – where the very nomenclature suggests a catch-all term for non-whites. But it is also important at broader regulatory scales where the new LSPs include significant representation of the 'community' (and voluntary) sectors. The resort to 'community' is significant in its recognition of the limitations of both state- and 'market'-led urban state agencies, and the new models of partnership which New Labour has introduced are a particular challenge both to more traditional Labour-elected councillors who do not accept their legitimacy, as well as to managerialist state bureaucrats whose assumption of the right to manage has been one result of neoliberal New Public Management.

So, LSPs and NDCs operate by constructing citizens as members of communities who then have responsibilities to work with government to tackle the problems of those communities. The whole process, however, is tightly controlled by central government through a framework of national floor targets that the local partnerships have to deliver, and they are regularly monitored and audited to ensure that they do so. It should be stressed, once again, that, despite appearances to the contrary, this control system is directed at enhancing the quality of life in the most deprived communities by the means of improving the public services delivered in or to those communities. For Labour, then, 'partnership', despite its weaknesses, played a key role in the fabrication of social order (Neocleous, 2000) by interpellating a variety of organisations, as well as communities, as both producers and consumers in a brave new market for public services.

Fuller and Geddes (2008) document a wide range of problems with NDCs that arise primarily from the 'command and control' character of the programme (for a critique of 'command and control' approaches generally, see Seddon, 2008). They question whether NDCs are sufficiently sensitive to local needs and priorities and even, in the case of LSPs, 'whether the transaction costs of partnership working outweigh any benefits', for example in terms of improved services (Fuller and Geddes, 2008, p 272). On NDCs, they conclude that 'there is growing evidence that few NDCs will achieve the wider objective of New Labour's neighbourhood renewal strategy of closing the gap between poor neighbourhoods and more prosperous areas' (Fuller and Geddes, 2008, p 272).[20] On the issue of community empowerment, they report:

> Even in the case of NDCs where community involvement is paramount, evidence suggests that partnerships have been fitted into existing nation state and urban state institutions and discourses, rather than the endogenous development of community-led structures and systems, or the development of local accountability. (Fuller and Geddes, 2008, p 272)

Given that the NDCs were established in 2001 but the Labour government did not begin to understand community development needs until 2004, this is not surprising. The government never showed any awareness, however, that this lack of understanding might have undermined the whole programme and never recognised that it might bear some responsibility for this undermining. There seemed to be no learning from past mistakes, but only a lurch from one initiative to another. Still, it is important to avoid concluding from this that there is no hope for the future. From the community's point of view, three positive options can be identified: first, there is the evidence that government intervention does bring some benefits, the costs of achieving these benefits do not appear to be very high in some cases and they can be a foundation for further progress; second, as we have seen in relation to managerial coordination, the government's capacity to exert effective control is very limited, so there is scope for communities to take the initiative in a number of ways, even inside the invited spaces of governmental decision making; and third, as argued by Davies (2007), there remains the possibility for communities to organise themselves outside of governmental structures and in direct contestation of those structures.

In considering its way forward in relation to any opportunity to work with government, therefore, each community has to ask itself a fundamental question: are the gains to be achieved in terms of linking social capital sufficient to make it worthwhile for it to take up the opportunity offered? In the case of the first option, then, the community must decide whether the benefits have occurred and will continue to occur in spite of or (in part) because of the community's involvement (if the former, then exit seems the logical decision to take; if the latter, then continued engagement with government seems reasonable). With the second and third options, the community must decide, in each case, whether it is more likely to succeed by working inside or outside the governmental structure concerned. Needless to say, the vast majority of communities are not in a position to make informed decisions of such a nature, and this is why community development is needed.

The choice for communities

The final question to consider is: why should communities, particularly poorer ones, trust government at all? Initially indeed, it seems that many communities were willing to give New Labour the benefit of the doubt. Later, however, there were suggestions that this goodwill might have been eroded in some areas. Blake et al (2008, p 51), for example, reported that: 'interviewers identified cases of deepening suspicion, on occasion, when decision-makers were thought to have restructured procedures and processes to avoid local challenges to official agendas, raising the question of whether there was a genuine desire to consult at all.' It should have become abundantly clear by now that New Labour's project was one of neoliberalisation, which can run counter to the interests of those in poorer communities. The government's position was unambiguously stated by CLG, setting out three priority outcomes for future expenditure on regeneration:

- improving economic performance and tackling worklessness, particularly in the most deprived areas
- creating the right conditions for business growth which could include investment in infrastructure, land use, and a better public realm; and
- creating sustainable places where people want to live and can work and businesses want to invest. (CLG, 2009, p 15)

In other words, everything was to be subordinated to the aim of economic growth, and economic growth was understood in terms of participation in the labour market and the expansion of profitable business. 'Economic performance' was identified with the performance of British capital – it took no account of unpaid labour, whether domestic or voluntary. 'Worklessness' meant the condition of those who are outside the labour market (the buying and selling of labour power), and is therefore a characteristic of millions of people who work very hard indeed, as parents, carers and volunteers of all kinds. Creating 'the right conditions for business growth' could include all manner of forms of exploitation, expropriation and other harms, just to satisfy the interests of investors. And of course, these places in which businesses want to invest were, by definition, the only ones that are sustainable within a capitalist system.

Neoliberalisation is therefore a fundamentally problematic and divisive project. It divides the so-called 'economically active' from the economically inactive, it destroys communities, it undermines existing social capital. It creates jobs, but many of these jobs are unfulfilling and poorly paid. It also creates insecurity, which then has to be regulated by a strong state.

Above all, neoliberalisation subordinates all forms of capital to economic capital, thus challenging and threatening democracy – because, ultimately, political power becomes just another commodity that can be bought or sold. Neoliberalisation therefore leads logically to the corruption of all our social and political institutions and of political community itself. In a society where all social relations are commodified, even common human respect has to be 'earned' (see Somerville, 2009a), and civility, sociability and even intimacy become matters of contractual exchange.[21]

It is interesting to compare this dominant New Labour project with its secondary project of securing social order. HMG (2008, p 21), for example, advocates what it calls 'the politics of the common good', where: 'People are willing to put their own interests second if they know they will not be exploited; they are willing to respect decisions that go against them if they are convinced that the process that led to those decisions was fair; they are willing to go to extraordinary lengths to help others if they know that help will be reciprocated in times of need'. This politics is therefore one of non-exploitation, due process and reciprocity – arguably, necessary conditions for a stable political community (see Chapter Three). Contrast this, however, with what happens under neoliberalism, in which labour is exploited, there is one law for the rich and one for the poor (Cook, 1989), and, instead of long-term reciprocity, market exchange is instantaneous and based on ability to pay rather than on need. By New Labour's own standards, then, a neoliberal society would be unfair and undesirable, yet this is precisely the kind of society that it aimed to create. And for good measure, if by chance anything went wrong (such as a major recession), it would be down to us ordinary citizens to put it right (with support from government, of course): 'in tougher economic times one of the most important demands will be that everyone who can work, does work. Those who cannot work, whether temporarily or more permanently, will still need to receive financial and practical support. To achieve this we need a fair system that focuses on what people can do rather than what they cannot, and offers them appropriate support' (HMG, 2008, p 24). So, even with three million unemployed, the government seemed to believe that jobs could be found for them all. And this nonsense came straight from the then Prime Minister Gordon Brown himself in his foreword: 'we expect people to work if they can, and access help and support if they can't' (HMG, 2008, p 3), a mantra he had repeated ad nauseam since 1997. Still, it expresses very clearly how the Labour government saw its role as primarily the handmaiden of capital and defender of the capitalist work ethic.[22]

Participatory budgeting – an illustration of a governmental approach

Participatory budgeting (PB) is perhaps the most important technique that the government selected to take forward the empowerment agenda implicit in CLG (2008b). Along with something called 'citizen governance' (roughly equivalent to public involvement in governmental decision-making bodies, as discussed above), it is the only empowerment mechanism that has been found to show clear evidence of spill-over from individuals to the wider community (Pratchett et al, 2009a, 2009b). The nature of this alleged empowerment may therefore be worth looking at more closely.

In its original form in Porto Alegre in Brazil, PB was a means to secure wider public participation in local government (see, for example, Gret and Sintomer, 2005; Wampler, 2007; Smith, 2008). The idea was that the public as a whole should be involved in the annual budgeting process of the city council, not merely in a consultative role but as active shapers of the pattern of the council's expenditure. This was achieved by means of a structure of popular assemblies at sub-municipal levels, and a process of deliberation in which locally generated priorities and ideas are translated into financial allocations. Local community groups are asked to rank different themes (for example, housing, schools, transport, environment, crime) against each other in order of their perceived importance in their local community. These rankings are then collated for each neighbourhood, resulting in a table known as the budget matrix, in which each neighbourhood appears as a row and each theme as a column. Adding up the ranking scores for each theme provides an indication of the relative priority to be attached to that theme across the city as a whole. This priority can be adjusted to take account of the population of the neighbourhood (more people means higher priority) and the needs of the neighbourhood as recognised by the people themselves (greater need means higher priority) (for detail on how the budget matrix works, see Hall, 2005, appendix 3). In this way, it can be seen that the investment priorities for the local authority are determined primarily by local citizens, working through deliberative assemblies structured specifically for this purpose.

The transfer of PB from Brazil to other countries, however, has resulted in something quite different from this (see, for example, Sintomer et al, 2008). It has changed from a process in which mainstream budgets are effectively allocated by the people for the people on the basis of deliberation to one in which selected (and relatively small) budgets are allocated on the basis of a system of competitive bidding. The shift is from what Pratchett et al (2009a, p 108) recognise is 'a transformative political model' (though they do not elaborate on what this transformation might mean) to what they describe as 'some successes in empowerment' (with 'empowerment' being defined in the meaningless terms mentioned above).

Typically, what happens in the PB 'experiments' in England is that a local authority tells community groups in its area that it has a budget available for spending on community-led projects. The groups are then invited to an event in which representatives from each community have a few minutes to make a case for funding a particular project. The meeting as a whole then decides which projects will get funded (typical examples, in Southampton and Keighley, can be found in CLG, 2008e, pp 25 and 30).

This can no doubt be a positive experience for those concerned and is, in some ways, an improvement on how such budgets are currently allocated (for example, on the whim of councillors or officers, or on some arbitrary measure of need).[23] It is, however, a classic case of depoliticisation and neoliberalisation disguised as deepening democracy and deliberative pluralism. It has three drawbacks in comparison with PB in Porto Alegre: first, it is separate from the mainstream working of local government and has, as yet, made no significant difference to how mainstream budgets are allocated; second, it reinforces the subordinate position of local people as supplicants or petitioners rather than citizens; and third, it sets community groups in competition with one another – although evidence so far suggests that, to their credit, community groups have resisted this push towards a quasi-market, preferring instead to develop their own needs-based sensibilities.[24]

The extent of community empowerment achieved by PB of this kind is strictly limited. Compared with PB in Porto Alegre, the lack of involvement by political parties is most striking (the Workers' Party played a key role in the PB process in Porto Alegre), and there is no clear support for community/citizen advocacy, with community groups being effectively left to fend for themselves (a laissez-faire approach). Indeed, within the current approach to PB, there is no clear conception at all of community development, as the latter appears to be viewed only as a means to support empowerment (see, for example, Pratchett et al, 2009a, p 173), which itself lacks clear meaning. The approach favoured in this book is the diametric opposite of this: empowerment, whatever it means, should be regarded as a means to community development. If the government's process of empowerment has no clear goal, then it follows that the government can attach the label 'empowerment' to more or less anything it chooses.

Conclusion

This chapter has explored the reasons for the increasing governmental emphasis on community, tracing its origins to the rediscovery of poverty in the 1950s and developing through an increasingly outward-looking and multi-faceted approach to tackling that poverty. Current governmental approaches (of all three main parties) can be characterised as a mix of neoliberal emphasis on choice and self-help, partnership working, social inclusion and community cohesion. The chapter has attempted to identify the purposes underlying these approaches. Until recently, the main purpose was clearly to improve public services (especially to poorer areas) but, since 2004, this has been overlain with a drive towards what Labour called 'community empowerment' and the Conservatives call 'Big Society'. There are reasons, however, to be sceptical about government motives and critical of its understanding of empowerment. Under Labour in particular, it ignored the causes of people's disengagement with politics, failed to take account of the fact that public participation takes place for different reasons in different contexts, related to different roles that people might play (for example, as service users, as members of particular communities or as citizens) and confused different kinds of coordination and different functions of social capital. It conspicuously and consistently failed to see issues from the point of view of particular communities and did not attempt to understand the causes of the deep divisions that exist in some of those communities. Finally, it presumed to act on behalf of the people and therefore assumed that the people should trust it implicitly, but did not appear to recognise sufficiently its responsibility to foster and nurture such trust. This helps to explain its tendency to offer patronising banalities and unhelpful homilies or gimmicks instead of realistic solutions to so many community problems.

Above all, both Labour and Conservatives appear to lack any concept of a beloved community. They believe in equality of opportunity but they lack understanding of the reasons for the differential take-up of opportunities. They recognise the need to enable the flourishing of all individuals but they do not understand the social causes of the lack of flourishing among so many of their citizens and so, in the case of Labour, it has not tackled those causes fairly and, in the case of the Conservatives, it seems unlikely that they will tackle them at all.

There remains the key question for communities, as for the public generally, namely whether it is worthwhile engaging with government or not. It is impossible, however, to give a general answer to this question: it all depends upon what is on offer, whether the offer is a genuine one, what the likely benefits are to the community and what the costs are to the community in taking it up. Although national government has shown itself to be generally untrusting, unreliable and micro-managing, there are examples of initiatives that can work to the advantage of deprived communities. One such example considered in this chapter has been that of participatory budgeting. This example clearly illustrates how communities can benefit from a government initiative, while at the same time the scope of the benefit is limited in such a way that nothing really changes.

Notes

[1] This was the same assumption as that underlying the largely destructive slum clearance and redevelopment programmes of the 1960s and early 1970s. But here the 'solution' was seen in terms of eliminating the physical 'problem' (the slums) and uprooting the 'cultural' problem (displacing the slum dwellers to more 'uplifting' environments). Later on, Dunleavy (1981) showed that these policies, particularly in relation to the provision of high-rise and system-built housing, were driven by the construction industry aided and abetted by professional architects employed by local authorities.

[2] This is not to say that earlier governments had necessarily been less keen on unleashing market forces – see Dunleavy (1981).

[3] Actually, the quality of housing built by local authorities in the 1950s has rarely been matched since, but the excesses committed by a minority of councils in the 1960s (creating new slums for old) left a baleful legacy from which local authorities have barely recovered even today.

[4] With the possible exception of planning, where consultation with the public on structure and local plans was required by the Town and Country Planning Act 1971 (see, for example, Heap, 1991).

[5] To use the jargon, there had been little 'bending' of mainstream budgets towards the poorer, more needy areas. This is hardly surprising because the Conservative initiatives never really aimed to do this – and indeed the practice of challenge funding militates against it, as those who rise better to the challenge tend to be those who are more capable in the first place.

[6] To give credit where it is due, this shift was first noticed by Rose (1996).

[7] Kearns (2004, p 21), for example, describes the Third Way as involving 'self-help within existing market and governmental structures'. Yet the 'free economy' beloved of liberals is essentially based on self-help, so an emphasis on self-help 'within existing markets' is a hallmark of neoliberalism. This is not to say, however, that there cannot be forms of self-help that are incompatible with neoliberalism – for example, see the discussions of community self-development in Chapter Two and communitarianism in Chapter Three.

[8] CENs were set up, with government funding, to act as equal partners with public authorities in local strategic partnerships.

[9] Community empowerment has been usefully defined by Adamson and Bromiley (2008, p 2) as: 'policy and service delivery change that more actively involves residents of communities in shaping what happens in their community'. This is sufficiently broad to include almost anything a government might do that results in community self-development. The government, however, prefers an even broader

definition of empowerment as: 'passing more and more political power to more and more people, using every practical means available' (Pratchett et al, 2009b). This definition is so wide that it borders on the meaningless. Most recently, the government has defined empowerment as 'the process of enabling people to shape and choose the services they use on a personal basis' (Agur and Low, 2009, p 4) – a narrower definition, but one that reduces the citizen to an individual service user.

[10] In the end, the only initiative here was to improve the advice and support available to facilitate the transfer of community assets, such as disused buildings, to community groups. These buildings could then function, for example, as a home for community enterprises, a meeting place for local groups, or an opportunity for local people to learn new skills (HMG, 2009, p 59).

[11] Rodger (2008, p 162) describes this phenomenon as '*inauthenticity*': 'confronted by the difficulties of the political administration of complex social and political systems, governments tend to conceal their manipulative and controlling activities by devoting considerable resources to appearing to be responsive to community and individuals. There is little evidence that the voluntary sector in the UK is actively engaged with government in shaping social policy or is genuinely embedded in policy networks ... The extent to which there is authentic community participation in the process of building community efficacy is questionable. The nature of the strategy is in reality one which has stimulated division rather than solidarity and is obfuscatory rather than illuminating about community involvement.' It is interesting to note that a similar approach seems increasingly to be adopted by employers in relation to the development of their employees – 'increased responsibility without meaningful discretion and authority' (Webb, 2004, p 719). This could be called 'inauthentic empowerment'.

[12] Again, whether the Cameron–Clegg government will do any better is not yet clear.

[13] '[N]one of the Pathfinders in the study appear to have a clear and comprehensive view on the extent to which different ethnic groups in their areas access, or benefit from, public services, partly because information on this is not readily and widely available' (SQW, 2008b, p 24).

[14] As in the example above, defusing tensions arising from BNP marches is certainly addressing the symptoms, but how far is it tackling the causes of those tensions? Some of these causes, for example, relating to institutional harms, will be discussed further in Chapter Nine.

[15] Community Chests were small grants for community groups launched in 2001, subsumed into the Single Community Programme (together with funding for CENs) in 2004, which was itself integrated into the Safer and Stronger Communities Fund in 2006.

[16] One example is that of the Community Forums in Newham (see also Blake et al, 2008, pp 21–4).

[17] This interpellation of community leaders can be taken to ludicrous lengths. Blake et al (2008, p 57) cite the example of community activist, F, who reports: 'If a lamp on my street is not working, people will walk 60 yards to tell me rather than phone the council.' Blake et al comment: 'Clearly, this is rewarding, but can also lead to stress. In F's case, this contributed to a heart attack, leading F to step down from chairing and shift into a less stressful area of responsibility.' A more appropriate comment would be: 'Clearly, this is *not* rewarding, because it results in a heart attack.' Why is it seen to be desirable that a community representative should act for someone who is perfectly capable of acting for themselves? This simple example vividly highlights the insidious nature of the New Labour project. Again, it remains to be seen whether the new government can, or even wants to, do any better.

[18] The legitimacy of a decision-making body lies in the recognition of its decisions as binding by those who are affected by them.

[19] Incidentally, a number of the 'invited spaces' in Barnes et al (2007) lack legitimacy by these standards. For example, there are cases where the methods of participant election/selection have not been democratically agreed, where the relevant publics have not even been clearly constituted or included in the election/selection process, and where the relationship between representatives and represented is otherwise unclear or disputed. As in other studies too, the burden of proving legitimacy tends to fall on the non-state representatives, this being a reflection of the unequal power between state and non-state actors.

[20] This has since been confirmed by Wilkinson and Noble (2010), who found that there has been 'little change in relative levels of economic deprivation in the NDC areas' (p 5).

[21] Needless to say, perhaps, this runs entirely counter to the idea of a beloved community.

[22] Unfortunately, it seems clear that the Conservatives' concept of the 'Big Society' is very much the same kind of beast. Citizens will be increasingly asked to do things for themselves that government would have done before. The main difference from New Labour could be that those citizens are given less support from government to do so.

[23] This suggests that PB of this kind could have a positive purpose in developing community learning, but this possibility does not appear to have been evaluated yet.

[24] In some cases, winning bidders have opted to receive a smaller amount of funding in order to allow the funding of other projects that they saw as equally if not more deserving.

Summary

Much of this chapter focuses on the approach of the New Labour government that was in power when the chapter was written. However, the criticisms of active citizenship and of illusory empowerment apply also, and perhaps with even greater force, to the policies of the current coalition government. There may be other aspects of New Labour, though, such as its approach to the coordination of services and to building social capital, that are not continued by the coalition. Given the conspicuous failure of New Labour on this score, as identified in this chapter, this possible abandonment of 'joined-up' government and governmentally prescribed social cohesion may turn out to be a welcome development. Arguably, however, it is important not to throw the baby out with the bath water, and it seems clear that poorer communities will continue to need targeted support from government and others for the foreseeable future – there is a key role for government in eliminating serious structural social inequalities.

Questions for discussion

- How do governments represent communities?

- In what sense was New Labour communitarian?

- Why did New Labour fail to develop communities?

- What should be the role of government in relation to community development?

Further reading

Fuller, C. and Geddes, M. (2008) 'Urban governance under neoliberalism: New Labour and the restructuring of state-space', *Antipode,* vol 40, no 2, pp 252–82.

five

Community economic development

Overview

Community economic development is a process of adding value to a community in such a way that further value is created, and so on – a process of self-expanding value. Approaches to community economic development can be:

- *'top down'*, where development is driven by government and other powerful organisations
- *'bottom up'*, where development is driven by communities themselves
- *'side in'*, where development is driven by a partnership of community groups/ members/representatives and professionals/officials/powerful organisations.

In recent years, criticisms of top-down and bottom-up approaches have led to increasing emphasis on side-in approaches, particularly co-production. Interest has also grown in building the capacity of so-called 'third sector' organisations to achieve community economic development. At least from 2004 onwards, the Labour government favoured an expansion of third sector organisations to deliver goods and services, taking over not only from the public sector but also from the private sector. Unfortunately, the government showed little understanding of how such an expansion was to take place, what form it ought to take, and how best to support it. Examples such as Hill Holt Wood (see **Box 5.1**), however, show that successful community economic development requires the creation of enterprises with clear vision of what economic activity is needed and why it is needed – an emphasis on value that is self-reproducing, that benefits the whole community and that is ecologically sound. The community entrepreneurs who are the creators of these enterprises are essentially economic, social and political activists.

Previous chapters in this book have explored a wide range of concepts relating to community and have examined the politics and government of community development. This chapter now looks specifically at community *economic* development, which can be understood in general terms as a process of the self-reproducing and self-expanding value of communities. Arguably, all community development involves improving the living standards of a community, for example, in terms of resources and assets, which can include not just income, property or wealth but also education, health, housing, leisure facilities, heritage – basically, anything that might add to the community's well-being. Community economic development, however, can be envisaged specifically as a process of adding economic value or wealth to a community, which itself can generate more value, for example, by creating jobs (which produce value) or enhancing skills (which are applied to produce value). Community economic development is therefore community development of a specific kind.

One way of making sense of economic development is in terms of the concept of capital, discussed in Chapter Two. Capital, understood as self-expanding value, can take a variety of forms, for example, economic, social or cultural. Community economic development is primarily about economic capital but this is not the whole story. It also involves social and cultural capital insofar as these other forms contribute to the development of economic capital. For example, as we have seen in previous chapters, social capital can be important for accessing employment and improving the quality of life for communities.

Approaches to community economic development (CED)

Broadly speaking, approaches to community economic development can be classified as top-down, bottom-up and side-in. 'Top-down' refers to CED that is driven from the 'top', that is, by government and other powerful organisations, whereas 'bottom-up' is roughly equivalent to autonomous development or self-development (see Chapter Two). Top-down CED is done *to* the community, while bottom-up CED is done *by* the community. 'Side-in' then refers to CED that is done jointly between the community and 'professionals' (public officials or private developers/businesses or powerful third sector organisations) – that is, development *with* the community.

Two sources of top-down approaches can be distinguished: private firms and government. Governmental approaches generally were discussed in detail in Chapter Four. In the 1980s, the myth of 'trickle down' was used to justify a form of development *in* the community that was not actually a development *of* the community at all: rather, forms of 'regeneration'[1] were implemented that typically involved redevelopment of land and buildings on the assumption that the new physical environment would be sufficient to improve the living standards of the local population. In later years, as we saw in Chapter Four, governmental approaches became more sophisticated, but the emphasis today continues to be primarily on securing profitable markets for economic capital. In particular, the drive for efficiency and uniformity favours development at national and regional levels rather than at community level, presenting significant barriers to CED (see, for example, McGregor et al, 2003).

Private firms clearly can and do provide jobs and investment in a community but this investment does not necessarily amount to CED as defined above. For example, jobs created may not be 'real' jobs in the sense of reproducing their own value or they may involve a level of exploitation whereby the value they produce accrues mainly to the investors and is not reinvested in the community. It is well established in the literature, for example, that poor people find that only poor-quality jobs are available to them (see OECD, 2006; North et al, 2007; Green and White, 2007).[2] In general too, poorer communities present a less attractive proposition for potential investors. The actions of private firms, particularly those from outside the community, can also result in increased inequality between different members of the community. This is because, as a matter of logic, those who are better able to take up opportunities offered by such firms tend to make more progress than those who are less able. Local enterprises can also find themselves priced out of the market by larger competitors, as has been seen, for example, in the case of supermarkets, who can offer greater economies of scale (see, for example, NEF, 2003). Such economies of scale work against many communities, resulting in the disappearance of corner shops, grocers, banks, post offices and pubs.

Top-down approaches to CED, therefore, lead to a number of problems for communities, and these will be considered further below in relation to New Labour. Bottom-up approaches are quite different. Traditionally, the concept of free enterprise expresses the thinking that lies behind these approaches, namely the belief that people should be free to develop economically as they wish, particularly through free trade and free exchange of goods and ideas. Free enterprise, however, has historically been associated with the exploitation of labour and the coercive commercialisation of human activity of all kinds, and this is not necessarily conducive to CED – for example, some enterprising individuals may benefit at the expense of others or some services may be provided at a price when they were previously performed for free.

One way of trying to make sense of CED is through the concept of social capital. Halpern (2005) is one author who takes the view that all economic development involves the mobilisation of social capital. Considering an individual firm or company, for example, it is arguable that bonding social capital is required to hold it together and to ensure its long-term survival. In practice, therefore, it is not surprising that the firm is commonly a partnership of individuals connected by strong mutual ties, such as a family. Such firms may well be examples of self-development (as in the notorious expression: the 'self-made man') but they are not necessarily examples of CED – see, for instance, Johannisson and Wigren (2006) on working-class community in Gnosjö in Sweden. Whether or not any strongly interconnected group in a community actually adds self-reproducing value to that community seems to depend on a variety of factors, including whether the social networks involved are enabling or restrictive, open or closed (see Taylor, 2008). The activities of some companies may indeed, at least in part, be described, from the community's point of view, as value *extracting* rather than value adding, insofar as, for example, the returns on their investments are not used to benefit the community but are spent or reinvested outside the community (Frith and McElwee, 2009).

Considering a plurality of firms operating in the same area, researchers have identified weak ties among firms in certain areas, known as *clusters* – for example, Silicon Valley in California, the M4 corridor in England, biotechnology firms around Cambridge, the Madchester culture, wine and food districts in France, car manufacture in US cities, glass and crystal manufacture in Bohemia. Clusters consist of owner-managed businesses, working in cooperative competition or 'co-opetition'. According to Porter (2004), a cluster creates an overall competitive advantage for the business community in the region where it has formed. Clusters are therefore a good example of bridging social capital leading to bottom-up CED. It should be noted, however, that cluster developments tend to be exclusive as well as inclusive: they are open to those who share their interests and can contribute to serving those interests but not to those, such as poorer people, who have different interests and may lack the capacity or willingness to cooperate with them (recall the discussion of Leonard, 2004, in Chapter Two).

Bottom-up community economic development therefore takes place through the mobilisation of bonding social capital in the form of enterprises and through the mobilisation of bridging social capital in clusters or networks of enterprises. It can also take place through the mobilisation of linking social capital, whereby community members access satisfying and well-paid employment, and other sustainable sources of income and political power – for example, government grants and contracts, election to political office and control of community assets.

Gorz (1980) argues that bottom-up approaches that remain within a framework of profit seeking are liable to reproduce and reinforce existing economic inequalities and therefore fail to develop the community as a whole. In order for them to succeed, he suggests, what he calls the needs-based economy has to be 'de-linked' from the global market economy. Essentially, for communities, this means a process of separate development outside of governmental and commercial structures and avoiding engagement with those structures (compare the 'exit–action strategy' for community groups discussed by Davies, 2007, and in Chapter Two). It is unclear, however, how communities can survive on this basis, except in the short term, for example as Temporary Autonomous Zones (Social Centre Stories, 2008).

Similar arguments have been made in relation to community entrepreneurship. For example, Lindgren and Packendorff (2006, p 211) suggest that, if bottom–up CED is to be successful in the long term, it must, to some extent, be working just *outside* the boundary of the culture, constructing and reconstructing the boundaries of everyday life. Otherwise, it risks being drawn back into the value-extracting and disempowering economic and political systems that caused the community's problems in the first place. Lindgren and Packendorff (2006, p 230) differ from Gorz, however, in that they describe community entrepreneurship as 'an eternal balancing act between deviation and belonging'. For them, therefore, community entrepreneurs must be somehow *inside* as well as outside the community, following the rules but also breaking the rules. They work from the bottom upwards but they aim to change the bottom in the process. They develop themselves as individuals and as collectives but they are about developing the community as well. This point will be illustrated later in this chapter in the case of Hill Holt Wood (see *Box 5.1*). It also seems to be the same point as that made by Bauwens (2005) in relation to peer-to-peer production, where the 'community' concerned is effectively a *virtual* community.[3]

For Halpern (2005), trust in strangers is the key factor for all community development, including CED. The problem, however, is that it is those communities that are most in need of development that are also likely to have low trust in strangers (for example, the encapsulated communities discussed in Chapter One). So how is a community that lacks trust in strangers supposed to gain that trust? How is a community that is relatively closed, inward looking and exclusive to become relatively open, outward looking and inclusive? This is the point at which the bottom–up model of CED tends to break down because it seems to be asking communities to haul themselves up by their own bootstraps, and this is just not a practicable option for many communities.

Adamson and Bromiley (2008) outline what they call a 'capillary' model of a bottom–up approach to community development, whereby community opinions are fed 'from highly localised structures to higher strategic partnerships' (p xxv) at district and county level – that is, from neighbourhoods through ward-based coordination mechanisms up to local authority-wide partnerships. This interpretation of scaling-up has potential but it needs considerable development, for example, in terms of the civic infrastructure required to enable it to happen and the communication systems needed to ensure its effectiveness. It is also unclear how such capillary action is to be effective at national level.

All these considerations suggest that the most promising ways forward, at least for the poorest communities and in the longer term, lie not with top-down or bottom-up approaches on their own but with approaches where it is said that 'top-down meets bottom-up' (Taylor, 2000) – or, more strictly, with side-in approaches where 'professionals' work with the community as equal partners. An example of a side-in approach here is what is known as '*co-production*', 'where users are equal partners with professionals in transforming services to suit their needs' (HM Treasury, 2007, p 49; Stephens et al, 2008).[4] Co-production is a growing phenomenon, where service users are regarded as *assets*, involved in mutual support and service delivery; developing generally outside nationally funded services, and usually *despite* public administrative systems (Boyle et al, 2006). Co-production is therefore not specifically private enterprise, nor is it public enterprise, nor can it be adequately characterised (like peer-to-peer production) as 'third sector' activity; rather, it is a form of economic development that cuts across *all* sectors. The breadth of its scope is, however, a source of weakness as well as strength, as it makes it vulnerable to increasing professionalisation (conspiracies against the laity by a new breed of professionals), managerialism (the emergence of new elites of super-managers) and governmentalism (increasingly intrusive apparatuses of state control). In short, co-production has potential to transform services in the interests of their users but also to transform them in the interests of service providers, managers and political leaders – and these interests may well be quite different in important respects.

In order to ensure that side-in approaches work as they are intended to do (that is, developing the community as a whole, and not just sections or elites of the community or other groups altogether), the New Economics Foundation has proposed certain guiding principles (see Stephens et al, 2008). These include:

- *Critical localisation*, whereby production should take place as closely as possible to the point of consumption, providing that this does not unfairly discriminate against producers in other communities (for example, through price subsidies, imposition of tariffs, embargos and so on). The point of this principle for CED is that it helps to ensure that the production of value takes place *in* the community and *for* the community, and hence it makes it more likely that surplus value will be reinvested in and for the community.

- *Reduced ecological footprint*, whereby new enterprises should be 'greener' than comparable existing ones, for example, by producing fewer greenhouse gas emissions. This principle looks to the future: in the longer term, CED has to be more environmentally friendly if communities are to survive and thrive.
- '*Three-leggedness*' (see Seyfang, 2006), whereby enterprises value social and environmental goals equally with economic ones, for example, by ensuring their organisational viability, helping disadvantaged individuals/groups, and building sustainable communities. This principle follows from everything else: if CED is to be sustained, the organisations responsible for it must be self-reproducing, the development must be of the community as a whole (not only, for example, of sections less in need of development) and the development must ideally put more back into the environment than what it takes out.

These principles chime well with the concept of the beloved community. The central idea is one of individuals cooperating freely and equally to achieve the flourishing of all. Such achievement, however, requires nothing short of a radical transformation of existing economic relations plus the striking of a difficult balance between private and public enterprise.

The 'third sector'

CED is commonly assumed to fall within what is known as the 'third sector', which can be understood as the part of the economy that is not privately or publicly owned. It includes a variety of types of organisation that all have economic value of some kind (see, for example, HM Treasury, 2007, p 89). A similar term that is used to label this part of the economy is the 'social economy' (for a detailed review, see Jones et al, 2007). Third sector organisations have been defined by government as: 'non-governmental organisations that are value-driven [as distinct, perhaps, from profit-driven?] and which principally reinvest their surpluses to further social, environmental or cultural objectives. It includes voluntary and community organisations, charities, social enterprises, cooperatives and mutuals' (HM Treasury, 2007, p 5, and, for a useful summary, see p 6).

Bickle (2006, p 14) provides a helpful model of third sector organisations based on two criteria: their ownership status (owned by no one or owned by their members) and their mode of governance (oligarchic or democratic).

This is illustrated in *Figure 5.1*. If the organisation is owned by no one (as is the case, for example, with a trust or a voluntary group), all value added goes primarily to advance the aims of the organisation. If it is owned by its members, then all value added accrues to the members. If it is oligarchic, that means it is controlled by only a minority of its members. If it is democratic, it is controlled by its members equally and collectively.

Figure 5.1: *The third sector (or social economy)*

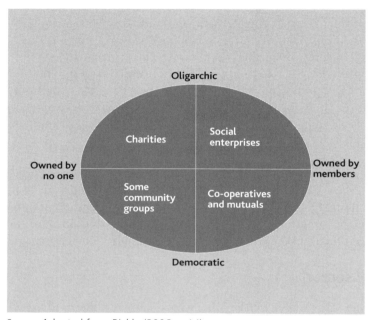

Source: Adapted from Bickle (2006, p 14)

This model leads to the identification of four types of organisation, though it should be emphasised that the boundaries between these types are fuzzy and permeable:

(1) *Organisations that are owned by no one and controlled by a minority of the organisation's members.* These are largely voluntary organisations, particularly charities, that is, organisations that rely on donations/ subscriptions and are set up to provide specific benefits for others. Such organisations may own assets but those assets are not owned by anyone in particular. The members of the organisation may simply be those who have signed up to the organisation's charitable aims, and who may

contribute periodically or occasionally towards those aims. Typically, the organisations are controlled by management committees or Boards of Trustees, whose members act on behalf of the organisation's intended beneficiaries. These committees or boards may or may not be elected by the membership of the organisation as a whole.

(2) *Organisations that are owned by no one and democratically controlled on the basis of one member one vote.* These are mainly voluntary and community groups and associations, mostly informal in the sense of not being legally constituted. Typically, the organisations have no assets other than the members themselves, who pool their assets (for example, their labour and skills) as they choose. Such organisations range from parent-and-toddler groups to political parties, from tenants' and residents' associations to trade unions and professional associations.

(3) *Organisations that are owned by their members and controlled by a minority of the organisation's members.* These are mainly social enterprises, broadly understood as member-owned trading organisations with social purposes – that is, purposes beyond those of benefiting their members. Such organisations can act as charities, though UK charity law requires that they distinguish between their charitable and commercial activities.

(4) *Organisations that are owned by their members and democratically controlled on the basis of one member one vote.* These are organisations whose assets are owned in common by the members, and the members could be staff, users or communities. Any trade surpluses are reinvested in the business or distributed to the members. This category of organisation therefore includes cooperatives and mutuals. These organisations are not necessarily social enterprises because they may be concerned only with benefiting their members, but they can be regarded as social enterprises if the membership is deemed to be a deserving group, for example, unemployed or low income, or if the membership is a community that is in need of development.

Organisations of all four types play an important role in CED, but this does not mean that third sector activities are to be identified with CED. Three differences can be seen. First, community organisations in general, and voluntary organisations, charitable foundations and those social enterprises that aim to benefit communities, can be seen to be well placed for adding value to communities, but this value is not necessarily self-reproducing. Second, third sector activities may add self-reproducing value but not to any particular community – in other words, their activities may legitimately be described as economic development but not as *community economic development*. Third, it is not only the third sector that can add self-reproducing value to communities. As noted above, both public and private sector organisations can also contribute to CED. It is important, therefore, not to be too precious about sectors and the boundaries that may or may not exist between them.

Further, specification of the third sector tends to exclude the roles of the domestic and what is called the 'informal' economy, which are particularly important for communities. It is not clear, however, why the boundaries of the third sector should be set in this way. Although the household (understood, for example, as a group of people living together, with substantial sharing of resources) may not be a charity or community group, it seems to be similar, in that it is also a type of organisation that is owned by no one. It can in fact be characterised as an enterprise: the assets of this domestic economy are huge, as is the labour involved, particularly childcare and housework, but domestic labour is largely unpaid. Such labour not only adds value but also, particularly in the case of childcare, that value can be self-reproducing, at least in the longer term (child rearing can be regarded as a form of investment, which results in adults who produce value in the future). The informal economy, defined as 'the paid production and sale of goods or services which are unregistered by, or hidden from, the state for tax, benefit and/or labour law purposes, but which are legal in all other respects' (Katungi et al, 2006) is also big business in many communities, with its value being estimated at £126 billion per year in the UK (Williams and Windebank, 2000). So, both the domestic and informal economies are of major significance for CED.

Currently, there is considerable interest, particularly from government (see below), in the capacity of the third sector, and of community enterprise generally, to develop communities – for example, by creating jobs, providing local services, improving the environment and building affordable homes. About a quarter of social enterprises are established specifically to support local communities (HM Treasury, 2006, p 29). A whole category of social enterprises, called 'social firms', are in the business of creating good-quality jobs for disadvantaged people (HM Treasury, 2007, p 58).

The track record of the third sector to date, however, is not particularly impressive. Amin et al (2002), for example, found that only 3% of the UK social economy operates without public funds, and the jobs provided are often poorly paid and unstable. In its annual business survey, the Small Business Service (2006) suggested that the social economy does not look like a viable alternative to private or public sector provision, although it can act as a bridge between them. None of this indicates that an emphasis on the third sector in itself is going to lead to any major transformation of the UK economy.

This is not to say that the third sector could not, in certain circumstances, have an important effect on the development of the country's most deprived communities. Currently, however, the prospects for such development do not look particularly favourable. Rodger (2008, pp 191–2), for example, has suggested that the 'cultural toolkits' assembled by young people in certain areas 'are not geared to facilitate their placement in the world of disciplined work. They live in and negotiate a local community environment dominated by illicit trades, which for some will provide entry into and tutelage in activities that may be episodic and do not build up a pension, but in the short-to-medium term are probably more financially lucrative than shelf-stacking, waiting on tables, or fetching and carrying in a factory. Informal working and dealing replace the mainstream economy, and the drugs trade is the main activity at the centre of the "*irregular economy*". The local working–class dealers are the foot soldiers of a global market system that reproduces in its hierarchical and reward structures all the worst excesses of the main economy' (see also Leonard, 2004, discussed in Chapter Two; MacDonald et al, 2005, discussed in Chapter One; and Chapter Nine). What these studies tend to show is that, for some people, the third sector does not (yet?) provide attractive alternatives to dead–end jobs and economic crime.

Governmental approaches to CED

Unsurprisingly, the approaches of governments to CED largely reflect their general approaches to community. In the case of New Labour, its approach had two key elements:

- A focus on reducing what it regarded as the key economic problem of worklessness, with particular emphasis on communities where rates of worklessness are highest, such as coalfields communities and neighbourhoods that score highest on the Index of Multiple Deprivation (CLG, 2007c). The government's aim was social inclusion, namely, the (re)integration of workless people into the labour market. It could be argued that this policy was having a modest degree of success until the recent economic downturn.
- Partnership with the third sector as the main way of tackling community economic problems generally. It was noted in Chapter Four that this approach developed largely following the publication of *Firm Foundations* (CLG, 2004), with an increasing emphasis on the role of community anchor organisations in particular – basically, organisations that can mediate between communities and government.

The clearest statement of the New Labour government's position on CED is to be found in its third sector review (HM Treasury, 2007). Here the government strongly endorsed what it called '*community capacity building*': 'the encouragement and provision of practical support to people to act together voluntarily to tackle problems, influence public services, meet social needs and improve the quality of life in their communities' (HM Treasury, 2007, p 48) (for a critique of the concept of community capacity building, see Craig, 2007). It described such an approach as bottom-up, but of course it was not because it was driven by government itself. It also clarified and developed the roles of community anchor organisations (HM Treasury, 2007, pp 5, 40–1). Apart from community capacity building itself, these were seen as:

- providing voice for under-represented groups (for example, through mentoring – HM Treasury, 2007, p 44)
- campaigning for change in how services are delivered (HM Treasury, 2007, p 52)
- promoting enterprising solutions to social and environmental challenges (HM Treasury, 2007, p 5)
- transforming the design and delivery of public services, for example through mutualisation (HM Treasury, 2007, p 5; see also Reed and Stanley, 2005).

Apart from the last point, this was largely rhetoric, in that the government provided little material support for such activities (for evidence on this, see Rodger, 2008, pp 161–2). The Labour government had long been keen, however, on the so-called 'modernisation' of public services, and it saw mutualisation as an attractive (because it's a 'Third Way' kind of thing) and effective means of achieving this aim. Mutualisation can be understood most simply as the transformation of a public (or even private) service organisation into a third sector body of some kind (for example, a co-operative or a trust), whose members are typically (though not necessarily) its users. Whether it be primary care trusts or Greenwich Leisure Ltd, the government saw the expansion of mutuals and other third sector organisations as a major plank of its agenda (an approach that continues under the current coalition government, with their concept of the Big Society). Moreover, it appeared to want to believe that these organisations would have secure foundations in communities, so that, in the course of time, it would be communities, acting through such organisations, which would take charge of schools, hospitals, public health, social housing, community safety, and so on. Nor did this revolution have to be confined to the public sector: the government was also interested in the potential of mutualisation for the private sector, citing the example of Supporters

Direct, which supports moves towards the democratic ownership of football clubs by their supporters (HM Treasury, 2007, p 47).[5]

To this end, the Home Office introduced two programmes in 2004: ChangeUp and Futurebuilders. The emphasis of these programmes was clearly on mutualisation, as defined above. ChangeUp gave funding to regional and local support providers to form partnerships to work to provide services to make frontline third sector organisations more effective, while Futurebuilders invested directly in those frontline third sector organisations that would otherwise not have access to commercial sources of finance, enabling them to bid for public service contracts. The total cost of these two programmes to 2011 will be £446 million. Evaluation of the programmes to date has criticised them for lack of clear focus on their objectives (for example, no measurable performance targets), poor management, inappropriate and costly applications processes and lack of attention to long-term sustainability (C&AG, 2009; House of Commons Public Accounts Committee, 2009). It seems that both programmes have made some impact but the extent of this impact is unclear.[6]

It may be significant that there is no effective representation of economic development on the boards of local strategic partnerships, which are, after all, the key partnership bodies at a local level (Fuller and Davies, 2005). The (possibly related) fact that most local authorities do not appear to be very interested in implementing the government's vision for the third sector also clearly presents a problem for government. Although a few councils, such as Hartlepool Borough Council (Audit Commission, 2003),[7] appear to be very effective, others appear to be struggling. Some have been described as trying hard but lacking coherence, for example 'Middlesbrough has more vision than Mother Teresa and more pilots than BA' (McGregor et al, 2003, p 26).

By far the largest amount of government funding for economic development work has not been directed specifically towards communities or towards any particular areas at all but has come in the shape of formal support to businesses, from Business Link and other business support providers. This support has cost £12 billion per year. Even so, it has been found to be inadequate and cost-ineffective (Hines, 2004; HM Treasury, 2007, p 70; see also Richard, 2008). In its 2009 budget, however, the Labour government launched the Future Jobs Fund, worth £1 billion, which aimed to create 150,000 jobs by 2011, and it expected 10% of these jobs to be created by social enterprises. The likely impact of this fund on communities is not yet clear at the time of writing.

The main source of spatially directed economic development work under the Labour government was Regional Development Agencies (RDAs), with a budget of £500 million per year. Unfortunately, however, according to at least one report, RDAs largely failed to connect with local communities and were found to be not delivering effective support for CED (Readfearn, 2005). The same could largely be said for the government's initiatives relating to communities with high levels of worklessness. There was certainly development *in* these communities but it is doubtful how far the communities themselves were developed. In the case of coalfields communities, for example, English Partnerships met its targets for reclaiming and developing land, and the Coalfields Regeneration Trust was on course to meet its targets for the provision of community facilities and so on, but high unemployment, poor health and education persisted, and some areas actually fell behind (see, for example, Johnson and Schmuecker, 2007; and Gore et al, 2007 – the Central Valleys in Wales). Basically, New Labour did not join up physical regeneration, and to some extent social regeneration, with economic regeneration. This is not to deny the existence of some success stories, for example, Sherwood Energy Village in Ollerton, and Meden Valley Making Places. The urban regeneration company of New East Manchester was also hailed as a success (Parkinson et al, 2006), but this is not a view that is universally held (see, for example, Ward, 2003).

Another important source of government funding for CED was the Local Enterprise Growth Initiative, which was launched in 2005 to foster entrepreneurial activity in deprived areas, for example, by providing business support for start-ups and helping existing businesses to grow. In the first two bidding rounds, £300 million was allocated to 20 local authorities, but no further round took place and the impact of this funding is not yet clear. The initiative is due to continue until 2011, but after that it is expected that funding will be channelled into boosting employment rather than encouraging new business. The difference between these two is important for communities: helping workless people into jobs may enable and encourage them to leave the area, whereas supporting enterprise and small businesses in a neighbourhood may make people more likely to continue living there.

This point highlights a tension in governmental approaches between what have been called 'people-based' and 'place-based' approaches to economic development. As noted above, the lion's share of government funding has gone towards 'people-based' approaches, specifically focusing on workless people and what might be called spatially insensitive forms of business support, but it is precisely these approaches that appear to have been least successful. Most research suggests that it is more fruitful to adopt 'place-based' approaches, which take account of an area's specific economic characteristics and then develop strategies to bring labour and capital together in such areas. Gore et al (2007), for example, studying labour market changes in three former coalfield areas, South Yorkshire, Lothian and the Welsh Central Valleys, noted how they differed in terms of their economic and physical context and transport links. The researchers concluded that these variations were crucial for understanding their economic development needs. This does not mean that there is no place for 'people-based' approaches, but only that a focus on individual workless people should be situated within a wider understanding of the 'place' or community in which they live, and it is this understanding that has been lacking in central government initiatives. It is interesting to note here the finding by Bailey and Livingston (2007) that, in spite of considerable opinion to the contrary, employment-related interventions targeted on individuals in deprived neighbourhoods do not generally result in people moving out of those neighbourhoods when their job prospects improve. However, it could be argued that this slightly misses the point that many people (particularly young people) do move out of these areas in order, for example, to go to university and/or to take up employment opportunities elsewhere, so interventions that generally increase such opportunities, and facilitate access to such opportunities, will tend to result in increased geographical mobility. It is not so much a matter of 'those who get on, get out' as 'they move out in order to get on'. What seems likely to contribute most to keeping people in an area is making that area a place in which they really want to live.

Another problem with New Labour's approach is what might be described as its lack of three-leggedness. It had no conception of the possible links between economic, social and ecological sustainability. It did not fully appreciate the importance of having an economy that ensures the local circulation and recirculation of the value being produced, for example, in relation to food. It had little understanding of how CED might relate to the wider economy, though this is essential for keeping inward investment in the community. Again, however, there were some notable exceptions, where local implementers seized the initiative. In Castle Vale Housing Action Trust, for example, the training of local people was geared to the skills requirements of potential new employers, and this approach was reported to be successful in reducing unemployment from 50% above the average for Birmingham as a whole to just less than the city average by 2004 (Mornement, 2005).

A harsh verdict on New Labour's approach overall would be that it promoted 'the self-interested profit maximisation of the private sector' whilst continuing 'the top-down bureaucratic and paternalistic approach typical of the public sector' (Levi, 2007, p 43). There is some truth in this, however. It helps to explain both why most of that government's resources went to business support providers, which are mainly private companies, and why those resources appear to have been largely wasted, because of its bureaucratic and paternalistic approach. And of course it also helps to explain why, in spite of its rhetoric to the contrary, relatively few of the government's resources were devoted to real CED.

The future potential for CED: community enterprise or community unionism?

This chapter has shown that CED is commonly associated with the third sector or social economy, but is by no means confined to that sector. Arguably, it has to embrace all sectors of the economy if communities are to be successfully and sustainably developed. Ideally, CED requires an entrepreneurial and three-legged approach, in combination with collective democratic organisation (see ***Box 5.1***). But how is this to be achieved?

Looking at the case of Hill Holt Wood (HHW) outlined in ***Box 5.1***, a number of points are worth noting:

- The community entrepreneurs originate from outside the community and work at the margins of that community, transforming both the community and themselves in the process – just as envisaged by Lindgren and Packendorff (2006).
- The lines separating the private, public and third sectors are blurred. HHW starts out as a private enterprise, then prospers due to support from the public sector and finally transforms itself into a community-owned enterprise or what I have called a 'community co-operative' (Somerville, 2007).
- The transition from a private to a social enterprise can occur for good business reasons, from the private owner's point of view.
- The links between the three legs of an enterprise (economic, social and environmental) can be very indirect and difficult to make – for example, woodland crafts may not be very profitable, the value added by training courses may be difficult to measure, the environmental benefits of woodland management may be difficult to determine and so on. Achieving all three legs simultaneously is very unusual for a social enterprise (Teague, 2007, pp 102–3).

What can be learned from this case is that CED requires a clear vision of what the enterprise is about and a certain single-mindedness to realise that vision. This means avoiding becoming sidetracked by issues of sector, funding sources and so on, and focusing on creating self-reproducing value, social and community benefit, and 'going green'. HHW is not a one-off: the potential for similar enterprises is enormous.

Box 5.1: Hill Holt Wood – a three-legged community enterprise

Hill Holt Wood (HHW) is a 34-acre ancient woodland in Lincolnshire which was bought by Karen and Nigel Lowthrop in 1995. At the time, HHW was in a very poor condition: most quality timber had been removed, invasive rhododendron had taken hold of large tracts of land and the drainage system had been severely damaged, leaving much of the surface area of the woodland waterlogged and inaccessible.

Karen and Nigel explicitly adopted a three-legged approach: economically, the new enterprise had to be a viable company; socially, it had to bring clear benefits to the local community and to society more generally; and environmentally, it had to put more (carbon) into the environment than it took out. First, they became part of the local community by selling their home, using the proceeds to buy an American Winnebago and then moving into it on site. To get the community involved in their enterprise, they took steps to open up the woodland to the public: they built a footpath through the wood for visitors to use as a dog-walking route, then they began attending local events, meeting their neighbours and generally publicising this new amenity. Visitors suggested the woodland would make a pleasant picnic venue, so Karen and Nigel created a small clearing at the edge of the wood and built a number of seating areas there. Soon the local community were arranging 'help days' in which around 20–30 people gathered together and spent the weekend camping in the woodland and helping with restorative activities.

In 1997 Karen and Nigel organised an open meeting, as a result of which a management committee for HHW was established which included representatives from the local community as well as local politicians and business people. Thus HHW became a social enterprise whose membership was open and free to all – members only had to sign their agreement with HHW's aims and objectives. However, HHW needed to look beyond the immediate rural community in order to ensure its long-term economic survival: it needed the support of major stakeholders in government and in the forestry industry. Through contacts developed in the community, Karen and Nigel secured a contract from the local education authority to provide on-site training in basic life skills, such as teamwork and responsibility for young offenders who had been excluded from mainstream education. This training developed into a series of courses, accredited to key stages 3 and 4, designed around improving, managing and maintaining the learning environment, that is, the woodland itself. Also, in 1998, the social enterprise Groundwork in Lincolnshire asked HHW to manage a government contract it had won under the New Deal for Young People programme. The numbers of learners grew steadily over the next few years, as did the number of people employed by HHW to carry out this work. HHW's economic viability seemed to have been secured and its achievements became increasingly recognised, as evidenced by a number of local, regional and national awards, and testimonials from a variety of agencies.

The key point in the transition from what might be described as a socially and environmentally minded private enterprise into a community enterprise occurred in 2002. Karen and Nigel both felt that the overall (three-legged) sustainability of HHW required that the business, and the wood itself, be fully owned and managed by the local community, not by themselves. Consequently, the Volunteer Board of Directors took full control in 2004. The new community enterprise has a membership of around 120 and they are elected to the governing body at an annual general meeting, with seats on the body being apportioned to corporate members (3), staff (2), individual members (7), faith (1) and funders (2). Members can be individual residents or local organisations such as businesses or parish councils.

Source: Adapted from Frith et al (2009)

One of the main obstacles to achieving CED is the widespread tendency to evaluate economic development in terms of the balance sheets of individual businesses. The problem is that a business with considerable social and environmental value may look economically unviable when viewed in these terms. In the case of HHW, for example, its dependence on government contracts may make it appear as if this is an unprofitable business being 'bailed out' by the state. This perspective, however, fails to consider three important factors: the savings to the public sector as a result, for example, of the diversion of young offenders from further offending (and other costs to the public purse, such as income support); the contribution made specifically to the community by the enterprise, which is generally not costed at all; and the value created in the long term as a result of the skills acquired by the young people involved, which may well not have occurred otherwise. This helps to explain why HHW is committed to evaluation in terms of what is called 'Social Return on Investment' (SROI) (see Aeron-Thomas et al, 2004; Lawlor and Nicholls, 2006; Lawlor et al, 2008).

None of this is to say that HHW is a beloved community, or that it forms part of a beloved community. There are undoubtedly inequalities both within the local community and within HHW itself. Rather, HHW points the way towards the possibility of a beloved community – it shows that such a community could be economically, socially and ecologically sustainable, that capitalist exploitation and state command-and-control are not the only ways in which modern economies and societies can be run.

Given the importance of community enterprises such as HHW for CED, it is important to give more thought to their nature and potential. Somerville and McElwee (2010) argue that community enterprise can be explained largely in terms of the balance of social capital functions served by its overall activity. Defining a community enterprise as an enterprise whose social foundation lies in a community of some kind, they go on to argue that the key questions to ask of a community enterprise are who participates in the enterprise, whom they represent and what is the nature of the community in which they move. The key participants are the entrepreneurs, who are seen as activists, in a triple sense: economic, insofar as they create assets and generate income; social, because their activity involves sections of the community in important ways, achieving benefits other than monetary ones; and political, in the sense that much of their activity involves mobilising the community as citizens and lobbying and advocating on their behalf in governmental arenas at local, regional and national levels. Their activism is indissolubly economic/social/political: their focus is on adding value, whether that value be understood in terms of money, social connectedness (community) or political/cultural change. Bourdieu's concept of capital as being economic, social and cultural is then used to explain how such activism can be generated (see Chapter Two).

Further, community enterprises can be understood, to some extent, in terms of the priority they give to different social capital functions (bonding, bridging and linking), how inclusive or exclusive their membership is, how democratically they are organised, how they relate to one another and to non-members, and how they construct community itself (as a polity, a network of interdependent actors, or a primary social group of some kind) (for more detail, see Somerville and McElwee, 2010).

It is also important to distinguish between the contribution made by each enterprise to the community and the total contribution made by all enterprises to the community: each community enterprise, considered in isolation, may serve only a particular section of the community, but all the enterprises together may have the effect of developing the community as a whole. Essentially, the social foundation of community enterprise can be interpreted as a community of equals, whether these be members of a cooperative, a community of supporters, or a community of some other kind, bound together by common residence, interest or identity. Any such community could spawn a variety of community enterprises. For any given community enterprise, then, it is not necessary (though it may be desirable in some cases) for all sections of the community to be represented within it, nor does it require high degrees of community participation, so long as the wider community within which that enterprise operates is democratically governed. The 'community' here must therefore be seen as in one sense a political community, with structures and processes of democratic government.

In the case of Hill Holt Wood, for example, this is seen in the criteria for membership of the enterprise and selection of the Board Directors by the members on the basis of one member one vote. The individual members are drawn from the local community but they also include parish councils, which are (in theory at least) representative of the local community. The governance of HHW, therefore, embraces not only the expected sectional interests within the community (dog walkers, picnickers, those interested in woodland crafts and so on) but also the interests of the community as a whole, as expressed through local political representatives (not only parish councils but also the local district council).

A very different approach from the above has come to be known as 'community unionism' (Wills, 2001, 2002; Wills and Simms, 2004). According to this approach, sustainable CED is to be achieved through some kind of alliance or coalition between trade unions and community groups, and particularly between producers and users of public services. Wills and Simms (2004) see this as a potentially effective way of mobilising workers who feel alienated from 'pale, male and stale' trade unions and who are less likely to be organised in their workplaces. They point out that such coalitions are common in the US and have proved to be successful, for example, in campaigns for a living wage. In the UK, however, such coalitions are few and far between. The outstanding example is that of London Citizens (see **Box 2.3** in Chapter Two): this started out as The East London Community Organisers (TELCO), which was strongly supported by local trade union organisations – in particular, UNISON. In general, though, the record of cooperation between trade unions and local communities is not good, and the prognosis could hardly be said to be favourable. Wills and Simms (2004) argue that a clear national strategy is required to sustain community unionism and make it effective, but the likelihood that such a strategy might be developed in the foreseeable future seems negligible. It could therefore be concluded that community unionism does not represent a significant national approach to CED in the context of the UK, though this is not to say that it cannot make occasional and important contributions in particular locations, as has happened in the case of London Citizens.

Finally, one could mention radical utopian approaches such as 'participatory economics' or 'parecon' (Albert, 2003). This is the creation of Michael Albert and Robin Hahnel. It involves self-managing workplace and consumer councils, remuneration based on effort and sacrifice, balanced job complexes and participatory planning. The beauty of parecon is that it involves the complete abolition of the labour market and its replacement by a system in which all work–related decisions are made democratically, so that exploitation and class divisions become impossible. The weakness of parecon, however, is that it offers no way to get from here to there. And even if it did, there would still be fundamental problems with it: for example, the emphasis on input measures of the value of work (in terms of the amount of effort or sacrifice) neglects the importance of output measures (in terms of product or service innovation, quality of design, aesthetic effect, greenhouse gas reduction, consumer satisfaction and so on); and it is not clear that anyone really understands how an advanced industrial economy could be practically organised on the basis of a system of participatory planning. Is it necessary, for example, to do without money? If so, then how is a system of sophisticated barter to be organised? And if not, what is to stop people paying whatever they think a thing is worth rather than what it has been judged to be worth in terms of the effort or sacrifice gone into making it? Either way, it would seem that making parecon work would require a powerful collective will that would inevitably be oppressive of its individual members.

Conclusion

This chapter has explored different approaches to community economic development, classified in terms of top-down, bottom-up and side-in. It has argued that all types of approach are problematic, mainly because of the structural inequalities between 'top' and 'bottom'. Certain types of side-in approach, however, where elements of the 'top' meet with elements of the 'bottom', seem to be capable of delivering CED. These are ones that can be shown to be 'three-legged', in the sense of being economically, socially and environmentally sustainable and cutting across private, public and third sectors. Since CED is commonly assumed to sit within the third sector, the chapter has provided an analysis of that sector and concluded that specifically *community* economic development does indeed occur within that sector, but also outside it and at the boundaries of the community itself. This finding echoes what other scholars have concluded about enterprise generally. Community enterprise, like all enterprise, is not to be restricted to any particular sector. Community enterprises can be owned by the community or by no one at all. For a beloved community, they have only to involve the flourishing of all their members equally in a cooperative endeavour.

The chapter has included an analysis and critique of government policy on CED. In particular, it has identified that governments mainly emphasise economic development regardless of community, and that specifically *community* economic development is secondary. The emphasis on community, however, has increased since 2004, and takes the form of encouraging 'communities' to take on as much responsibility for public services as possible, and maybe for some private services as well – an approach that is largely continued under the present coalition government. The main problems with this approach are that it may not be either attractive or desirable for communities to take on such responsibilities in many cases, and that the process of such take-overs seems to be part of a wider neoliberal project, in which the interests of poorer communities in particular are subordinated to those of commerce and outside investors. In any event, the approach barely succeeds in being more than one-legged. Given this finding, the prospects for achieving the beloved community on a wider scale are not looking good.

The final section of the chapter considered the future potential of CED and argued that there seems little alternative to the approach of building, developing and supporting a wide range of three-legged community enterprises, where such enterprises are committed to developing a beloved community (a community of equals, in which the flourishing of every individual member is achieved through the cooperation of all). Hill Holt Wood was described in detail as an example of such an enterprise. In contrast, few prospects were seen for community unionism, and none at all for participatory economics.

Notes

[1] The term 'regeneration' is essentially vague, not just because it includes physical, social and cultural as well as economic development, but because it confuses capital with mere expenditure. Regeneration may add value but it does not necessarily produce self-expanding value – it could involve consumption (or even waste) rather than investment. The all-embracing character of the term allows the government to claim, for example, that it plans to spend as much as £36.5 billion over two years 2009–10 on regeneration (CLG, 2009).

[2] See conclusion from a review of JRF research: 'The quality of jobs, and whether in economic terms they offer realistic incentives for people to return to work, remain fundamental challenges even if transport connections and other measures to connect disadvantaged areas to jobs are addressed' (Taylor, 2008, p 13).

[3] Peer-to-peer production is a form of economy that involves distributed networks, which are 'networks in which autonomous agents can freely determine their behavior and linkages without the intermediary of obligatory hubs' (Bauwens, 2005). Bauwens characterises peer-to-peer production as a 'third' mode of production, a 'third' mode of governance and a 'third' mode of ownership. In practice, it is a form of cooperative enterprise in which membership is open to everyone equally who wants to participate in the (virtual) community.

[4] Bovaird (2007, p 847) defines co-production as 'the provision of services through regular, long-term relationships between professionalised service providers and service users or other members of the community, where all parties make substantial resource contributions'. For the latest thinking on co-production, see Slatter (2010).

[5] In this respect, the current coalition government could be different, as they appear to include the private sector within their 'Big Society'.

[6] Unsurprisingly, the Conservatives have now announced that they are to be abolished (Queen's Speech, 25 May 2010).

[7] Hartlepool Borough Council was described by the Audit Commission as making an excellent start with excellent prospects for improvement. The council ensures a good choice of sites and buildings for businesses, it encourages inward investment, it supports businesses by offering advice and support, it supports sector development in relation to tourism and it underpins these activities by regional and local partnership working.

Summary

Community economic development is a key feature of community development generally. The main approaches therefore reflect those described in Chapter Two. This chapter, however, contains further discussion of how, in particular, governments and other powerful organisations work *with* communities, and the problems that are commonly associated with such collaboration. The relatively uncritical and unregulated expansion of the third sector under New Labour looks set to continue under the coalition, subject, of course, to the expenditure cuts that are expected to affect all public sector economic activity. In the long term, however, it is hoped that more strategic attention will be given to how best to encourage, nurture and reward community entrepreneurship.

Questions for discussion

- What is self-expanding value? How can we recognise it when we see it?

- What is the third sector? Why is it deemed to be preferable to the first and second sectors for developing communities?

- What is the appropriate role for government in relation to community economic development? How can governments be persuaded to adopt this role?

- What is community enterprise and community entrepreneurship?

Further reading

Frith, K., McElwee, G. and Somerville, P. (2009) 'Building a "community co-operative" at Hill Holt Wood', *Journal of Co-operative Studies,* vol 42, no 2, pp 38-47.

HM Treasury (2007) *The future role of the third sector in social and economic regeneration: Final report*, Cm 7189, London: HM Treasury.

Somerville, P. and McElwee, G. (2010, forthcoming) 'Situating community enterprise: a theoretical exploration', *Entrepreneurship and Regional Development.*

Community learning

Overview

Community learning is a process of developing understanding of our connectedness with one another, leading to the deepening of that interconnectedness. The key to community learning is the *recognition of common purpose*. Learning is distinguished from schooling, which is to do with achieving uniformity and predictability of activity. Schooling is not incompatible with understanding but it tends to place arbitrary limits on the possibility of understanding, for example through command-and-control structures and the commodification of learning itself.

The chapter considers how schools can become more 'community-friendly', it draws a distinction between community learning and family learning, and it suggests that the government's Sure Start programme is not sufficiently rooted in local communities to achieve community learning that can be sustained after the programme has come to an end. In contrast, some community-led initiatives, by ensuring that learning is passed on from one community to another, and reinforced through processes of simultaneous teaching and learning, have greater potential to endure.

The nature of community learning

Learning can be considered as a process of developing knowledge, skills and understanding. Understanding is key because without it knowledge is just lists of facts, and skills are merely cleverness. The nature of understanding, however, or rather of the capacity to understand, commonly known as intelligence, is the subject of considerable debate:

> Individuals differ from one another in their ability to understand complex ideas, to adapt effectively to the environment, to learn from experience, to engage in various forms of reasoning, to overcome obstacles by taking thought. Although these individual differences can be substantial, they are never entirely consistent: a given person's intellectual performance will vary on different occasions, in different domains, as judged by different criteria. Concepts of 'intelligence' are attempts to clarify and organize this complex set of phenomena. Although considerable clarity has been achieved in some areas, no such conceptualization has yet answered all the important questions and none commands universal assent. (Wikipedia – http://en.wikipedia.org/wiki/ Intelligence – accessed 17 August 2009)

Given this variation in the capacity of individuals to understand and learn, it follows that the learning capacity of communities is also likely to vary greatly. Community learning, however, while encompassing individual learning, is of a qualitatively different order. If community is understood as meaningful interconnectedness, as argued in Chapter One, then understanding is at the heart of what community is all about, and it is an understanding that is essentially shared with others. Understanding here signifies nothing more or less than a mental grasp of meaningful interconnectedness.

All learning adds to our value as sentient beings (learning is not limited to the human species!). One way of making sense of this is in terms of the concept of human capital (Becker, 1964), whereby an individual's learning is seen as an asset that can be set to work (by themselves or by others) to produce added value. Learning in this sense is a kind of economic capital (see Chapter Five), and learners can therefore be seen as producers and entrepreneurs. This interpretation of learning, however, is overly narrow for our purposes, not only because of its inherent speciesism (it assumes that only human labour can be productive of value) but also because the value that learning adds is not merely economic. Learning develops social and cultural capital as well as economic capital: as we saw in Chapter Two, much of the value associated with higher status, distinction and influence is produced by particular forms of knowledge, skills and educational credentials (cultural capital), and increased understanding within and across social networks can help to build social capital.

Community learning is concerned specifically not so much with learning *in* the community as with learning *by* the community, as a whole. Some advocates of community learning see it as a bottom-up process, a process of community self-development, involving cooperative lifelong self-learning (see, for example, Ellis, 2003, 2005). They believe in a fully inclusive sharing of learning within and across communities based on open communication, in which communities take ownership of their own learning through dialogue, self-evaluation and self-development. They are critical of forms of institutional learning, particularly schools, and tend to support homeschooling movements. They want to break down unnecessary barriers between teachers and learners, between 'experts' and 'non-experts'. They have a vision of learning as one that is, in Bourdieu's terms, geared to the habitus of individuals and communities, and not subordinated to governmental agendas of employability and the production of 'good citizens'.

Community learning can therefore be seen as an essential aspect of building meaningful interconnectedness, that is, of community development. Community learning is the name given to the process whereby communities learn *that* they are meaningfully interconnected, *how* they are meaningfully interconnected and how they become *more* meaningfully interconnected and more *purposeful* in their activities. This does not mean, however, that communities necessarily become more homogeneous or less diverse in terms of their beliefs or values – on the contrary, community learning is more likely to lead to greater cultural richness and diversity.

Although it may overlap with it to some extent, community learning is not to be equated with the 'anything goes' approach associated with anarchist 'free schools', in which the distinction between teachers and learners is blurred, there is no set curriculum and no set timetables for learning. Community learning is indeed open-ended and democratic but this does not mean that it rejects all structured approaches to learning. Rather, it involves structures that enable learners to develop their own sense of purpose (and consequently, their own beliefs and ways of acting), both as individuals and as a community: for example, through how learning is organised, the shape and content of the curriculum, and the methods and styles of learning adopted.

Schooling versus community learning

Schools would appear to be the main formal community-based agency for learning activities, and learning can be said to be institutionalised in such organisations, insofar as learning activity is officially recognised as such, only to the extent that it fits into the curriculum and work routines that the school follows. The school as an institution can provide valuable structure for learning processes but it also has limitations from the point of view of community learning, especially if not grounded in learners' communities outside the school, for example, in the home, the street, the neighbourhood, friendship networks and so on.

'Learning' is sometimes contrasted unfavourably with 'schooling', which is said to mean 'to be conditioned, to believe, to perform and to act in a given way' (Meighan, 2004).[1] The key question, however, is whether schools necessarily involve such top–down regimentation and, if so, what repercussions this has for students' learning. In practice, it could be argued that whether a school is primarily enabling or disabling of community learning will depend largely upon what it is aiming to do – what is sometimes called the ethos of the school.

Notwithstanding this argument, it must be admitted that schools tend to be top–down, hierarchical structures, where each class teacher rules over their class and the head teacher rules over all. It is this authoritarian, command-and-control structure that enacts 'schooling' and produces a general sense of uniformity in a school. Moreover, these structures are firmly embedded within an all-encompassing and corrupting capitalist system, where schools function as factories for the production of knowledge and credentials that raise labour productivity and reproduce class distinction.[2] The disadvantages of such structures for learning of any kind, let alone community learning, have long been documented by writers such as Illich (1973), Holt (1964) and others. In Illich's view, for example:

> Schooling – the production of knowledge, the marketing of knowledge, which is what the school amounts to, draws society into the trap of thinking that knowledge is hygienic, pure, respectable, deodorized, produced by human heads and amassed in stock.... [B]y making school compulsory, [people] are schooled to believe that the self-taught individual is to be discriminated against; that learning and the growth of cognitive capacity, require a process of consumption of services presented in an industrial, a planned, a professional form;... that learning is a thing rather than an activity. A thing that can be amassed and measured, the possession of which is a measure of the productivity of the individual within the society. That is, of his social value. (Cited by Gajardo, 1994, p 715)

Illich, then, saw schools as an integral part of a system dedicated to the commodification of all aspects of reality, including knowledge. Learning, which was for Illich an aspect of being in the world (part of the habitus of every individual and community), becomes corrupted into the acquisition of knowledge, seen as a possession to be exploited (part of a global capitalist economic field).

John Holt was equally scathing about 'education', but for rather different reasons:

> Education ... now seems to me perhaps the most authoritarian and dangerous of all the social inventions of mankind. It is the deepest foundation of the modern slave state, in which most people feel themselves to be nothing but producers, consumers, spectators, and 'fans,' driven more and more, in all parts of their lives, by greed, envy, and fear. My concern is not to improve 'education' but to do away with it, to end the ugly and antihuman business of people-shaping and to allow and help people to shape themselves. (Cited by Wikipedia – http://en.wikipedia.org/wiki/John_Holt_(educator))

Where Illich objected primarily to the industrialisation and marketisation of knowledge, Holt saw the education system as fundamentally coercive. In crude terms, both were libertarians, but Illich was a socialist (or at least anti-capitalist) while Holt was a liberal (and maybe pro-market in some sense). Illich was not opposed to schools in principle but claimed only that, once a certain threshold of institutionalisation had been reached, schools made people more stupid (in Habermasian terms, we could say that this institutionalisation represents a colonisation of their lifeworld by the system – see Chapter One). In contrast, Holt lost faith in the possibility of school reform and rejected the education system entirely. Both of them, however, came to advocate forms of homeschooling, family and community learning, and so-called 'informal education' (for more on informal education, see www.infed.org).

Since Illich and Holt, the commodification of learning has progressed by leaps and bounds – see, for example, Leadbeater (2000). Traditionally, students have been seen as passive consumers in the sense of empty vessels into which teachers poured knowledge, but now they (or at least their parents or guardians, acting on their behalf) are increasingly viewed as active consumers, choosing the schools to which they go and even running schools for themselves.[3] Holt might be pleasantly surprised by what is to be found in some schools today, whereas Illich would be horrified.

The work of Illich and Holt has been largely neglected or ignored, let alone critically evaluated. An obvious point to make, however, is that the evidence on which their critiques of schools are based is, at least in Illich's case, very thin. A number of awkward questions need to be asked. For example: Does institutionalisation actually reduce the value of learning and, if so, how and why? Or: If schools are so oppressive of children, why is it that so many students of all ages regularly express positive feelings about the school they attend?[4] Or again: Granted that schools have certain inherent faults, are the alternatives to school necessarily any better?

For this book, the acid test of a school is how it performs in relation to the community in which it is based, particularly a poor or encapsulated community. Does it, for example, merely reconcile the younger members of that community to their lot in life, expecting little by way of academic achievement and doing nothing to raise their aspirations? Does it focus attention mainly on the brighter students and tend to neglect the rest? Does it see itself as part of the community, working with local people to improve their quality of life and so on, or does it see itself as set apart from the community, enabling young people to escape to what it regards as a brighter future for them?

Over the years, such questions have moved up the political agenda, for a number of reasons. First, the working-class comprehensive schools of the 1960s and 1970s were criticised for their low standards of educational attainment (particularly compared with Britain's main competitors) and therefore for 'failing' their pupils. Since then, the primary purpose of government education policy has been to improve school performance. Second, the importance of parental involvement in children's learning has been increasingly recognised by government and, to facilitate such involvement, a more open and communicative approach by schools towards their surrounding communities is required.

The problem here is that there is a certain tension between hitting performance targets and being more 'community-friendly'. Increased emphasis on school performance can increase this tension (Crowther et al, 2003). For schools, the dilemma is that they are under pressure to raise pupil attainment levels (as reported publicly in school league tables) but also to be 'inclusive', for example, of children with learning or behavioural difficulties. An obvious way of improving league-table performance is to be more 'exclusive' in terms of selecting more promising pupils and excluding more 'difficult' or troublesome ones, but most schools have little freedom for manoeuvre here. Needless to say, however, the adoption by any school of such a more 'exclusive' approach would show a lack of responsibility towards the needs of the community.

With increasing emphasis on 'parental choice' and the growing diversity of specialist schools (technology, language, sports and so on), school Trusts and city academies, schools also run the risk of becoming more disconnected from their local communities. At the same time, however, they may become more connected with communities of other kinds, such as regional, national and even global communities of faith, business and learning. Their catchment areas may be larger, and they may be more closely linked with other schools and education institutions in other areas. Cantle

(2008), however, is firmly of the opinion that faith schools in particular are divisive on a local scale, though evidence to support this opinion is lacking (but see ICC, 2009[5]). Arguably, schools are disconnected from their local communities in other ways, for example, because they have to deliver a national curriculum, much of which will have little of relevance to local communities. Admittedly, citizenship studies has been introduced partly to counteract this,[6] but Ofsted (2006) reports continuing poor teaching of this subject in a quarter of schools.

Homeschooling, that is, the organisation of learning for children in their families and communities, was the norm until the 19th century. Typically, it was geared towards the type of work that children would pursue throughout their lives, for example, in the fields or in the home. Today, however, homeschooling is very different. It is largely a reaction against the negative effects of formal schooling and takes many different forms, using a wide variety of methods and materials – for more information, see Wikipedia on 'Homeschooling'. Homeschooling is a significant movement in the US, where in 2003 there were 1.1 million homeschooled students. Numerous studies in that country have found that homeschooled students on average outperform their peers on standardised tests. However, these studies may not be comparing like with like, as the parents of homeschooled students are likely to have more formal education and higher incomes than the average parent; also, the homeschool testing is usually voluntary, while the public school testing is compulsory. Overall, it is not yet clear what advantages, if any, homeschooling may have over formal schooling. The most likely conclusion to be drawn is that it all depends on the nature of the schooling provided in either case. Such a conclusion would be reminiscent of debates about whether childcare is better provided by two carers than by one – that is, it all depends on the quality of care being provided.

The relationship between school and community

Arguably, the purpose of a school is, first and foremost, to serve the children and young people in its care. Such service, however, can be interpreted in a variety of ways. Does it mean, for instance, giving top priority to ensuring that they get the best grades in examinations, leading to top positions in adult society? Or does it mean giving them the best possible preparation for the adult life that they are most likely to lead? Or does it mean ensuring that their experience of school is as enjoyable as possible, including intellectual stimulation as well as a circle of friends and pastoral support? Or does it mean treating them all fairly, fostering their sense of justice and fair play, so that they become 'active citizens' in a positive sense, contributing towards making the world a better place? The answers to all these questions help to determine what the elusive ethos of a school might be.

Part of this ethos has to do with how the school relates to the community in which it is based. For community learning, it is necessary for schools to be open and accountable to their communities. A school that sees itself as set apart from its community is likely to have an elitist ethos, in the sense that it is concerned with cultivating 'leaders of the future', in which leadership is understood in a traditional hierarchical sense rather than a distributed sense. This ethos is often reinforced by the leadership style of the head teacher, which can be autocratic rather than democratic. The unaccountable school, therefore, has an inevitable tendency towards elitism and autocracy. Traditionally, this tendency was supposed to be held in check by the local education authority (LEA), who ostensibly represented local communities and who had considerable powers to determine school budgets, open and close schools, hire and fire school staff and decide school policies generally. Following the implementation of the policy of Local Management of Schools (LMS) in the late 1980s, however, many of these powers, particularly the control of budgets, were devolved to individual schools. Suddenly, the governing board of the school became the key body for holding the head teacher to account.

LMS stipulates that each school governing body must include elected parent and teacher governors and nominated governors from the LEA and from the local community (the latter is not specified, so it could be a local shopkeeper or a representative of a local residents' association or other interest group). The only significant group of stakeholders that does not have to be represented on the governing body is the pupils. With this exception, however, the composition of the governing body can be seen to ensure a certain degree of accountability of the school to the local community: apart from the actual community representative, parents mostly live in the community, so do many of the teachers, and the LEA governors typically live locally too or represent the local community in other ways (for example, as local councillors). So here we have an example of what has been called a 'learning democracy with over 350,000 local people legally responsible for the conduct and direction of their schools and large amounts of public money' (Allen and Martin, 2002, p 9).

The question is, however: how successful has LMS been in holding head teachers to account and connecting schools with local communities and businesses? What difference has it really made to the policy, practice and performance of schools generally? It is worth pointing out that LMS does not define any strategic role for the governing body in relation to the community. The agendas of governing bodies are almost entirely focused on the school itself, and it is arguable that LMS has had the effect of co-opting parents and community to these agendas. The governors identify with the common interest of the school but do not necessarily have a clear idea of what this is (Dean et al, 2007). Further, the membership of governing bodies does not reflect the make-up of the population of either parents or local communities: school governors are disproportionately white, female and professional (Dean et al, 2007).

There are signs now that the agenda may be moving on from LMS. For example, the Welsh Assembly Government published the School Councils (Wales) Regulations in 2005, which require the governing bodies of local authority maintained schools (except nursery and infant schools) to establish school councils to which one student from each year is elected. The council must meet at least six times a year to discuss matters relating to the school, their education and any other matters of concern or interest, and to make representations to the head teacher and governing body, who must consider the matter and respond accordingly (National Assembly for Wales, 2005). An increasing number of schools in England have set up similar school councils. It looks, therefore, as if schools are becoming more democratic.

Another example is that of trust schools. Following the Education and Inspections Act 2006, school governing bodies can opt to set up a trust, which is a charity, owning the assets of the school and employing staff. One purpose of setting up such a trust is to allow for the federating of several schools within a single legal entity. The trust partners can be a variety of public, private and voluntary organisations who are responsible for appointing some school governors, known as foundation governors. Trust schools are based on the model of foundation schools, which are part funded by religious organisations (mainly) (for more detail, see DCSF, 2009a). Arguably, this model represents a further step in the disconnection of schools from local communities and towards greater connection with other schools, businesses, universities and faith and other voluntary organisations. The advantages of this move, in terms of possible increased collaboration, diversity, enterprise and innovation, have not yet been demonstrated.

Policy makers generally assume that a school contributes, or at least can contribute, value to its local community (see, for example, the policy on extended schools discussed below). This is, however, an issue that does not seem to have been much considered by researchers. One exception is Clarke et al (2007), who studied an area in Bristol that had lost its secondary school – see *Box 6.1*. As a result, children had to attend schools elsewhere and: 'This leads to the disintegration of school-based networks which often involve mothers. It also increases mobility and transitoriness among the local population, as families may move to get their children into the secondary school of their choice. This fosters a sense that the community cannot offer residents what they want and therefore they are willing to put less into the community' (Clarke et al, 2007, pp 91–2). The general lesson is clear: schools can act as an important and relatively stable focus for the growth of meaningful interconnectedness, that is, community, and the closure of a school can therefore be seriously damaging for community.

Box 6.1: The value of a school to a community

You feel 'us against the world', that sort of attitude develops, when you attack a school, you attack its community as well. I can't think of anyone I've met who's had an involvement with the school in the past who's not felt a real sense of loss from it closing. And obviously especially the kids that were going there until a year or so ago, they've not got anything good to say about the change at all, but are very negative about it ... The expression I keep hearing from a number of people is that it seemed to sort of rip the soul out of the area for a lot of people.

Source: Bristol respondent, cited in Clarke et al (2007, p 91)

Extended schools

Another way in which schools can serve their local communities is through extended provision within the school outside of normal school hours. According to current government policy (see DfES, 2005), such provision can be wide ranging, and includes wraparound childcare, parenting support, family learning and widespread community use of school facilities, not just for learning but for other health and recreational activities. A school that provides all of these services is known as a full-service extended school.

'Wraparound childcare' essentially means childcare 'wrapped around' the usual core provision by the school. It is defined as 'care for 3–4 year olds provided before and/or after an early years education place and directly facilitated by the provider' (Smith et al, 2004). In addition to the 2.5 hours' free early education place as core provision, the child receives so-called 'extended provision', which parents have to pay for. Effectively, this enables full-time childcare from 8am to 6pm on all school days. Such wraparound care has been found to be both popular with parents, particularly working parents (affordable, good value and accessible) and beneficial for children (in terms of stability, familiarity, continuity of care, smoother transition to full-time schooling, and improved social skills) (Smith et al, 2004). Most nurseries also provide wraparound care, but this is not usually linked to schools (Smith and Lee, 2005).

In itself, wraparound care is a form of social care rather than community learning. However, it is clearly important for supporting children's learning and therefore for facilitating community learning. In addition, as part of a full-service extended school, it frees up time for parents to take part in a range of activities, which include community learning. The evaluation of the government's Full Service Extended Schools Initiative, launched in 2003, found that it was improving pupils' educational attainment, impacting positively on family stability and generally enhancing the life chances of local people – for example, adult learning classes have enabled unemployed adults to gain qualifications leading to work (Cummings et al, 2007). Community Learning Centres on school sites in many areas now provide a full service: early years education, childcare, positive parenting initiatives and study support.

Evaluation suggests that the policy of extended schools is helping to make schools more 'community-friendly', with most parents and pupils rating the extended services positively, particularly where those services are provided as part of a 'cluster' of schools working together (Wallace et al, 2009). This comes at some cost to the school itself, but this seems to be outweighed by the benefits for both individuals and communities. A report by the Audit Commission (2006a) provides many examples of schools working well with other organisations to achieve community learning and development. One of these examples is reproduced in ***Box 6.2***.

Box 6.2: The role of schools in regeneration and renewal in Hartlepool

Hartlepool New Deal for Communities (NDC) has carried out detailed work and established governance structures to enable residents to understand, define and propose action in their own communities. A wide range of engagement methods were employed including local street meetings and focus groups to reach specific groups such as ethnic minorities, older people and children. Community conferences have included groups of primary and secondary school children from across the town who have effectively helped to influence the contents of plans for their areas.

Stranton and Lynnfield primary schools have had Community Learning Centres built on site, funded using NDC capital, to provide early years education, childcare, positive parenting initiatives and study support. These two schools have also both recruited two social inclusion assistants and pupil attendance has improved significantly as a result. But while only these two schools are located in the NDC area, all schools in the town with substantial numbers of NDC resident pupils are engaged in NDC funded projects, aimed at raising their educational attainment.

Schools are also making a contribution to regeneration and renewal in other ways. For example, Dyke House secondary school has recruited and trained 70 non-teaching staff from the community, engaged in roles such as teaching assistant and learning mentor, and has its own training scheme for technicians. Schools are also well-developed in relation to extended school activities, with all schools running breakfast clubs and at least five extended activities. These activities enhance links with the community as well as providing enrichment opportunities for children.

Source: Audit Commission (2006a, p 24)

Governmental area-based initiatives

Over the decades, governments have launched numerous area-based initiatives that have impacted on community learning. In recent years, the most important of these have been Education Action Zones, Excellence in Cities and, above all, Sure Start. It is probably fair to say that Sure Start has completely eclipsed all the others, but there are still some lessons to be learned from the others that are worth noting here.

Education Action Zones (EAZs) aimed to develop new ways of raising standards and enriching children's educational experience in areas with underperforming schools. They were run by forums or committees of parents, local communities, national and local businesses, and local education authorities. Excellence in Cities Action Zones were a follow-up to EAZs but smaller, each being built around one secondary school and a cluster of 'feeder' primaries.

In terms of community learning, a notable finding related to the use of family centres in EAZs. Research by Ranson and Rutledge (2005) revealed that such family centres could transform traditional values and child behaviour – from blind obedience to parental authority and stereotypical gender roles to basing relationships on respect and dialogue and commitment to lifelong learning and service to a wider community. Tisdall et al (2005) found similarly that parents and children expressed increased confidence, improved child behaviour and development, improved finances (for example, reduced worklessness), faster access to services and improved community relationships. On the down side, however, families with multiple difficulties (in particular with housing) did not perceive positive impacts. Since then, the government has funded an increasing number of intensive family support projects with similar aims and using similar methods (see **Box 6.3** for an example).

Box 6.3: Learning how to live in community

Jane is a single mother with three children. Problems arose when she moved into a neighbourhood with a good reputation. The neighbours were described as 'highly motivated, educated people'. Her elder daughter, who was pregnant, was in a violent relationship with a drug dealer; her younger daughter was exhibiting poor behaviour at school and was bullying others. Her son had spent time in care and, when he returned to live with the family, he did not get on with her new partner and as a result the partner moved out. Shortly afterwards, her elder daughter lost her baby due to a cot death. Over the following 18 months neighbours made numerous complaints to the police, the local MP and the local paper: noisy parties, alleged drug dealing from the premises, people threatening neighbours with baseball bats, and cars coming and going at all times of the day and night. The neighbours wanted the family moved.

The Intensive Family Support project worker worked closely with each member of the family to address the underlying problems. Jane was provided with support in developing parenting routines and structures; her son was assisted with budgeting skills and in getting a job as a YTS [Youth Training Scheme] mechanic; and a system of rewards was established to address the younger daughter's aggressive and bullying behaviour. Following six months of intensive work with the project, the changes that were achieved were remarkable and resulted in neighbours writing to the local beat officer saying: 'I don't know what you've done, but it's marvellous.'

Source: Adapted from Nixon et al (2006, pp 7–8)

This is a particularly interesting example for community learning because, although it appears to be a success story, it is clear that the community (understood as the highly motivated, educated neighbours) has actually learned nothing from this experience. On their own admission, they do not know what has been done and are, consequently, not in a position to be able to learn from it. This is therefore a good example of family learning but not of community learning. It is not even clear whether the family concerned has even been accepted as part of the community now. Yet, without the support of networks of friends and relatives in the community (social capital and so on), it seems likely that this family's problems will eventually re-emerge.

Another initiative perhaps worth mentioning is that of Community Learning Chests. These were funded through the Neighbourhood Renewal Unit's Skills and Knowledge programme (based in what is now the Department of Communities and Local Government). £10 million was made available to distribute in small grants of between £50 and £5,000 to help individuals and residents' groups to access the learning and advice they needed to play an active role in delivering neighbourhood renewal in their local area. Activities could include training programmes or other learning opportunities, exchange visits, attendance at conferences, use of a neighbourhood renewal adviser, magazine subscriptions, reference books, and support for black and minority ethnic communities to explore and share their culture and traditions so as to promote racial harmony and community cohesion. Anecdotal evidence indicates that Community Learning Chest grants are very much welcomed by community groups (probably for much the same reasons as noted in **Box 2.2** in relation to the JRF Neighbourhood Programme – Taylor et al, 2007), but no formal evaluation seems to have been conducted.

A further relevant government initiative is the Active Learning for Active Citizenship (ALAC) programme, launched by the Home Office in 2004. This was focused on delivering the learning required to enable people to become 'active citizens' (see discussion in Chapters Three and Four). It is a strange initiative because it purports to develop the skills and knowledge required to engage effectively with governmental bodies but it contains no coherent analysis or understanding of how these bodies work and does not even pose the question of why people would want to engage with them. Its vision of active citizens is devoid of any clear political content. As a result, one cannot be sure what is being learned here, let alone whether it might count as community learning. It pays lip-service to Freire but it seems to lack his critical acumen. It would appear to be an example of participationism (see Chapter Three). The programme has since been succeeded by Take Part (see www.takepart.org). Some useful community development is no doubt being carried out under this programme, but its contribution to community learning is currently very difficult to determine. It may be that its main effect is in helping to develop social capital, but it lacks any clear focus (for example, is it really concerned with building linking social capital, or what?). There has been an evaluation of ALAC (Mayo and Rooke, 2006), but this was relatively uncritical and no evaluation of Take Part has yet been published.

Similar comments could be made about the government's introduction of citizenship education into the national curriculum. France and Meredith (2009, p 88) make the point so well that it is worth reproducing their argument in full:

> This is aimed at preparing young people to be citizens by teaching them their social and moral responsibility, about what community involvement means, and about political literacy (Advisory Group on Citizenship, 1998). However, what is absent

in this debate is a recognition that citizenship is a 'lived' state, in which being a citizen is a social process where individuals are active in constructing themselves as citizens through norms, practices and meanings in everyday life ... Citizenship in this context is a more dynamic and negotiated process that can involve power struggles over who is to be included or excluded. It is therefore important to recognise that citizenship is not simply a legal status but also a social–political practice of being recognised ... Policy fails to actively acknowledge this in terms of the young, with the focus being on the making of future citizens ... Policy sees young people as 'between' childhood and adulthood and 'in transition' towards adulthood, therefore the lived daily experiences of the young are given little attention. Citizenship education is concentrated on 'responsibilising' young people, making sure they understand what their core responsibilities are in being citizens ... For example, within these discussions the emphasis is on participation as volunteering, where individuals are encouraged to 'give back' to others ... Government's approach to both participation and citizenship is, then, very narrowly focused and does not acknowledge young people's lived experiences of citizenship.

Sure Start is by far the largest governmental initiative related to community learning, and it dwarfs all the other initiatives. It was launched as a 10–year programme in 1999 by what were then the Department for Education and Skills and the Department of Health. It provided funding of up to £3 billion for 524 Sure Start Local Programmes (SSLPs), each with a budget of up to £1 million per year and typically serving a population of 400–800 children. Later on, a further 45 mini Sure Starts were established in rural areas, each typically serving 150–170 children. SSLPs were administered by local partnerships between local authorities, primary care trusts, and voluntary and private sector organisations, with the aim of bringing together core programmes of health (child and maternal), early education and play, and family support for children below the age of four. In practice, their core services have been: outreach and home visiting (for befriending, delivering health/development services, acting as a gateway to other services and providing specialist services); primary and community healthcare (for example, for postnatal depression, pregnancy, breastfeeding support and smoking cessation); support for good-quality play, learning and childcare; and other support to families and parents (Allnock et al, 2005). The emphasis on outreach work was important for two reasons: to access difficult-to-reach families and to ensure autonomy for local projects.[7] SSLPs were required to involve parents in their governance structures (management boards and parent forums), in determining local needs and priorities and in assessing the impact of the interventions made.

SSLPs are currently in the process of transferring to 3,500 Sure Start Children's Centres, a process that was due to be completed in 2010. These Centres are funded through local authorities (instead of directly by government) and managed by Children's Trusts. According to the Department for Children, Schools and Families website (accessed 20 August 2009), the government expected to see a change in the core services being provided, as it specifically mentions helping parents into work (with links to the local Jobcentre Plus and training) and sees its national childcare strategy as enabling all families with children to have access to an affordable, flexible, high-quality childcare place for their child.

The National Evaluation of Sure Start (NESS) is reputed to be the largest evaluation ever carried out by a UK government. Its main reports so far have been Melhuish et al (2005) and Melhuish et al (2008). In 2005, the evaluation found only limited evidence of the effects of SSLPs, and these effects were only small ones. The evaluators also reported that SSLPs were not reaching the most severely disadvantaged (such as lone or teenage parents or workless households or disabled children),[8] but only the 'moderately disadvantaged'. Similarly, the National Audit Office (NAO) (2006a) reported that most of the new Sure Start Children's Centres were in relatively disadvantaged areas, but only a third of them were proactively seeking out the most disadvantaged families in their area. An evaluation of parental participation in Sure Start in 2004 found that parents were attracted by the opportunity to gain new skills and improve job prospects but needed a degree of social confidence to engage with Sure Start services and were discouraged by the perceived targeting of Sure Start at the poorest areas or the worst parents (hence they might be less likely to participate if they felt that they might be labelled as bad parents) (Avis et al, 2007; but see also Pemberton and Mason, 2008, p 23 – 'the majority of interviewees highlighted that their primary motivation for becoming involved in service delivery or service planning was non-economic and more focused around increasing their own self-confidence and on enhancing opportunities for their children').

By 2008, however, the national evaluation reported that things had changed. The evaluators now found 'almost no evidence of adverse effects of SSLPs' and modest evidence of positive effects (Melhuish et al, 2008, pp v–vi). Most parents and children were said to have benefited, leading to fewer behavioural problems and better social skills among children. In general, health-led SSLPs were found to be more effective, for example in relation to maternity services, with relationships being established with parents at the pre-natal stage (Anning et al, 2007). Researchers also noted some good practice in involving black and minority ethnic communities, though they concluded that SSLPs could do better here (Craig et al, 2007). With regard to parental involvement generally, however, Pemberton and Mason (2008) concluded that little change had taken place and that there continued to be a lack of male participation in particular. The issue of user involvement in decision making is particularly important here, as some studies have found that it increases self-confidence, which is crucial for community learning (Williams and Churchill, 2006; Pemberton and Mason, 2008).

From the point of view of community learning, although Sure Start has many good points, there are problems with its overall approach, and also with the perspective adopted by its official evaluators. These problems were first identified by Norman Glass, who is credited with being the originator of Sure Start itself. In theory, he said:

> Sure Start was run on community development principles – that is, it was structured to allow local people, particularly parents, to participate fully in determining the content and management of programmes, in the light of their perceptions of what their areas needed ... The statutory agencies were seen as helping the programmes to get off the ground and then handing them over to local, parent-dominated management boards. (Glass, 2005, p 2)

In other words, Sure Start was envisaged as a process of community self-learning and self-development, with the role of government being to facilitate this process – a classic case of co-production (see Pemberton and Mason, 2008, and Chapter Five of this book). In practice, however, Sure Start has been driven by governmental agendas, in particular relating to childcare and employability – 'a sort of New Deal for Toddlers' (Glass, 2005, p 2; for a clear statement of the government's agenda here, see HMG, 2009[9]). In general, SSLPs have not been judged in terms of their contribution to community learning or development but on the basis of what they have done to improve health and social care services for children and to make their parents (or at least their mothers) more healthy and employable. This can be seen in NESS's approach, which is based on a so-called 'theory of change', whose connection with community development is difficult to determine. The approach seems to make assumptions about what counts as healthy child development and family functioning and then assesses SSLPs in the light of these assumptions. However, the assumptions remain largely unstated. Even where the health benefits are clear and uncontested, as in the case of smoking cessation, it is difficult to be sure about the factors that have produced such an effect. There are some examples of SSLPs being run by community groups, but the significance of this has not been highlighted by NESS. Finally, with the move to local authority-run Sure Start Children's Centres, the possibility of parent or community control or even co-production seems to disappear altogether (see Pemberton and Mason, 2008, p 20), to be replaced by 'more traditional models involving the planning and designing of services involving either "distributed commissioning" or "user consultation"'(Pemberton and Mason, 2008, p 23).

Gustafsson and Driver (2005) provide an interesting explanation of Sure Start in Foucauldian terms. They argue that Sure Start cannot be understood solely as a form of *disciplinary* power, whereby the state induces people to accept and even embrace its rule (as in its policy of 'active citizenship', criticised in Chapter Four). It is also a form of *pastoral* power, whereby the state supports people with knowledge and skills to shape their own lives for themselves. The exercise of such pastoral power can involve genuine empowerment, in the sense that it can increase people's capacity for self-action and self-development, which can lead to challenges to state power. By the same token, however, it can help legitimate the state as a benevolent, and indeed beneficent, 'welfare' state and thereby make people more trusting and accepting of state power. In the case of Sure Start, parental participation has led to changes in how SSLPs work, taking on board some of the suggestions that parents have made, and this partly explains the diversity of practice to be found in SSLPs. Gustafsson and Driver (2005, p 541) conclude that: 'Sure Start may serve as a constructive route to self-actualisation among parents who take an active part as well as among parents who choose not to participate in the programme. Either way, parents are taking part in some form of governance of the self.'

This conclusion needs to be treated with caution, not least because there are no examples in the literature of any parent achieving some form of self-actualisation through involvement in Sure Start. Given Sure Start's emphasis on childcare and employability, it seems more likely that the long-term impact of the programme will be to secure more effective inclusion of both children and parents into the work routines and daily rhythms of capitalist society (as indeed does seem to be the underlying intention of the policy). Nevertheless, it cannot be denied that the programme offers certain opportunities that did not exist before, so there is at least an increased potential for self-actualisation as a result of Sure Start. The main problem is that, in the absence of any framework for community self-development, Sure Start is unlikely to have any lasting effect on the most disadvantaged communities, as described in Chapter One. It can be thought of, without too much exaggeration, as a less intensive version of an intensive family support project, and is unsustainable for much the same reason, namely that it is not sufficiently rooted in the community in which it has been seeded.[10]

Community-led initiatives

In principle, and also mainly in practice, community-led initiatives are most suited to community learning. This is for the fairly obvious reason that, if a project is a community project, the members of the community who are so committed to that project that they play leading roles in it are almost bound to be learning collectively from that experience. There are so many such initiatives that it is difficult to single out any one in particular. One type of project, however, seems to epitomise the principles of community learning, and that is residents' consultancy.

Residents' consultancy involves 'learning through shared experience' (Amion Consulting, 2004) or, more precisely, through people from one community sharing their experience with people from other communities. The value of residents' consultancy stems from the uniqueness of the backgrounds and experiences of residents involved in community development. Such experiences result in the consultancies having a particular affinity with 'clients', both within the residents' own communities and in similar communities elsewhere. Clients are able to draw confidence and self-belief from the consultants' own experiences of dealing with similar issues. A particularly successful residents' consultancy is run by Royds Community Association (see www.royds.org.uk). The concept was later taken up by government in the shape of the Neighbourhood Renewal Unit's Guide Neighbourhood programme, where people experienced or trained in certain areas (for example, Bromley-by-Bow) act as mentors or 'guides' for residents in other areas.

It is interesting to compare this approach with Freire's (1996) concept of '*conscientisation*' (see Chapter Two and **Box 6.4**). In the case of the latter, community members are assisted by educators to become aware of the capacity they have to take action collectively. Conscientisation therefore involves a kind of partnership between learners and teachers, in which the latter help the former to become collectively more self-aware and purposeful. In residents' consultancy, however, communities act as both learners and teachers: they learn by experience in one community and then share this learning with other communities. In Freire's approach, communities have to learn to translate their already existing understanding into the language of 'experts' and professionals, whereas in residents' consultancy it is the residents who are the acknowledged experts and, if professionals really want to help them, then the onus is on those professionals to communicate in plain English (or Portuguese or whatever!).

This is not to say, however, that there is any incompatibility between the two approaches. A partnership between learners and teachers could well develop in such a way that the learners take on responsibility for their own learning and provide assistance to learners elsewhere. Indeed, this is a key aim of Freire's approach.

Box 6.4: The Tassibee Project – a case of conscientisation

This project, based in Rotherham, used faith as a starting point for Mirpuri Punjabi speaking women, with the women meeting every Friday for prayer sessions. This enabled them to develop confidence and self-esteem, overcoming resistance from their husbands and from community leaders, and learning to act as a group. Basic literacy and personal development training was introduced by the community worker, and the women eventually established their own steering group for the project. In the course of time, their skills became sought after by other organisations, and some of the women volunteers moved on to paid employment.

Source: FCWTG (2002)

Conclusion

Community learning is a complex and little-understood process but is crucial for community development and for ensuring that such development endures. The motivation and purpose of community learning comes from within the community itself, and cannot be manufactured from outside, although outsiders can play an important role in stimulating and guiding the process. Community learning approaches are critical of authoritarian, command-and-control approaches to learning (known as 'schooling'), but this does not necessarily mean that they reject institutional learning of any kind (although some do, for example, Holt). Rather, it seems that the possibilities for schools and other educational institutions as sites for community learning have not yet been fully explored.[11] In practice, all such institutions are subject to economic and political pressures, for example, to ensure that their learners will be employable and will become 'good citizens' as the state requires. There is an increasing variety of ways, however, in which those institutions can respond to such pressures. For community learning to take place, the institution's response must be guided first and foremost by the experiences, needs, demands and aspirations of the community itself (although, as mentioned above, outsiders also have a part to play). This is rarely the case at present, and this perhaps helps to explain the growing popularity of homeschooling as an alternative to schools.

This chapter has also considered governmental initiatives beyond schools that impact upon community learning, but has criticised them either for their lack of effectiveness for community development (for example, Sure Start) or for an apparent lack of sound evaluation (for example, Community Learning Chests and Active Learning for Active Citizenship). Either way, the track record of governments on community learning can only be regarded as poor.

Finally, community-led community learning initiatives were examined, with a distinction being made between those facilitated by what might be called professionals from outside the community and those facilitated by community members themselves. The distinction may be important insofar as it reflects a difference in the social background of the facilitator. Where the community is working class, it may be that someone who shares its habitus (for example, as social housing tenants) will be in a better position to facilitate its collective learning. In the case of the Tassibee project, it was important only that the facilitator was a woman, and it did not seem to matter that she was white and non–Muslim. For these initiatives, therefore, the key thing is to achieve a good fit between facilitator and learning community. Obviously, this is more easily done where a social affinity already exists between the two.

It has to be said that the prospects for community-led approaches to learning in England are uncertain. Under New Labour, the Department for Children, Schools and Families was the main government department for learning but it was not committed to community learning. The Home Office understood community learning only in terms of learning for 'active citizenship', which is essentially an ideological construct, associated with a depoliticising participationist agenda. The Department for Communities and Local Government alone was committed to community learning (as a means to neighbourhood renewal), but it took no real account of schools in its agenda (for example, it saw no role for schools in community cohesion – CLG, 2010, in stark contrast to DCSF, 2009b). Consequently, it can be seen that the Labour government had no coherent approach to community learning. Its most recent innovations, such as school trusts and children's trusts, would not have been likely to change anything because their main focus was on the traditional role of schools as places of schooling. There was always a risk, anyway, that such trusts would be led by elite groups of parents rather than by communities as a whole – a risk that has now become real under the coalition government's proposals. Sure Start Children's Centres look more promising in that they tackle a variety of cross-cutting issues affecting community learning, but it seems likely that they will continue Sure Start's emphases on improving employability and childcare rather than move towards a community learning approach. Unless governments of whatever colour begin to take community learning more seriously, as a process of building mutual understanding both within and across communities, in which all governmental institutions are involved (that is, as a mainstream process, not just an add-on to existing activity), the chances of moving towards a beloved community will continue to be remote.

Notes
[1] Donzelot (1979), among others, has argued that, historically, compulsory schooling was introduced in order to discipline families, particularly working-class families, to become docile subjects of capitalist rule.
[2] On the latter point, see, for example, Ball (2008), on how schools reproduce rather than challenge social inequality and injustice.
[3] This was written a year before the coalition government's proposals to so 'empower' parents.
[4] In one state secondary school in which I conducted focus groups recently, participants in different groups volunteered the observation that 'we are like one big happy family here'.
[5] 'Recent newspaper reports suggest that some Church of England schools in cities in the north of England now have a majority of Muslim pupils. As a result some Christian parents have decided to send their children to secular schools' (ICC, 2009, p 18).
[6] It includes, for example, 'our rights and responsibilities at school and within the wider community' (OCR, 2009, p 19), but it should be noted that this section of the curriculum (para 3.3.1) does not actually say anything about the relationship between the school and its local community (for a useful critique of citizenship education, see Kisby, 2007).
[7] It is also perhaps related to a renewed focus on the role of health visitors, as recently highlighted by the Conservative Party.
[8] This was true also in the mini Sure Starts (Glennie et al, 2005). In some SSLP areas, black and minority ethnic groups were not being reached at all (Pascal and Bertram, 2004).
[9] This White Paper on social mobility makes clear that the primary focus of the government's efforts is on achieving 'an upwardly mobile society' (HMG, 2009, p 8), which is not at all the same thing as a beloved community. The flourishing of individuals that the government envisages is to be achieved not so much through cooperation with other individuals on an equal basis as through mainstream economic development and reformed public services or 'social investment' – that is, through inherently unequal capitalism and state bureaucracy. Needless to say, perhaps, this attempt to turn working-class children into middle-class adults is doomed to failure.

[10] For example, being focused only on 0- to 4-year-olds, it ensures that the duration of membership of the group is limited to the number of years for which the children of any given parent fall within this age group (namely, five years for one child, though this can be extended for each younger sibling).

[11] Although this chapter has focused on schools, much of the argument applies equally to other learning institutions, such as universities (although in the case of universities the nature of the community they are supposed to serve is far less clear).

Summary

This chapter has explored the complex relationship between a school and the community in which it sits. Competing interpretations of the purpose of a school are outlined and assessed. Under Local Management of Schools, schools have become more autonomous but they receive mixed messages as to how they should exercise such autonomy. The standpoint of community learning provides a yardstick against which the ethos and practice of a school can be assessed. Basically, are the students enabled to recognise a common purpose in all that they do?

No government has had a coherent approach to community learning, and the new coalition government is no exception. The coalition's proposals for parent-run schools are, in principle, only an extension of the previous government's proposals for school trusts. This development risks leading us ever further away from the ideal of a beloved community.

Questions for discussion

- What value does a school contribute to a community?

- What value can a community contribute to a school?

- What is the appropriate role of government in relation to community learning? How can governments be persuaded to accept this role?

- Why is community learning essential for a beloved community?

Further reading

Ball, S.J. (2008) *The education debate*, Bristol: The Policy Press.
Clarke, S., Gilmour, R. and Garner, S. (2007) 'Home, identity and community cohesion', in M. Wetherell, M. Laflèche and R. Berkeley (eds) *Identity, ethnic diversity and community cohesion*, London: Sage, pp 87–101.

Gustafsson, U. and Driver, S. (2005) 'Parents, power and public participation: Sure Start, an experiment in New Labour governance', *Social Policy & Administration,* vol 39, no 5, pp 528–43.

seven

Community health and social care

Overview

Health is a complex and contested concept. Essentially, it has to do with positive, life-affirming, joyful activity. Arguably, it is a matter of life lived in balance or equilibrium or harmony, affording a sense of well-being. Where this balance is to be struck, however, is difficult to identify precisely, and is subject to wide differences of opinion. The concept of a beloved community, for example, suggests that the balance is to be achieved through cooperation among all the community members, based on mutual equal respect. This chapter examines what might be meant by a healthy community and how such a community can be developed.

A healthy community can be described as one that is liveable, sustainable, equitable and empowered. The Alma Ata Declaration in 1975 set out a vision of a process of co-production and co-learning in which communities shape health priorities while professionals develop practices to meet those priorities, with an emphasis on developing community and preventive services and tackling the social determinants of poor health.

In practice, co-working between health professionals and communities rarely lives up to this vision and health priorities continue to be dominated by professionals. Most countries lack even the capacity to put the Alma Ata approach on their agendas. In the UK, in spite of (or perhaps because of) numerous attempts at reorganisation, the NHS stubbornly remains a command-and-control system, with little community input, and continuing (and even growing) insensitivity and unresponsiveness to that input, particularly in relation to so-called secondary care (basically, hospitals).

The nature of a healthy community

It seems to be generally agreed that health and well-being have material, psychological and social dimensions:

- *Material*, that is, the health of the body, which involves not only a lack of physical impairments, diseases and so on, but also access to whatever that body needs to sustain itself, for example, food, shelter, relevant skills.
- *Psychological*, that is, the health of the mind, which similarly involves not only lack of mental impairments, disorders and so on, but also understanding of one's state of being, one's needs, drives and aspirations.
- *Social*, that is, the health of society, in which the material and psychological aspects of health are given meaning through relationships among actors (see, for example, Vaitilingam, 2009, p 6).

Each of these dimensions can be seen as indispensable for healthy living: material conditions that enable the sustaining of life itself; psychological conditions that enable a sentient being to determine for itself how its life is lived; and social conditions that shape and integrate material and psychological conditions. A *healthy community* has been characterised as one that is liveable, sustainable and equitable (Barr and Hashagen, 2000, p 23), and empowered (Wilkinson, 1999; Marmot and Wilkinson, 2001) – see *Table 7.1*.

From *Table 7.1* it can be seen that a healthy community has characteristics of the three dimensions identified above. Materially, it is a community that is environmentally and economically resourceful, diverse and sustainable, meeting the lifelong needs of *all* of its members.[1] Psychologically, it is self-directed and self-organised, with a diversity of experience and imagination, built on a foundation of mutual respect, esteem and trust. Socially, it is well connected, internally and externally, supporting and caring for its own members and strongly influencing the powers-that-be outside the community.[2]

Arguably, these characteristics of a healthy community require that it be *positive* about health and well-being. This involves being open minded about different life-styles, promoting healthy norms (for example, eating a balanced diet, taking a moderate amount of exercise, being polite and considerate to neighbours) and limiting health-damaging or harmful behaviours (for example, smoking, abusing drugs, binge drinking, unsafe sex).

Community health, then, can be understood as involving meaningful interconnectedness in a number of different ways: among community members (the social dimension of a healthy community) and across health dimensions (material, psychological and social). It can also, as discussed below, involve meaningful interconnectedness between community members and health professionals, between the habitus of so–called 'lay' people and the field of healthcare systems.

Table 7.1: *Characteristics of a healthy community*

Healthy community	Characteristics (adapted from Barr and Hashagen, 2000, p 23; Marmot and Wilkinson, 2001; Wilkinson, D., 1999; Wilkinson, R., 1996)	Dimensions
Liveable	Clean, safe physical environment (1) Meets community needs (1) (2) (3) Everyone lives to a ripe old age (1) Contains wide variety of resources (1) Contains wide variety of experiences (2) Provides public health care services (3)	(1) = material (2) = psychological (3) = social
Sustainable	Has a diverse economy (1) Has a negative carbon footprint (1) Has an innovative economy (1) (2) Is self-organised (1) (2) (3) Is a well-connected, self-supporting community (3)	
Equitable	Inclusive, meets needs of all (1) (2) Mutual respect, trust and esteem (2) (3) Resources are fairly distributed (3) Mutual support, caring and non-exploitative (3)	
Empowered	Has economic resources (1) Controls its own destiny (1) (2) (3) Has support networks (3) Has political power and influence (3)	

Developing healthy communities

The story of community health really takes off with the Alma Ata Declaration in 1975 (WHO, 1978). This set out a global strategy for Health for All by 2000. Its vision was one of communities (including patients and carers) and health professionals working and learning together – that is, a process of co–production and co–learning, where communities shape health priorities, while professionals develop practices to meet these priorities. The emphasis was on developing community services and preventive services (so–called primary healthcare), and on tackling the social causes of poor health, including the prevention/resolution of armed conflict and social injustice.

The Health for All approach has been proved to improve health outcomes (see, for example, McPake, 2008; WHO, 2008). In the 1980s, for example, dramatic improvements were found in health outcomes in China, Costa Rica, Sri Lanka and Kerala (in India) as a result of emphasising the provision of primary healthcare within an overall social welfare-oriented development model, where services were provided to everyone who needed them, free at the point of use. The focus therefore needs to be on what it is about this approach that produces healthy communities.

The difficulty here is that much activity that is represented as co-working between health professionals and communities does not appear to meet the Alma Ata standard. Rifkin (1986), for example, reviewing 200 case studies of community participation in health, identified three different approaches (see De Vos et al, 2009, p 24):

- the *medical* approach, in which health professionals foster community participation in order to reduce individual morbidity and to improve sanitation;
- the *health service* approach, which aims to improve the delivery of health services by mobilising community members to participate in that delivery;
- the *community development* approach, which aims to empower community members by involving them in decisions that are related to the improvement of the social, economic and political conditions that affect their health.

The first approach is concerned with getting communities, as individuals and as collectives, to take responsibility for their own healthcare. The second is to do with targeting potential beneficiaries of health services to participate in different ways in order to improve service effectiveness. Only the third approach involves community members as more or less equal partners in the development of healthy communities, as envisaged by the Alma Ata Declaration. Rifkin (1986) also recognised that this approach, involving community development through community empowerment,[3] does not necessarily require the active participation of all community members in all public decision-making processes (see criticisms of participationism in Chapter Three and of governmental approaches to community empowerment in Chapter Four).

The problem with the first two approaches to community participation appears to be that governments that failed to make significant improvements in primary healthcare came to see them as ways, respectively, to cut healthcare costs and to neutralise any unrest that might result from such failure. By the 1990s, partly due to pressure from the International Monetary Fund and the World Bank, many countries had moved away from the Health for All model of co-produced universal healthcare by introducing user fees, insurance mechanisms and greater private sector involvement. The effect of this change was to undermine access to health by the poorest people in the poorest countries, and in some not-so-poor countries. This can be seen from Oxfam research in 2006, which found that states where services remained publicly financed and free at the point of use (such as Kerala in India and Sri Lanka), provided far greater universal protection from health risks (McPake, 2008; see de Vos et al, 2009, p 31, for a similar verdict on Cuba). In countries without such state-funded universal health services (countries that include the US), large numbers of the population have no access to any effective healthcare that they can afford.

Surprisingly, perhaps, the *value* of the Alma Ata approach remains under-specified. In practice, health priorities continue to be determined by professionals rather than by communities and health services continue to be dominated by target-oriented approaches. Rather than challenging this agenda, participationism may actually have reinforced it, for example, because of a catalogue of perceived failures of community participation. A variety of studies in the UK have uncovered evidence of participants being burnt-out, labelled as a 'grass', threatened or attacked (Kagan, 2006; Barnes et al, 2007). Halabi (2009) provides a particularly stark example from Indonesia, where the introduction of decentralised arrangements for public participation has been an integral part of the move away from universal healthcare, which has resulted in a significantly deteriorating quality of service, particularly for the poor. So the health benefits of community participation in health services may have been exaggerated, at least in countries not following the Alma Ata approach (see, for example, Wayland and Crowder, 2002).

De Vos et al (2009), for example, emphasise the importance of a *class* perspective, where the poor make their own decisions through their representatives. They cite the issue of land reform, which is critical for developing healthy communities in the Philippines (as in other countries) ('communities that are able to take control of their own land are able to take control of their lives' – p 27), but which cannot be addressed adequately at the community level. Political organising, within and across communities, is therefore necessary for developing healthy communities.[4] Halabi argues similarly that a different approach to developing healthy communities is required, based on a 'progressive realisation of the right to health' (Halabi, 2009, p 54), spearheaded by a partnership between Indonesian government agencies and Western and Indonesian NGOs. The argument seems to be that, in countries that are not following the Alma Ata approach, national healthcare reform programmes are required, tailored to the circumstances of the individual countries concerned, before lasting development of healthy communities can take place.

A further important argument by Yamin is that placing health users on an equal footing with health providers and funders in deliberative processes may not be sufficient to develop healthy communities because 'the rules of the game may have already been set' (Yamin, 2009, p 10). (This echoes the arguments of Taylor, 2003, discussed in Chapter Three.) What is also required, therefore, is a fair, democratic process of determining how healthcare priorities should be set. Yamin argues that this process is currently lacking in many countries because of the disproportionate influence of pharmaceutical and insurance companies, the World Bank and a variety of NGOs, as well as the distorting effects of foreign aid. One exception, however, appears to be Brazil, where 'constitutionally-created health councils ... have allowed for a genuine transfer of control over priority-setting and budgeting to affected populations' (Yamin, 2009, p 12).

Even this is not enough. Developing healthy communities also requires that steps should be taken to tackle the social determinants of poor health. As Yamin (2009, p 12) says: 'if participation in health is limited to the local community level or to delivery of health programs, key decisions that take place at a district or central level relating to resource allocation, health care workforce, structuring of health systems, and the like ... are never "up for contention"'. Moreover: 'devising strategies for participation cannot be confined to the health sector when we have abundant evidence that social determinants of health, including workplace and neighborhood characteristics, education, and income inequalities, have a far greater impact on population health than "downstream" questions relating to health care' (Yamin, 2009, p 12) – evidence such as in the case of land reform in the Philippines discussed above. The process of developing healthy communities is therefore closely bound up with programmes for wider political emancipation.

Governmental approaches to health and social care in the UK

In the UK, a National Health Service (NHS) was established in 1948. Basically, it was a command-and-control system, with all health services being accountable to the Secretary of State for Health for everything they did. Although the first such Secretary, Aneurin Bevan, famously declared that he did not want to hear the clatter of every falling bedpan, the legislation that set up the NHS made no provision for him or his successors to wear earplugs. What happened instead was the adoption of what is known as a 'biomedical' model of health, in which the focus is almost entirely on addressing the biological causes of ill health, with major health policy decisions being left to the (clinical) judgement of hospital consultants, general practitioners and so on. Issues of community health and social care, insofar as they were considered at all, were seen as largely a matter of individual behaviour, choice and responsibility, outside the NHS system. An unhealthy alliance between health professionals and the state therefore developed (see Copeland, 2004) – what George Bernard Shaw would have called 'a conspiracy against the laity'.

The first – and possibly only – major change in the NHS's command-and-control system was the introduction of market-based approaches from 1983 onwards. These involved the introduction of competition among health service providers (a so-called 'internal market') in order to counteract what was regarded as the monopoly power of the health professions. The purpose was to challenge but not necessarily tame these professions. The central emphasis was on increasing the choice of patients (as 'customers') and improving the responsiveness of service providers. Improving health was understood, rather narrowly, in terms of increasing the effectiveness of personal health (and social) services, and health as a *community* issue continued to be largely ignored. This remains the key emphasis of health policy in the UK to this day (see, for example, DH, 2009a).

With the NHS and Community Care Act 1990 came a new emphasis on health and social care in the community rather than in institutions such as hospitals. This so-called 'community care', however, should not be confused with care *by* the community. The focus was essentially on the meeting of individual needs by health and social care agencies working in the community. As Twelvetrees (2002, p 132) put it: 'The approach taken by governmental and voluntary agencies to the needs of these people and groups was the development of individual care plans in the context of an overall plan designed by these agencies together.' Examples of such 'community care' are legion: Care and Repair, carer support schemes, community transport, 'good neighbour' projects, day centres, Home–Start and so on. As Twelvetrees (2002, p 133) says, they are generally designed to build and/or provide networks of support for people living in their own homes. Some of them are actually grassroots initiatives based in the community, so could be described as care by the community, but probably the majority of them are not. Many of those that are community led rely on government support and/or funding for their continued existence.

From 1997 onwards, the approach of the New Labour government was more strategic. It aimed to reduce health inequalities across the country, deploying a mix of centralised and market-oriented models of provision, working with and through communities, and retaining a strong emphasis on 'customer' (or patient) choice and voice. The inequalities it aimed to reduce were across geographical areas, across socio-economic groups, between men and women, across different BME groups, across age groups, and between the majority of the population, on the one hand, and vulnerable groups and those with special needs, on the other (DH and HM Treasury, 2002). The strategy set numerous targets and adopted, as its key measures of success, increases in life expectancy and reductions in infant mortality. This represented a strategic centralisation, reinforcing the already well-established command–and–control structure of the NHS.

Following the adoption of this strategy in 1998, NHS spending nearly tripled (from £33 billion in 1996–97 to £92.6 billion in 2007–08), leading to substantial increases in the numbers of doctors and nurses and substantial reductions in waiting times for surgical operations, out-patient appointments and emergency treatment. Overall, life expectancy increased, infant mortality reduced and the general health of the population improved. At the same time, however, the gap between the worst-off and the average did not narrow, so overall health inequality was not reduced (see DH, 2009b).

At a tactical and operational level, the government transferred the responsibilities for healthcare to *trusts* of different kinds: primary care trusts, which controlled 80% of the NHS budget; NHS trusts, which were responsible for secondary, hospital care; and NHS foundation trusts, whose governors were mainly elected by staff, residents, patients and carers. As we saw in Chapter Five, a trust is a free-standing body that is owned by no one but is managed by a board of trustees on behalf of others. It was the government's intention that, in the course of time, all trusts would become foundation trusts.[5]

Since 1975, the activities of the NHS have been scrutinised by watchdogs, whose job it is to act on behalf of the community and patients – essentially, a complaints-driven service. The first of these watchdogs were the Community Health Councils (CHCs), which were abolished in 2003 and replaced by Patient and Public Involvement (PPI) forums. The weakness of these forums, however, soon became clear, and they in turn were replaced by Local Involvement Networks (LINks) in 2008. It is difficult to know what, if any, importance to attach to any of these bodies, as they have few powers of redress for their complainants and their opinions appear to carry little weight in relation to health trusts or professionals. CHCs did at least play an advocacy role, but the role of PPI forums was basically only consultative; LINks have been given some powers to hold NHS bodies to account, but it is not yet clear how effective these powers will be. The main problem, though, is that the whole approach of relying on watchdogs to improve a service is flawed. The proper role of such a body is to take action when occasional injustices occur, not to be a vehicle of continuous improvement or system reform. In this sense, PPIs were particularly misconceived, but even the LINks seem to have been set up to fail. The kind of thinking that lies behind such policies is what Seddon (2008) has criticised as a focus on failure demand (typical of a command–and–control approach) instead of on getting it right in the first place.

In other ways, however, the government appears to have moved towards a more locally focused approach. Apart from programmes such as New Deal for Communities and Sure Start (discussed in earlier chapters), which contained a strong emphasis on health improvement, the New Labour government launched a range of locally based initiatives specifically on health, most notably Health Action Zones (see ***Box 7.1***) and Healthy Living Centres. In 2003, local social services authorities were given power of scrutiny over health services, and under the Local Government and Public Involvement in Health Act 2007, PCTs (but not NHS trusts) were required to consult with local people and to produce, together with local authorities, a Joint Strategic Needs Assessment. In general, from the early 1990s onwards, there was a shift towards more personalised services, which tended to favour local communities (DH, 2006; Healthcare Commission, 2007), and by 2006 the government had become convinced that community–based interventions were most effective in improving health (and also social care) (DH, 2006).

Box 7.1: Health Action Zones (HAZs)

HAZs were seven-year partnerships between the NHS, local authorities, community groups and the voluntary and business sectors. They 'were established with the explicit aim of influencing policy development; they were designed to mobilise support for action to address health inequalities and promote equality of access to services' (Bridgen, 2006). Twenty-six HAZs were set up in England in 1998 and 1999, lasting until 2005–06, covering over 13 million people in some of the most deprived areas, including inner cities, rural areas and ex-coalfield communities. They typically addressed both healthcare issues and the determinants of health such as housing, the environment, employment and income.

The national evaluation of HAZs (Barnes et al, 2001; Benzeval, 2003) identified the community involvement objectives of HAZs as: improving public accountability, improving health, improving services, accessing lay or experiential knowledge and increasing public knowledge and support. They found varying degrees of satisfaction with the extent of community involvement in the development of HAZ plans. Most community capacity-building effort was focused at the project or sub-local level, with little evidence of it at the strategic level, and resources for it were insufficient across a range of groups and areas. Three constraints on community involvement were: the pressure to achieve early wins; the plethora of government policy initiatives; and the centralised performance management framework. Examples of improvements included: Labyrinth in Sandwell HAZ developed a shared community involvement framework where none had really existed; Bradford HAZ supported the development of a multi-agency community development strategy; and Primary Care Groups (now PCTs) had been influenced to involve communities in their work.

Detailed evaluation of three HAZs by Benzeval (2003) found that reducing health inequalities was not generally thought to be an achievable goal, because:

• HAZ resources were not sufficient to make significant changes in the lives of their populations
• the timescale of the HAZ initiative was too short to achieve changes in the long-term causes of inequalities.

Consequently, the role of the HAZ was usually seen as one of developing the local capacity to address health inequalities, and there was a widespread belief that HAZs had done this. The direct impact of HAZs on health inequalities was seen to be minimal, but there was also a feeling that HAZs had: pushed reducing health inequalities up the local agenda and made it more visible; broadened the understanding of the determinants of health; contributed to the development of local partnership structures to tackle health inequalities; contributed to developing systems and processes that will support more effective planning in the future; and improved some mainstream services. HAZs were viewed as 'drivers for change'.

Community-based interventions happen where local people are active in their design and implementation (including in assessing needs, and in planning and management arrangements). Successful interventions include training and support for volunteers, peer educators and local networks – for example, Sure Start (see Chapter Six), Warm Front, Jamie's school dinners (for further examples, see ***Box 7.2*** and Halpern, 2005). Potential for successful community action on many health issues has also been identified, for example on alcohol misuse, drug misuse and accident prevention, but the value of much of this action remains unclear.

Box 7.2: Home-Start

Home-Start is a voluntary organisation, founded in 1973. Since its first Volunteer Preparation Course in 1994, Home-Start has trained 40,000 volunteers to visit and support families in their own homes, of whom 11,000 currently do so. Volunteers live in the same community as the families they support.

Shinman (2005, p 6) found that services for socially excluded and vulnerable families with young children needed: to be open, trustful and respectful; not to 'fob them off'; to be responsive and act promptly; to give accurate, relevant information in small chunks by word of mouth; and to work together and know what the others are doing.

Home-Start works by building a relationship between the volunteer and the family, with the aim of befriending and mutual practical and emotional benefit for as long as needed. Families are referred to Home-Start by a variety of agencies, including social services and GPs, and are also contacted through outreach work. Nearly all mothers in Shinman's evaluation reported positive effects of Home-Start, including increased confidence, new interests, rehousing, new partner, job training and so on. It could take three or more years to overcome difficulties (Shinman, 2005, p 31). Portage received unequivocal praise (portage offers practical help and ideas to parents of pre-school children with additional support needs, to encourage the child's interests and make learning fun for all the family, thus equipping parents with the necessary skill and confidence) (Shinman, 2005, p 33).

Source: Adapted from Crispin et al (2005) and Shinman (2005)

It might be thought that foundation trusts in particular represent a significant step towards the adoption of an Alma Ata–type approach – devolving power and ownership of health services to local communities, thus achieving a situation where communities and health professionals can work together on a more equal basis (as appears to be envisaged by Blears, 2003). Unfortunately, however, this is not the case. Such a trust can be understood as a classic Third Way option, being proposed as an alternative to both public ownership and private ownership, but such alternatives are not necessarily community friendly. Foundation trusts are actually an example of pure spin, a con and a sham. The board of governors, to whom community (and all the other) representatives are elected, is an advisory body only, with the key decision-making body being the board of directors, who are obliged to take note of what the board of governors says but not to follow it. So the governors do not actually govern at all. And the trust is not a trust either, in the usually understood sense of the word, because the real decision makers, the directors, are not trustees but NHS employees. Furthermore, foundation trusts have a significant degree of freedom in deciding the composition of the board of governors – for example, a majority of the board must be elected by 'members in the public constituency' (DH, 2005), but it is up to the trust to determine how this membership is recruited (from residents, patients and carers). Finally, there are no plans for increasing direct participation by patients or public in the trusts' decision-making processes. It can be concluded, then, that foundation trusts represent an *illusion* of community governance, which is unlikely to fool anybody. Real power remains firmly with the board of directors, who are answerable only to the Secretary of State for Health. The government's much-trumpeted revolution in how the NHS is governed leaves power relations almost exactly the same as they were before, but with greater room for discretion and manoeuvre for local healthcare managers.

In general, in spite of the moves towards localisation discussed above, the NHS continues to be community insensitive and community unresponsive (Emmel and Conn, 2004, p 11). 'Community' tends to be defined by the NHS in terms of a plurality of lay people, who are consulted in order to hit pre-set targets of efficiency and service delivery.[6] This is not consultation proper, however (Emmel and Conn, 2004, p 7), and professionals can feel free to ignore what these lay people say if it is seen to conflict with clinical judgement or to undermine clinical autonomy. Typically, those consulted are self-appointed 'community leaders' who misrepresent their communities by excluding marginalised groups, and these latter groups either lack power to have a voice or intentionally ensure that their networks are invisible to those in authority (Emmel, 2004, pp 6–7). The gap between the concerns of the NHS and those of the community appears to be huge and growing (see also Barnes et al, 2007), and it is difficult to share the optimism of commentators such as Bridgen (2006), or even to see what evidence can be adduced to support it. True, governmental agencies continue to recognise the importance of community action for improving health and social care, but the work of such agencies also continues to remain peripheral to the main concerns of the NHS, and indeed also of local authority social services departments.[7] In spite of possible erosion at its edges, the NHS (much like government in general) remains an unstoppable juggernaut that simply gobbles up everything that crosses its path.

Another growing problem with the NHS goes by the name of *giantism*. This term is used to describe the way in which NHS trusts, in a misguided pursuit of 'efficiency' and economies of scale, have closed smaller hospitals and built increasingly large ones, which are inevitably less accessible or accountable to local communities. The change has enabled the trusts to make savings from bulk purchasing and commissioning, and from the introduction of new technology. On the down side, however, it has increased the burdens and costs for people to access hospital services, particularly for those who rely on public transport (Boyle et al, 2004, p 13). It also appears to have facilitated a wider spread of dangerous bacteria such as MRSA and clostridium difficile. Declining standards of hygiene, cleaning and catering in hospitals, attributed largely to increased 'efficiencies' particularly related to the contracting out of these services, have also contributed to the rise of these 'superbugs'. In 2002, the World Health Organisation reported that a patient admitted to a UK hospital had a 1 in 10 chance of ending up suffering 'measurable harm' from mistakes (clinical or otherwise, for example, food poisoning), microbes, faulty equipment or drug side-effects, with resulting additional hospital stays valued at £2 billion per year (WHO, 2002). Finally, although malnutrition has long been recognised as a common and serious problem among hospital patients in the UK, the latest national in-patient survey has reported worsening problems with regard to hospital food (The Patients' Association, 2009, p 6).

Possible pathways to health policy reform

Comparison of UK government performance on health with the principles of Alma Ata reveals that the UK has a long way to go on this issue. The main gaps would appear to be as follows:

• The government needs to show that it understands and endorses the concept of the social determinants of health. Much of what the NHS does, however, not merely ignores the social determinants of health inequality (largely income and social class) but actively reproduces and reinforces that inequality, for example, through the status differences between doctors and patients, and through command-and-control and market-oriented approaches. Consequently, it is no surprise that health inequalities persist.
• Related to this point, the emphasis of the NHS continues to be overwhelmingly on curing illnesses rather than preventing them in the first place. A classic example is cancer, where the age-adjusted mortality rate remains about the same as it was 50 years ago – survival rates have more than doubled in 30 years, but over the same period the incidence of cancer has increased by a quarter, even allowing for increases caused by the ageing of the population (Marqusee, 2009).
• Also, partly related to the first point, health policy is still not joined up with other policy at any level, even though it is well known that well-paid,

satisfying employment, good education, decent housing, and so on, all contribute to healthy lives and healthy communities.

- Currently, the extent to which the government, and health professionals generally, work with communities to identify problems and implement solutions is minimal. On the rare occasions when they do talk to one another, the conversation tends to be one-sided (the government health spokesperson or professional talking to the public) – very much a case of the 'expert' explaining things to a 'lay' person. This is not a dialogue based on equality and mutual respect and trust – all of which are themselves required for healthy communities and, of course, for the beloved community.

- Other government policies actually work *against* Alma Ata principles, for example, the increasingly punitive policies favoured by the Home Office (at least up to the change of government in May 2010) may cause harm unnecessarily (Commission on Families and the Wellbeing of Children, 2005). Also, right across government, there is an emphasis on so-called 'independent living', even though it may be more healthy, not only for communities but also for their individual members, to recognise and embrace their dependence on one another (see Oldman, 2003, for a critique of independent living).

An important nettle that has still to be grasped is that of the regulation of health professions. It should be abundantly clear by now (Copeland, 2004), particularly after the Harold Shipman case, that self-regulation is not enough to ensure that doctors can be held to account by their patients and by the public generally. Yet the General Medical Council (GMC) has only recently reaffirmed the principle of self-regulation by introducing a revalidation of all registered doctors based on a five-yearly scrutiny of competence (see GMC homepage – accessed 15 August 2009). What is needed, of course, is a completely independent regulatory body.[8]

There are also many ways in which the NHS could be made more locally accountable. Local authorities have a duty to promote the well-being of their area and could be given more say over the commissioning of health services in that area (Morley and Campbell, 2003). Primary care trust boards (or the GP governing bodies that will replace them) could be composed of directly elected local residents (Morley and Campbell, 2003). Foundation trust boards of governors could be empowered to instruct trust directors. As may be proposed by the coalition government, more decisions on primary care could be devolved to neighbourhood health centres, perhaps working together with children's centres. Patients' and health users' groups could be represented on the governing bodies of such centres – with rules to ensure the effective involvement of marginalised groups – as equal members of the community of users of health and social care. And so on.

Finally, and perhaps most importantly, more attention needs to be given to the development of productive partnerships between NHS staff, patients and the community (that is, co-production of health). Co-production suggests a more organic and dialogical relationship between the NHS and the communities it serves. A good example of an attempt to develop such a relationship is the Expert Patients' Programme (Boyle et al, 2004, p 7). Essentially, this programme enables patients to develop the skills and knowledge required to manage their own chronic health conditions.

Conclusion

It is a matter of disappointment and indeed disquiet that it is so difficult to identify clear examples of successful community health initiatives, at least in the UK, that meet the Alma Ata standard. One can speculate about the precise causes of this but probably the most important factors militating against a community-health approach are:

- the continuing and deepening medicalisation and unhealthy professionalisation of health and social care issues;
- the escalating costs that arise from this medicalisation and professionalisation;
- the continuing pressure to treat health as a private rather than a public good, for example, the market dominance and political influence of large pharmaceutical companies;
- the dominant command-and-control approach of the NHS, which sees 'communities' as entities to be managed rather than respected.

One can point to a small number of initiatives with community-health potential, such as HAZs, but it appears that these initiatives have not been developed strongly enough or for long enough to make any lasting impact on the way in which mainstream health services are delivered. Consequently, the social determinants of health remain largely unaddressed and there is no joined-up approach to dealing with them, whether at a national or a local community level. The ideal of a healthy community, and therefore of a beloved community, remains far beyond our reach.

Notes

[1] The emphasis is on 'all' because the needs of some sections of the community, such as psychiatric patients, tend to be neglected (Halpern, 2005, p 90).

[2] Evidence of the importance for health of being socially connected comes, for example, from Sherbourne et al (1995), who found that people who are isolated and lack intimate social support are more likely to suffer from depression when under stress, and to remain depressed for longer. More widely, of course, powerful social connections can help to improve health services and generally attract resources that can help people to live more healthily.

[3] According to Rifkin (1986), 'empowerment can be defined as creating opportunities and inspiration to enable those without power and/or influence to gain skills, knowledge and confidence to direct their own lives'. This affects community health outcomes directly, through healthier social interaction (improved community support, and feelings of empowerment among community members), and indirectly, through a community's improved ability to exert social and political influence (Bridgen, 2004; Laverack, 2004).

[4] This finding from the Philippines has lessons for the encapsulated communities in England discussed in Chapter One. But how are they to organise across the boundaries of their community?

[5] This has now been overtaken by the coalition government's decision to abolish PCTs and devolve most of their functions to GPs. At the time of writing, however (July 2010), the details of this restructuring remain unclear.

[6] 'Community care', for example, still tends to mean care that goes on outside of institutional care (see, for example, HMG, 2009) – typically at home. Contrary to popular opinion, however, there is no a priori reason why care provided outside an institution should be any better than that provided in an institution. In general, community care approaches also tend to emphasise the independence of the individual client and to downgrade the importance of community, which involves interdependence (Oldman, 2003). Rather than the individual flourishing through their involvement with others, they are made to feel that they must learn to cope on their own, with as little help from others as possible – a recipe for (increased) social isolation, not community.

[7] It is telling, in this respect, that Morgan and Swann (2004), for example, see the issue of public or community health mainly, if not entirely, in terms of developing social capital – Alma Ata has been all but forgotten.

[8] Given the impending transfer of functions from PCTs to GPs, this need for external regulation becomes even more pressing.

Summary

Perhaps the most astonishing thing about community health and social care is the enormous gap between what needs to be done and what is actually done. In spite of what is commonly believed, none of the main advances in health and well-being in the last hundred years or so (for example, clean air, traffic accident reduction, smoking cessation, balanced diet) have come from health services or health professionals. On the other hand, untold thousands of people every year are the victims of iatrogenic harms, whether this be from over-prescribing or mis-prescribing, lack of hygiene, medical errors, malnutrition or murder (for example, in the case of Harold Shipman). Meanwhile, social determinants of ill health remain largely unaddressed, leaving us a long way from the ideal of a beloved community. Of course, simply transferring the powers of primary care trusts to general practitioners, as now proposed by the coalition government, will make little difference to this.

Questions for discussion

- Is the Alma Ata vision of health for all equally identical with that of a beloved community?

- What are the main obstacles to realising this vision?

- Is health too important to be left to the health professionals?

- Do we get the health service that we pay for and that we deserve?

- Where does social care fit into all this?

Further reading

Barnes, M., Newman, J. and Sullivan, H. (2007) *Power, participation and political renewal: Case studies in public participation*, Bristol: The Policy Press.
Emmel, N. and Conn, C. (2004) *Towards community involvement: Strategies for health and social care providers. Guide 1: Identifying the goal and objectives of community involvement*, Leeds: Nuffield Institute for Health.
Emmel, N. (2004) *Towards community involvement: Strategies for health and social care providers. Guide 2: The complexity of communities and lessons for community involvement*, Leeds: Nuffield Institute for Health.

eight

Housing and community

Overview

This chapter looks at the relationship between housing and community action, focusing in particular on housing-related social movements. Collective resident action is seen as taking a number of different forms, such as:

- the defence of habitus against perceived external threats, for example gentrification, privatisation and unwanted new development
- action for resident management and control
- the 'tenants' movement', which encompasses, in addition to the above, organised campaigning for improved living conditions and political influence for residents.

Governmental approaches to housing and community reflect those outlined in Chapter Four, namely neoliberal, neo-colonial, communitarian and partnership approaches. The Right to Buy is interpreted as a classic example of 'roll-back' neoliberalism, while housing market renewal is understood as a case of 'roll-out' neoliberalism.

The relationship between housing and community is often taken for granted. It is commonly assumed, for example, that to live in a housing area of some kind is to live in a community. This is not necessarily the case, however, and this chapter therefore looks more closely at the relationship between housing and community, in order to consider in general how communities based on or around housing are formed and sustained through time, and in particular the effects of government action on this relationship.

Perhaps the most distinctive feature of housing is that it is a *private* good, unlike public goods such as health and learning. Unlike these other goods, housing is an asset that can be owned or rented. In advanced capitalist societies, it has typically been treated as a commodity and its provision has been dominated by market forces, as exemplified by the continuing obsession with house prices in the media and among the public generally.

Notwithstanding these arguments, it appears that housing is indeed closely related to community through the fact of *shared residence*. In any given housing area, even if the residents do not live together in the same house, they still share a common space of some kind, such as a boundary with a neighbour, a street, an open space for leisure and recreation, a corridor and common entrance in a block of flats and so on. More importantly, perhaps or partly by virtue of their residence, they may share a common attachment to the area in which they live – giving rise to a community of place, as described in Chapter One. Housing is therefore associated with certain kinds of interaction resulting in mutual recognition of a common experience of living conditions, giving rise to the possibility of collective action. Housing therefore provides a foundation for habitus (singular or plural), understood as (a) distinct, durable way(s) of living. It is through such habitus that the meaningful interconnectedness of community emerges.[1]

Housing tenure, understood as a distinct bundle of property rights and obligations, is particularly distinctive of housing as a *field*. In other fields, such as health or education, goods and services are broadly viewed as being provided in three different ways: through the market, through the state and through voluntary effort. These three ways are equated with three different sectors: the private sector, the public sector and the voluntary and community sector, respectively. The main cleavages in welfare provision are therefore regarded as sectoral. With housing, however, tenure presents a complicating factor because it gives rise to a different kind of cleavage, between those who *own* housing (as owner-occupiers or landlords) and those who *rent* housing. Some commentators, such as Saunders (1990), argue that tenure cleavages are more important than sectoral cleavages, and it is at least plausible that those who rent their homes (whether from a private, public or voluntary sector landlord) have more in common with one another as tenants than they have with their landlords.

Housing tenure presents a significant issue for community development. Owner-occupation, for example, can work either for or against community. Ownership of such a valuable asset can be a source of security and stability for the owner, thus helping to ensure their continued residence in a community. On the other hand, the owner can regard and treat their asset more instrumentally, as an investment and potential source of profit to themselves and their families, which could work against community in a number of ways. Much of the debate in Britain over the Right to Buy for public sector tenants centred on its pros and cons for community (see further below). On the whole, it can be said that the benefits of owner-occupation for community have not been conclusively demonstrated.

Collective resident action

Much of the literature relating to housing and community focuses on what could broadly be described as collective action by residents. At least three types of such action can be identified in the literature (see Somerville, 2011). The first is action for neighbourhood defence, using forms of protest and resistance, where the primary purpose of the action is to defend a neighbourhood community against a perceived threat. The second is action towards resident management and control, where the primary purpose of the action is that the residents should run their own affairs in some sense, and, third, there is the so-called 'tenants' movement', where the primary purpose is for different groups of residents to work together in order to improve the conditions for all. Some, perhaps most, forms of collective action involve combinations of these different types of activities, that is, combinations of localised resistance, taking control, and cross-community campaigning.

Historically, a common form of neighbourhood defence action was that of rent strikes (withholding of rent as a protest against rent increases that were regarded by tenants as unacceptable or excessive). These rarely seem to have proved successful (Grayson, 1997), but a notable exception was that of the Glasgow rent strike of 1915 (see *Box 8.1*).

Box 8.1: The Glasgow rent strike of 1915

The conditions during the First World War meant that no new housing was provided in Britain, but large numbers of workers moved into Glasgow to work in its munitions factories. This resulted in a substantial increase in demand for housing, which prompted landlords to impose huge rent rises. The rent strike was a direct response to these increases, which were seen as unjust. This strike involved over 20,000 tenants, with the number increasing rapidly up to the time of state intervention. The government felt that it had to respond decisively because of the risk that such civil disobedience might damage the war effort. Consequently, all rents were frozen at their existing levels and a system of rent control was introduced that lasted, on and off, for more than 40 years.

Source: Adapted from Grayson (1997); see also Somerville (2011)

Two further examples of the defence of poorer neighbourhood communities are worth noting, in view of their recurring significance. One can be described as *anti-gentrification*, involving organised resident opposition to a threat posed to their communities by an influx of 'a different class of person'. What has happened in many cities, but also in some rural areas (see, for example, Midgley and Bradshaw, 2006), is that traditional working-class neighbourhoods (or peasant villages) have become 'colonised' by more affluent people with different tastes and a different culture (see, for example, Allen, 2008, and Chapter Two of this book). The result has been a rise in house prices, squeezing less affluent local residents out of the housing market and, in some cases, riding roughshod over long-standing local customs and practices (for example, complaining about the noise of church bells on Sundays). Rather than curbing gentrification, government policies in many countries have facilitated and encouraged it through various policies of regeneration and renewal – in particular, in England, the policy of housing-market renewal (Allen, 2008).

The other example is the defence by public sector tenants against the transfer of the housing in which they live to other landlords. Such transfer is seen as a threat because it paves the way towards the privatisation of public rented housing and a return to the dark days of private landlordism. In England, this action has been led by the pressure group Defend Council Housing. It is unclear, however, exactly what is being defended here: is it a community and, if so, what is this community? And if it is not a community, what is it? If it is council housing as a tenure that is being defended, as the name of the pressure group suggests, why should it be considered desirable to defend what is, after all, a form of landlordism? Defence of such a tenure may serve to bring together those who share the same tenure but, by the same token, it may serve to divide council tenants from those living in different tenures (private tenants, housing association tenants, owner-occupiers, and so on).

There are also many examples of the defence by those living in more affluent neighbourhoods against threats to their property values and affluent life-styles. Some of these residents are known disparagingly as 'nimbys' ('not in my back yard') and the range of possible threats that they perceive is probably infinite: low-cost housing, hostels for the homeless, wind farms, travellers' sites, industrial units and so on – virtually anything that could have the effect of reducing the value of their assets or neighbourhood amenities. Such defence, usually organised through community and residents' associations, can prove to be remarkably effective (depending, as it does, mainly on the degree of power wielded by the associations' members), even against what an impartial observer might judge to be in the public interest (see, for example, Boudreau and Keil, 2001).

Action for resident management and control has been spearheaded by organisations such as tenant management organisations, housing cooperatives, resident–controlled housing associations, community development trusts and other community enterprises. Such action is concerned that residents should, so far as possible, run their own neighbourhoods, employing staff as necessary to provide a wide range of services and selling their expertise to groups of residents in other neighbourhoods. Some of these organisations, such as Coin Street Community Builders (CSCB) in London, The Eldonians in Liverpool and Royds Community Association in Bradford, have been remarkably successful (see, for example, Somerville, 2010).

A third kind of resident collective action has been identified as the '*tenants' movement*', which incorporates defensive action but also includes campaigning, within durable tenants' and residents' associations, for improved living conditions and political influence for residents, particularly those living on council estates. This movement is based in residents' own communities but also involves concerted action across communities. Over a period of many decades, the struggle has been for public housing with low rents, free from damp and disrepair, and for community facilities of various kinds. Traditionally, at least since the Second World War, its strength has lain in its connections with the Labour movement and, in particular, with the Labour Party. This movement of council tenants has had notable achievements, such as the Tenants' Charter (in 1980) (which gave tenants a number of rights, in particular security of tenure), the defeat of the government's proposals for housing action trusts (which, in their original form, would have changed the tenants' landlord without consulting them at all), the right to a ballot of all council tenants to decide on proposals to transfer their housing to other landlords (in 1988), and ensuring the government's commitment to a 'decent homes standard' (in 2001). No doubt partly as a consequence of such activism, the government has sought to involve tenants in an increasingly wide range of policy formulation and implementation.

Somerville (2011) suggests a way of explaining collective resident action in terms of Bourdieu's concept of habitus. Collective action to defend neighbourhood community, for example, is geared towards protecting working-class or middle-class habitus. Distrust of private landlords, for example, is a strong characteristic of working–class habitus, from the 19th century right up to the present day, and this helps to explain both the rent strikes of the early years and the popularity of Defend Council Housing today. The only partial success of actions to defend council housing could also be due, in part, to the fact that the changes proposed for council tenants do not appear to significantly threaten their habitus. In contrast, middle-class movements to defend their assets and amenities tend to be more successful because their members are more powerful and are often defending their habitus against weaker groups whom they do indeed see as threatening their habitus.

Similarly, action for resident management and control typically grows from within working-class habitus, aiming to change its nature from what Crossley (2002) calls a 'resistance habitus' to one that is more in charge of its own destiny. Successful examples of such action, however, are few and far between, and this suggests that very special conditions are required – for example, a tightly knit group of highly committed residents, a clear and visible threat (for example, in the case of The Eldonians, the threat to destroy their homes), a decisive repulse of a potential threat (for example, Royds' winning of Single Regeneration Budget funding in competition against Bradford City Council), a golden opportunity (such as the Greater London Council's gift of the OXO tower to CSCB), a strong spirit of social enterprise and an enduring constituency of support. The habitus is still that of a working class, but it is one that is self-confident and proactive, not merely reacting to the whims of markets or governments.

Again, both the successes and failures of the tenants' movement can be attributed to its embeddedness in working-class habitus: successes, such as security of tenure, low rents and decent homes (both testimony to the strength and durability of working-class ways of everyday living in council housing); and failures, arising from the subordination of working-class habitus to the field of housing investment flows and other market forces, pushing for the commodification of working-class housing and amenities. Like the Labour movement or trade union movement, the tenants' movement seeks only an accommodation within an existing field, namely, that of landlord–tenant relations (compare the field of capital–labour relations associated with the trade union movement). It does not seek a transformation of that field (which would involve the abolition of landlord–tenant relations). Consequently, it seems destined to continue to occupy a subordinate, but nevertheless significant, position within the field itself.

Governmental approaches

Government approaches to housing and community broadly follow those outlined in Chapter Four, namely neoliberal, neo-colonial, communitarian and pragmatic partnership approaches. Examples of neoliberal policies are those that promote owner-occupation as the tenure of choice, that emphasise the importance of choice for tenants and for housing consumers generally and that give priority to 'renewing' the housing market where it is perceived to be failing or underperforming. Examples of neo-colonial policies are those that assume that it is possible to build communities *ex nihilo*, on the assumption of an absence of pre-existing communities, that such communities can be *planned* to be 'balanced' and 'sustainable' and that existing communities can be (re-)engineered to make them conform more closely to the desires of more powerful groups. Examples of communitarian policies are those that attempt to build communities more 'organically', through deepening of resident involvement and promotion of 'strong, active communities' (see Chapter One). Examples of partnership policies are those that emphasise cooperation between landlord and tenants, between housing organisations of different kinds, and between housing and other services. There are clearly areas of significant overlap between these approaches.

A classic example of a *neoliberal* housing policy is that of the Right to Buy, which was introduced into Britain by the Conservative government in 1980. This policy gave council housing tenants a right to buy their homes from the council at substantial discounts, which increased according to the length of time they had been public sector tenants. This has enabled the sale of around 2.5 million council homes to their tenants up to December 2009. The possible implications of such a policy for community can be analysed as follows. First, it should be noted that the policy exacerbated a long-term process of residualisation of council housing, according to which it tended to be the more desirable housing in the more desirable locations that was sold off, to the more affluent tenants (Forrest and Murie, 1990), so that council housing increasingly came to be seen as a 'second best' tenure, for those who could not afford to buy their own homes. Second, many of the tenants who bought their homes under the Right to Buy would have otherwise had to move from their homes and away from their home areas in order to become home owners. For these households, therefore, the introduction of the Right to Buy encouraged them to remain in their existing communities. For other tenants, however, particularly those living in less desirable areas, the Right to Buy had precisely the opposite effect: it allowed them to move away from their homes on a long-term basis, either by selling their home on to someone else after a few years (early resales were penalised by requiring discounts to be paid back) or by letting it out privately.

The effects of these transactions on community are complex but appear to have done more harm than good overall (see, for example, Forrest et al, 1996). Jones and Murie (2006) in particular argue that the Right to Buy has resulted in more overcrowding (because of the sale of larger and better council housing – p 211) and greater transience of population ('council housing has become a staging post for many tenants on the way to buying on the open market' – p 212). There have been continual problems in managing relations between tenants and owner-occupiers living on council estates (p 215) and resales of properties purchased under the Right to Buy have attracted a range of households not necessarily with local connections (p 213). Many better-off Right to Buy purchasers have moved away and let their properties to poorer households, particularly in the least desirable estates, and these 'new tenants' have to pay higher rents than their council tenant neighbours (p 213). All of these factors, taken together, indicate that Right to Buy has resulted in less healthy, less stable, poorer and more divided communities (divided between owners and tenants, and between council tenants and private tenants).

The Right to Buy is an example of 'roll-back' neoliberalism (see Chapter Four), where the state facilitates withdrawal from non-marketed provision (in this case, housing provided by local authorities) and the expansion of marketed provision (here buying and selling for owner occupation). An example of 'roll-out' neoliberalism, where the state actively intervenes to change the way that markets work, is New Labour's policy of housing market renewal (HMR). This policy was launched in 2002 'in response to concerns expressed by local authorities and their partners about the emergence of problems of low and changing demand for housing – reflected in very low house prices' (Leather et al, 2009, p 4). Between October 2003 and March 2008, over £1 billion of government funding was allocated to nine housing market pathfinders across the Midlands and north of England, with a further £1 billion to cover the period up to March 2011 (Leather et al, 2009, p 5). The main aim of this policy was to eradicate 'low demand' by 2020.

It is pertinent, therefore, to question what is meant by low demand and why it should be seen as a problem. There is a notable lack of evidence, for example, that communities in these areas recognised the existence of such a problem. Indeed, it might be expected that poorer communities would regard high demand, not low demand, as a problem because it results in lower affordability of housing to buy and longer waiting lists for affordable housing to rent. Unfortunately, we do not really know what residents of these areas thought about this key issue because it appears they were never asked. The general approach towards community engagement taken by the pathfinders is illustrated in *Box 8.2*.

Box 8.2 Housing market renewal

In Manchester Salford Partnership, community engagement was undertaken by local teams. This involved door-knocking and contacting specific households affected by the proposals and consulting them before beginning development so as to raise awareness of the programme and of issues such as relocation packages and financial support. Households were also invited to join residents' groups set up as part of the masterplanning process, over such issues as large compulsory purchase order schemes. The respondent interviewed claimed that any challenges to schemes had come from individual residents rather than community groups and had been resolved, although often after intensive consultation.

Source: Leather et al (2009, p 60)

This shows that all the key decisions on the programme had already been taken before residents were 'consulted' and the purpose of the 'consultation' was then simply to ensure that the programme went ahead as smoothly as possible. It is clear that community groups were not even contacted by the programme managers (who preferred to set up their own residents' groups), and the claim that no challenges came from any community groups is not supported by any evidence. As for 'intensive consultation', given the power differences between the two parties, this is probably just a euphemism for brow-beating.

Given the relative helplessness of residents in this situation, it is not surprising that some had recourse to the media in order to make their case heard. Wise to this, the pathfinder teams employed their own media managers to minimise negative coverage, and this proactive approach was directly linked to making the areas more attractive to developers and other commercial bodies. As one respondent reported for the national evaluation:

'… we will actually look at it from a developer prospective [*sic*], I mean we will talk about the importance of HMR in terms of business benefits and what we can do is actually alert them to the resources going in and challenge more negative stories …'. (Cited in Leather et al, 2009, p 61)

In other words, negative stories need to be rebutted, not so much because they may be false, but because they may be damaging to the creation of the markets that the pathfinders want to see. Ultimately, what the pathfinders want to do (and this is what roll-out neoliberalism is all about) is to provide increased opportunities for capitalist exploitation, where firms will come into the area to raise the value of property generally, yielding profits for themselves and perhaps attracting higher-income households into the area, resulting in gentrification. In other words, insofar as they are focused on communities at all (which is doubtful), housing-market pathfinders are an outstanding example of 'top-down' community development (see Chapter Two).

More generally, policy approaches in housing have tended to concentrate on its built form (so-called 'bricks and mortar') rather than on the people who inhabit that form. One thinks in particular of policies to clear slums, to renovate housing and to raise housing standards (most recently, the Decent Homes Standard for council housing). Such policies have not been renowned for their sensitivity to the needs of communities (see, for example, Dennis, 1970). With the arrival of area-based policies such as General Improvement Areas and Housing Action Areas in the 1970s, and Renewal Areas in the 1980s, however, housing policy gradually became more community focused in certain respects (see, for example, Atkinson and Moon, 1994).

Mention should perhaps be made here of town planning. Much of post-war planning policy ignored the needs, wishes and knowledge/expertise of existing communities and imposed on them ideologies and prejudices that were not based on any sound research evidence. Examples of such policies included the building of new towns, the separation of human activities into separate 'zones', the restriction of new development to 'key settlements', and so on. It is not the purpose of this book to provide a detailed critique of the planning system (see Minton, 2009, for an example of such a critique), but it can be argued that the general approach of that system has been neo-colonial and communitarian. New towns, for example, were designated by the government in Westminster without any consultation with local authorities or with the residents in which such towns were to be built. People and jobs were then relocated to these areas from large cities such as London, Liverpool, Glasgow and Birmingham in a planned process of resettlement. In this process, the national government was the colonial power and the settlers came largely from urban working-class communities. New towns were also based on a concept of balanced community, in which it is assumed that it is desirable for a community to contain a mix of different kinds of household. In practice, this meant a mix of people of different ages or different generations, and different tenures, but not of different social classes or ethnic groups, as the settlers were overwhelmingly white working class. It was further assumed that new towns could be divided into clearly delineated neighbourhoods, each of which would contain such a balanced community (Heraud, 1968). In this way, the new towns policy expressed a communitarian view that the world consists, or ought to consist, of a 'community of communities' (see Chapter Three).

More recent policy on so-called 'mixed income communities' or 'MINCies' echoes the earlier new towns policy, though it springs from rather different concerns (see CLG, 2006c). Both policies aim to provide well-designed housing, planned neighbourhoods and an integration of different tenures. In the immediate post-war period, however, the main concern was to raise the housing standards of the working class, whereas in recent years the focus has been more on achieving community cohesion, sustainable neighbourhoods and social order. There has now been a considerable amount of research on MINCies – for a summary, see Holmes (2006); for an interesting discussion, see Tunstall and Fenton (2006); for a thoroughgoing critique, see Cheshire (2007); and for an up-to-date survey of residents' views, see Bretherton and Pleace (2009). In general, MINCies can be defined as residential neighbourhoods that contain a mix of household incomes, and this is assumed to occur when a certain proportion of the housing is affordable to those on low incomes. Basically, there are two kinds of MINCies: new-build MINCies and regenerated MINCies. In the former case, the idea is, as in new towns, to create a 'balanced' community from scratch, whereas in the latter case, the expectation is that better-off households will take up residence in what is currently an area of low-income households.

Predictably, in view of all the evidence so far adduced in this book, research reveals that residents are often unhappy about different tenures in the same development (Bretherton and Pleace, 2009). This is not surprising, because it is unreasonable to place very different people cheek by jowl and simply expect them to get on with one another. It is yet another example of a neo-colonial and managerial mentality. Rather than solving any problems of social order or cohesion or unsustainability, it merely serves to reproduce these problems within the development itself. The concept of MINCy is not based on any proper understanding of community or community development. In its evaluation of the government's 'sustainable communities' policy, the Sustainable Development Commission has commented that it is basically a policy for building houses and is not joined up with other community services, in particular employment (SDC, 2007). For all these reasons, MINCies are vulnerable to erosion in the long term, for example, due to buy-to-let or buy-to-mothball, where home owners rent out their homes to lower-income households or leave them empty altogether. It may be that planning mixed-income communities within a free market just does not work (Cheshire, 2007).

With regard to regenerating existing communities to achieve a mix of resident incomes, the picture looks hardly any better, even though greater effort has been made to join up housing with other services (for example, in New Deal for Communities – see Chapter Four). A number of studies have shown that regeneration initiatives targeted at poorer communities over the years do not appear to have improved their position relative to other communities (Dorling et al, 2007; Leunig and Swaffield, 2008).[2] Leunig and Swaffield (2008, p 23) suggest why this should be: 'current policies mean that poorer towns will continue to get poorer relative to the rest of the country. When the national economy is doing well, and money for regeneration is plentiful, they will get gradually poorer. When the national economy is doing badly, and money for regeneration is hard to come by, they will get poorer much more quickly.' Dorling et al (2007) reported evidence of increasing polarisation, with rich and poor living further apart. It is unclear whether regeneration programmes have reduced the rate of this polarisation, made no appreciable difference to it or actually contributed to it (for example, by enabling better-off households to move out of the area) (Thornhill, 2009, p 48).[3] These findings would appear to suggest that the problem for many poorer communities, particularly urban ones, is not so much gentrification as social isolation. Rather than being made to receive an influx of more affluent households, they have been left largely to their own devices.

Housing policy has also been increasingly infected by the New Labour government's emphasis on developing active citizen-consumers (as discussed in earlier chapters). Examples of initiatives here include: the requirement to involve tenants in the governance of housing organisations (CLG, 2007b; Housing Corporation, 2007), partnership bodies, for example, for housing regeneration, and 'wider neighbourhood services' (CLG, 2007b); partnerships between landlord and tenants, for example, through tenant management organisations, estate agreements, tenant participation compacts, good neighbour agreements and so on; increasing involvement of tenants in the monitoring and auditing of housing services; and representation of tenants on national bodies, namely, the National Tenant Voice.[4]

It is not clear that any of these initiatives (with the possible exception of efficiently run tenant management organisations – see ODPM, 2002b) have led to significant improvements for the tenants concerned, for those whom they represent or for communities generally. Overall, the Labour government's approach to tenant participation, or what it increasingly called 'tenant empowerment' (CLG, 2007b), was part of a participationist agenda that has been extensively criticised in Chapters Two, Three and Four of this book. Tenants were triply constructed by government: neoliberally, as free consumers in a housing market; neo-colonially, as needing to be 'civilised' in the ways of the world (that is, they were expected to be 'responsible' actors in the housing system – see Flint, 2004; McKee, 2008); and in a communitarian fashion, as members of local communities who should be actively involved in working with their landlords and with government for the benefit of their communities. The reality, however, is that social housing is not a free market, most tenants will never be both able and willing to adopt the activist roles that the Labour government expected (for the reasons described in previous chapters – and see also McKee, 2008), and the concept of a community of *tenants* is inherently problematic, because a tenant is defined in terms of their relationship with a landlord (which involves occupying a position in a field of positions with other tenants, rather than being in a habitus shared with other residents).

A major policy that perhaps should be mentioned here is that of the large-scale transfer of council housing to other landlords. Originally promulgated under the Conservatives in 1988 as a means towards privatisation of the public housing stock, this policy was enthusiastically embraced and encouraged by New Labour as a classic 'Third Way' option, whereby decent, affordable housing becomes provided mainly by housing associations, which are 'third sector' bodies (see Chapter Five). To date, well over a million homes have been transferred under this policy.[5] It has been argued (for example, by Defend Council Housing) that such transfer is against the interests of tenants because it removes the possibility of local democratic control over what happens to their homes. Historically, however, it is clear that council tenants have rarely been able to exercise such control over their local authority landlords (see, for example, Cole and Furbey, 1994). In practice, it appears that the housing associations to whom council housing has been transferred have, on the whole, been more accountable and responsive to their tenants than their predecessors, and possibly also more community minded (see, for example, Pawson et al, 2009). It is possible, however, that at least some of this advance may have been due to the government's favourable treatment of housing associations in comparison with local housing authorities (for example, higher investment for decent homes and grants towards building new housing). Consequently, the benefits (if any) of this policy for community and community development are not at all clear.

The long-term failure of housing policy to deliver sufficient affordable housing has had major repercussions for communities. Basically, it results in an intensification of competition for housing, which finds expression in increasing conflict within communities. This conflict takes two main forms. One is where groups within a community have succeeded in preventing the provision of more affordable housing in their area (which could be for other local people or for outsiders). These are examples of the nimbys mentioned earlier. The other is where groups from outside the community have outbid local people in buying the housing that is available, forcing the latter to remain in unsatisfactory housing or to leave the area altogether.[6]

Encouraging more bottom-up approaches

An interesting finding by Uguris (2004), based on research in Lewisham and Islington, is that collective action by tenants and residents tends to reinforce rather than challenge complex existing divisions of class, sex and race, and creates new divisions based on 'turf'. This is a salutary reminder that bottom-up approaches have their flaws and should not be idealised or romanticised. Nevertheless, it is clear that the serious problems with top-down approaches identified in the previous section call for the development of more vigorous and comprehensive bottom-up approaches, at least as a counter-balance. Examples of such bottom-up approaches include: building community-owned and controlled housing such as resident-controlled housing associations, housing cooperatives, self-help housing projects and co-housing communities (see Dearling, 2003);[7] and new initiatives such as community right to buy, community land and housing partnerships and trusts, and Community Gateway.

Housing cooperatives are the most obvious solution to the problem of the divide between owners and renters, but there are few of them in the UK, in contrast to many other countries (Coles, 2009, reports that only 0.2% of the UK's housing stock is mutually owned/managed, compared with 18% in Sweden, 14% in Norway and 25% in Turkey). This could be changed radically if the government were to be more active in supporting the development of housing cooperatives,[8] for example through community land trusts (CLTs).[9] Such trusts facilitate sustainable community development and protect the community against land speculation.

Community right to buy currently operates only in Scotland (under Scotland's Land Reform Act 2003). It allows a community to register an interest in fixed assets (land or buildings) and have first right of refusal when those assets come on the market. For this to work well, the community needs to be clearly defined as a geographical entity, and it is no accident that the only significant purchases under this right have been Scottish islands (Eigg, Gigha and Western Isles). It seems feasible, however, as proposed by the Conservatives in their 2010 manifesto (Conservative Party, 2010), that the right could be drafted so as to apply to any community group wanting to invest in and run a local asset, for example, developing land for a housing cooperative or buying a local shop or pub or even forming its own energy company (as achieved by the community of Ashton Hayes in Cheshire). The group could identify one or more suitable sites or bases for such an enterprise and be given first right of refusal when the relevant asset or assets are put up for sale.

Community Gateway is the brainchild of the Confederation of Co-operative Housing. It is an arrangement whereby tenants of a social landlord can become members of a community gateway association, which then decides what to do about the housing they live in. They could, for example, choose to continue to be tenants of their landlord, or to become a housing cooperative or something else. The key advantage of Community

Gateway, therefore, is that it extends the scope of collective choice for social housing tenants. So far, however, only six housing associations have chosen to go down this road (see CCH, 2010). It might be a good idea if all housing associations were required by law to set up such community gateway associations, whose membership would be open to all tenants of the housing association.

More recently, there is evidence of housing organisations working more in partnership with other organisations at a local community level, for example, schools (Thornhill and Kent-Smith, 2009) and health and social care organisations (Davis et al, 2009). The significance of such developments for community, however, is not entirely clear.

Conclusion

It seems that the dominant view of the field of housing in the UK, as in other advanced capitalist countries, is that it is a 'space of positions' (Bourdieu), and this is not at all integrated with housing as a space of 'dwelling' together, which is a characteristic of community. Increasingly, housing is seen in terms of its market value and its potential for capital accumulation rather than in terms of its contribution to community. This is a serious problem that current housing policy largely fails to address.

This chapter has reviewed the history of collective action around housing and governmental approaches to housing and community. This review suggests that there are grounds for both optimism and pessimism, but the latter seem to outweigh the former. On the positive side, there are examples of significant community-led successful housing development, often in the face of hostility from powerful bodies. On the negative side, however, mainstream housing development, policy and management continues to promote and follow a two-tenure market model that has conspicuously failed to deliver real community for residents in this country. In contrast to the current situation, a beloved community would be one where home owners and tenants are valued equally, where the production, use and enjoyment of their homes and of the living space that they share with others is made possible through cooperation with others on an equal basis and where no community member profits (from their housing) at the expense of another.

Notes
[1] Note that community here does not arise directly from residence itself, but only indirectly, through habitual interactions among the residents of a place and through shared attachment to a place by its residents.

[2] Much so-called regeneration is of course not aimed at helping communities at all but simply at making profits for capital (see, for example, Minton, 2009), even if this rides roughshod over community needs and interests.

[3] Some commentators go further, pointing out that regeneration in some cases involves the actual removal or exclusion of certain groups from the area, for example, bans on 'hoodies' (from the Bluewater shopping centre), elimination of rough sleepers from the streets of London (in preparation for the Olympic Games in 2012) (CLG, 2008f) and so on (the so-called 'eliminative ideal' is discussed in Chapter Nine).

[4] The coalition government has now (July 2010) announced that it will abolish the National Tenant Voice.

[5] The transfers are called 'voluntary' because it is left up to each individual local authority to decide whether or not it wishes to transfer its stock. If it does so decide, it then has to consult its tenants and move towards a ballot of all the tenants. Unless a majority of votes in the ballot are cast against the transfer, the authority can proceed with it, subject to approval from the Secretary of State.

[6] This is particularly so in the case of young people in rural areas – see Midgley and Bradshaw (2006).

[7] Co-housing is a form of collaborative community housing where individual homes are clustered around a shared common space.

[8] For a useful summary of the advantages of cooperative housing, see Handy (2010).

[9] CLTs are currently empowered by the Housing and Regeneration Act 2008. The Act enables land to be held in trust for the benefit of a local community so that the community can retain control in perpetuity of any housing that is built on that land.

Summary

The relationship between housing and community is complex and poorly understood. Paradoxically, housing is both an indispensable building block for community of a certain kind (what might be called 'residential community') and a largely private-built form that functions to set individual households apart from their community. In addition, differences of tenure (owning versus renting) and sector (private versus public) can result in divisions within the community itself. It is argued in this chapter that much of this can be explained in terms of class divisions in habitus. Governmental approaches are also criticised for their lack of understanding of the relationships involved and their unrealistic expectations in relation to what they choose to call 'tenant empowerment'. The 'Big Society' now looks set to deepen this lack of understanding and is therefore likely to add further to the problems that already exist in this policy area.

Questions for discussion

- How important is the ownership and control of housing for community?

- How can community action be based on residence?

- What is the appropriate role for government in relation to residential community?

- Could cooperative housing be an essential ingredient of a beloved community?

nine

Community order

Overview

This chapter considers the preconditions for the existence of a beloved community. These include mutual respect among all members, on the basis of their equal worth. All policy is concerned with policing, understood as a function or process of maintaining order, enabling patterns of production and reproduction (of community, society or whatever). A distinction can be made, however, between policing that merely keeps order of any kind and policing that aspires to 'fix' the beloved community. The chapter explains how this latter ideal form of community policing involves a balance between public self-policing and special kinds of policing practice.

The chapter strongly criticises crude divisions of people into two types, such as 'law-abiding' and 'deviant'. Such stereotypes are characteristic of governmental approaches but are also reflected in much of the academic literature. They undermine the very possibility of moving towards a beloved community because they legitimise and reinforce mutual disrespect and social/moral inequality. The process of labelling involved infects, and perhaps reflects, the ways in which we think about and treat people generally, thus tending to exacerbate divisions of class, race, gender, generation, and so on. This division between 'us' and 'them' is then expressed in a bifurcation of government policy, with the 'law abiding' being increasingly held responsible for policing themselves and the 'deviants' being increasingly targeted for policing interventions of all kinds. The rest of the chapter is concerned with exploring the nature and implications of this bifurcation, and evaluating government policy on community safety and anti-social behaviour. It is concluded that much of this policy is not only ineffective and wasteful but actually counter-productive, being likely to increase rather than reduce disorder.

The word 'order' conjures up a number of different images and ideas. One thinks, for example, of 'law and order', but also of quite different meanings, such as hierarchy and tidiness, regularity, security and safety. In this chapter, 'order' will be taken to mean a dynamic state that tends to equilibrium – due to the following of rules or other regular patterns of behaviour in space and time. Following the argument of this book, two types of such order can be distinguished. The first type is the order of a 'field' (Bourdieu). Thus one can talk of 'a new world order' or the political economic order of the global capitalist system or the Westphalian order of the global interstate system or any one of a wide variety of governmental orders established around the world.[1] The second type is the order of a 'habitus' (Bourdieu), and this order can be understood most simply as an alternative expression for meaningful interconnectedness. Since meaningful interconnectedness within habitus is what this book understands by community, it follows that order lies at the heart of what makes a community. The order of a community can be identified with the form of its meaningful interconnectedness. It is the nature of this form that is the concern of this chapter.[2]

A particular difficulty in investigating the nature of community order is that it is, to use Habermas' term, so thoroughly 'colonised' by the system.[3] That is to say, the order of the field so dominates community life that it is difficult to identify the order that is distinctive of the community itself. Insofar as the habitus of a community is integrated with a field, then it may even become part of the same order. This chapter will therefore attempt to identify how community order differs from order more generally and, in particular, how it comes into conflict with, challenges and resists established order.

A key question for community order, as for order more generally, concerns what is required to ensure such order. The short answer to this question, however, is that it depends on the nature of the community. In Chapter Three, for example, I argued that political community, and hence political order, requires decision-making authority, but it does not follow from this that communities of other kinds cannot be ordered in the absence of such an authority. In this chapter, I will consider the possibility of what might be called spontaneous order, where a community essentially polices itself.

The chapter will focus mainly on issues of policing, respect and anti-social behaviour, since these are key issues relating to communities.

The forms of community order

Since the time of Aristotle (1976), if not earlier, it has been recognised that there exist forms of what might be called moral order, which involve methods and techniques whereby the behaviour of a society's members is characterised by a certain level of peace and productivity. The number of such forms of moral order, however, is potentially infinite. At different times in history, it has been viewed as perfectly 'in order', for example, to own slaves, to kill disobedient wives and children, to commit incest, to invade neighbouring territories without provocation and to rape, enslave and kill their inhabitants, to kill those of a different religious faith or ideology, to steal from the poor and defenceless and evict them from their homes, and so on. A moral order is therefore not necessarily a 'good' order in the way that term is understood today. This raises the question, however, of whether we do actually have a common sense of a moral order today, or whether the form of that order might vary from one community to another.[4]

Sayer (2005, p 948) argues that such a common moral sense does exist and he calls it 'lay normativity' or 'lay morality'. At the heart of this conception is the principle of valuing, caring about and being concerned for oneself and others – that is to say, respect (Somerville, 2009a, p 140). It is important to bear in mind that this lay normativity may not involve *equal* valuing of others and may be compatible with a wide variety of discriminatory constructions such as classism, racism, sexism, heterosexism, disablism and so on. However, it does seem to include at least a general principle of non-harm to others, providing those others do not pose a threat to oneself. Arguably, this represents an advance over the 18th century, for example, when the slave trade was in full flow and aggressive imperial wars were fought with little apparent consideration for the huge loss of life involved.[5] It is to be expected, in any event, that lay normativity will vary according to the nature of the 'laity'. In modern consumer society, therefore, it appears that only those who *consume* are really respected (Millie, 2009, p 208).

Whatever the reality (or lack of it) of lay normativity on the world stage, Somerville (2009a, p 245) argues that mutual respect on the basis of equality of citizenship is necessary for orderly interaction in a democratic society. Otherwise, some citizens would be considered as being of lower value than others, which, apart from being disrespectful, would mean that their voices would carry less weight. As Dee Cook (2006, p 21) points out, this can lead to a sense of injustice and therefore to conflict and disorder:

> If a society cannot guarantee 'the equal worth of all citizens', mutual and self-respect and the meeting of all needs, it cannot expect that all citizens will feel they have an equal stake in abiding by the law.

This statement is perhaps slightly misleading, in that abiding by the law does not require that all citizens must feel they have the same stake in it (some will have more to gain than others from abiding by the law – or more to lose from not abiding by it), but the important implication of what Cook says is that *unequal* valuing of citizens tends to create a situation where disorder is more likely. This could help to explain why, if we exclude states that are failed or are experiencing open civil war (such as Somalia, Democratic Republic of Congo, Iraq, Afghanistan, Sudan and so on), crime and disorder are highest in countries such as South Africa (with its history of apartheid), India (with its caste system) and Brazil (with its continuing oppression of indigenous peoples).

In the beloved community, which is a democratic community, every member is valued equally with all the others. The concept of the beloved community also makes clear that freedom and order are mutually constituted – the flourishing of every individual member secures the order of the community as a whole.[6] This is the only true basis for an ethical community order. A distinction can therefore be drawn between this ideal form of community order and that which actually exists, namely different forms of lay normativity or different ordered ways of 'going on' in habitus.

Public self-policing and the co-production of social order

The maintenance of order of any kind, whatever its context (such as the family, the community, the market or the state) can be called 'policing' (see Loader, 2000, p 334). The term 'policing' therefore has a much wider connotation than activities carried out by the public police. As Neocleous (2000, p 10) argues, the terms 'policing' and 'policy' have the same root, and all policy is, to some extent, concerned with the maintenance of order. For example, as Rodger (2008, p 5) reports, following Squires (1990), the Poor Law Amendment Act 1834 'was a system of welfare that was primarily concerned to *police* entitlement to benefits in a context of building a disciplinary society that would complement the needs of the growing and developing capitalist economy' (my italics). This has been the role of 'welfare' ever since, with the result that all the government policies considered in previous chapters of this book have been formulated, developed and implemented with a view to establishing, maintaining and/ or improving order, whether this be public, social, political, economic, moral, aesthetic, community or whatever.

Corresponding to the distinction made in the last section between ideal and real forms of community order, one can distinguish between real and ideal forms of community order maintenance or community policing. Put simply, the ideal form of community policing is one that aspires to maintain a beloved community. Following Somerville (2009a, 2009b), this chapter argues that this ideal is one of democratic community self-governance, as described by Somerville (2009a, pp 152–5), or 'public self-policing'

(Somerville, 2009b), combined with co-governance (Somerville, 2009a, p 156) or the co-production of social order (Somerville, 2009b, p 264).

Perhaps the earliest exponent of a concept of public self-policing was Jane Jacobs (1961). She pointed out that routine mutual monitoring and surveillance of one another by people going about their daily business tended to reduce the incidence of behaviour that might commonly be regarded as transgressive, anti-social or criminal – behaviour that is literally 'out of order'. Since then, a number of attempts have been made to explain her findings. These attempts can be summarised in the argument that potential transgressors are deterred by the perceived risk that others might intervene or might bear witness against them later on, or perhaps by the shame that might be attached to being seen as a transgressor. Readiness to intervene is a key factor in public self-policing. Studies have shown, however, that this readiness is actually quite low – bystanders do not generally intervene where transgressions take place (assaults, damage to property, dropping litter and so on). This is because they have difficulty, first, in noticing the incident, then in interpreting it as a transgressive act that calls for intervention, and finally, in actually intervening to provide help (for example, because of the risk of harm to themselves) (Latane and Darley, 1970). Deciding to run this risk is more likely where the transgressor is known to the witness and also where the witness is known to them; where it occurs in the witness's own immediate neighbourhood (Harris, 2006, p 64); where fellow bystanders are seen as people like them (Levine et al, 2002, p 3); where the authorities are perceived as responsive, effective, supportive or trustworthy (Silver and Miller, 2004, p 558); and where the witness recognises a responsibility/duty to intervene or an intrinsic value in intervening (Hawdon et al, 2003; Barnes and Baylis, 2004, p 101).

The lessons from this body of evidence are that the decision to intervene is conditional upon having trust that other people and the authorities will support, or at least not undermine, one's intervention, and upon having a certain social status or reputation in a community and responsibilities associated with that status. In many situations where a transgression takes place, however, such trust is lacking and there is no witness with sufficient 'clout' in the community to risk challenging the transgressor. In these situations, therefore, public self-policing is of limited value in maintaining order. What are needed in addition are dedicated policing organisations who will work with the grain of local community self-policing in order to achieve successful interventions. This is called co-governance, or co-production of community order.

There can be a wide measure of agreement on what counts in general as a transgression, but considerable disagreement about whether or not any particular event is transgressive. Also, even when there is agreement that the event is transgressive, there may still be disagreement about the appropriateness and proportionality of any action taken in response to that transgression. It should not be assumed that intervention is necessarily well intentioned or beneficial in its effects. Some forms of public self-policing can be actually harmful for the community – for example, where the community is dominated by criminal gangs (such as drug dealers – May et al, 2006), whose rule is typically reinforced by an 'anti-grassing' culture (see references in Somerville, 2009b, p 264); where members of the public take the law into their own hands (that is, vigilantism); and where communities are deeply illiberal, unequal, hierarchical or divided, for example along racial lines, or ignorant and insensitive, for example, on drugs issues (Shiner et al, 2004, p 9). In all these cases, intervention by members of the public tends to have harmful effects, whether these be in terms of punishment or retaliation by gang members and vigilantes, or open conflict between different social and ethnic groups (who may themselves be organised into gangs). For all these reasons, public self-policing has to be governed by an independent, impartial 'rule of law' – an ideal of 'natural justice' (Rodger, 2008, p 11).

None of this should be taken to imply that public self-policing cannot or does not play an important role in maintaining order in many, perhaps most communities. It is interesting to note, for example, the studies of how communities have acted in the face of disasters such as earthquakes, hurricanes and floods, not to mention 9/11 (see Solnit, 2009). Rather than a Hobbesian war of all against all in the absence of any clear authority, with widespread panic, mob rule, looting, arson, rape and so on, one finds a feeling akin to joy among the survivors, as people pull together in the aftermath, spontaneously gathering, socialising and helping one another. The problems after the disaster come not from the people but from the elite, whose claim to authority has been undermined by the disaster itself and who are prepared to use armed force to regain that authority (for an excellent example of this in the aftermath of Hurricane Katrina in New Orleans, see Mooney, 2009). These appear to be excellent examples of public self-policing, all the more important for occurring in such desperate circumstances.[7] One could contrast them with the episodes of huge destruction of human life – genocides, wars and so on – that have universally been carried out at the express command of political and military elites.

On its own, therefore, public self-policing has both benefits and drawbacks when measured against the community policing ideal. Basically, it works well only in communities whose members value, respect and trust one another equally. One could add that this respect and trust also need to be extended to those *outside* the community if order within the community is to be maintained. Where human beings do not respect and trust one another equally, however (which is invariably the case in practice), public self-policing can produce consequences that are far from the ideal. What are needed, therefore, are organisations, institutions and practices that *both* promote and advance greater equality of trust and respect *and* intervene to address the harmful effects of public self-policing in unequal societies; that is to say, that act as both prevention and cure. These can be broadly described as forms of *policing practices*. They are not in themselves forms of self-policing, but they work on and with public self-policing to make it fairer, either from within the community or from outside the community. This close collaboration between public self-policing and certain forms of policing practices is what I call the *ideal* co-production of social order.

Who is a transgressor?

Popular opinion tends to assume a clear and unproblematic division between a law–abiding majority and a transgressing minority. This opinion is reflected in the speeches of leading politicians, for example Blair's division of the people into the 'innately decent' and the 'others' (see Stephen, 2008, p 329).[8] It is assumed that people simply choose either to comply with the law or to break the law. The reality, however, is typically more complex. In Chapter One, we saw that people growing up in encapsulated communities find that their choices are restricted in determinate ways, and these restrictions can lead them into adopting transgressive forms of behaviour as a means of surviving in those communities. It seems that transgressors differ from others, not so much in terms of their *dispositions* to action as in terms of the *contexts* within which they act.[9] This contextual variation has led to the stereotyping of certain neighbourhoods, communities and social groups as problematic for social order.

Rodger (2008, p 113) describes an example of this binary opposition (identified here as a division between 'decent families' and 'street families') from Anderson's (1999) research in Philadelphia:

> The 'street families' perceived conventional society as a social order that had humiliated them through racist practices and disadvantaged them through social and economic policies that left them isolated in communities without welfare support or opportunities for well-paid and dignified work. In those circumstances, conventional society lost its legitimacy and the 'street families' adhered to an 'outlaw culture' in which working class values of social solidarity and unionism were replaced by a 'code of the street' ... the young men of the lower–class community adopt styles of behaviour, language and codes that

> embrace criminality, and sexist and abusive attitudes to non-family females, in order to preserve integrity on the streets.

This is similar to the distinction discussed in Chapter One between 'roughs' and 'respectables', but here the argument is even more insidious because it appears to attribute a wide range of characteristics, behaviours, values and even identities to an entire social group, namely 'young men of the lower-class community'. It cannot, however, be assumed that all young men, or even a majority of young men, living in the same community respond in the same way to changes in the economy and wider society. Such an assumption is potentially harmful because it can be used to justify enforcement interventions against whole communities or social groups. This is not to imply, however, that there is not a problem here: Squires (2009), for example, is clear that the code of the street involves the use of violence, and this is inherently self-destructive.[10]

Related to this, Rodger (2008, pp 188–91) introduces a concept of 'inverted fear' to explain how young men behave in what he calls a 'disorderly community' (p 189) such as that studied by Anderson (1999). He accepts that 'the world does not divide into those who are law-abiding, and are therefore assumed to be burdened with the fear of the deviant minority, and those presented as the deviants, who are typically presented as being "fearless", brazen and lacking in moral scruples' (p 189), but he argues that this is because: 'Criminality as an enterprise is full of dangers and risks, and engaging in anti-social behaviour is not necessarily prompted by an absence of conscience or a disregard for others' (p 189). Rather, he goes on to argue, transgression arises as an adaptation (mainly out of fear) to 'a socially disorganised environment' such as 'in inner-city areas and peripheral housing estates': 'a by-product of a strategy of survival in the sense that to remain aloof from the incivility and criminality of peers can present significant risks to the non-participant because it might suggest that one is not to be trusted' (p 189). What this argument seems to imply is the retention of a binary opposition between a law-abiding majority and a transgressing minority, but with the minority being conceived no longer as demonic 'others' (Young, 1999) but instead as *victims* of their environments, who *have* to transgress in order to survive in those environments.

This approach, which sees transgression as explicable within victimology, is problematic on a number of grounds. First, the binary opposition is as questionable as ever. It is not clear that all, or even the majority, of young men in encapsulated/disorderly/disorganised communities behave in the ways described, nor does it seem likely that different kinds of communities can be distinguished on the basis of the existence or non-existence of such behaviours within them. The identification of inner-city areas and peripheral housing estates in particular, without any qualification, sounds like negative stereotyping of a most unfortunate kind. Second, the exclusive focus on 'disorderly' or 'lower-class' communities serves to highlight transgressions of a particular type (for example, public violence, and the threat of violence, against the person) and ignores the possibility of all kinds of other transgressions that occur in all types of community – in particular, it ignores the 'crimes of the powerful' (Hall, 2009, p xv). Third, the treatment of transgressors as fearful victims diminishes their responsibility for their actions and therefore diminishes their humanity – in short, it disrespects them or reinforces or justifies their lack of self-respect. This approach, therefore, involves a significant distortion of the overall picture on community order and transgression, and has negative implications for policy or appears to imply policies that would have harmful effects.

The fairest answer to the question of who is a transgressor is: anyone. We are all capable of transgression, including serious transgression. We all begin our lives transgressing, and life itself can be represented as a process of learning to desist from some transgressions and to succumb to others (possibly even the same ones at a different time) (see, for example, Williamson, 2006). We are much more likely to transgress in some contexts than in others, but, in any given context, given the choice, some of us will transgress and others will not.

Policing practices

To return to the issue of community policing, the next question to ask is: what are the forms of policing practice that will advance the community policing ideal by working on and alongside of public self-policing? Fundamentally, this is a question about how power can be used to help us achieve the beloved community. Fortunately or unfortunately, there is a wide variety of possible answers to this question.

First of all, it seems appropriate to be reminded of the wide range of harms that result from situations where mutual and equal respect and trust are lacking. Coleman et al (2009) provides a useful source of material on this. Examples of the harms considered in the latter book alone include those arising from disrespect related to gender (Ballinger, 2009 – particularly on rape, domestic violence and the state's reinforcement of gender stereotypes), race (Burnett, 2009 – particularly the 'new racism' of an assumed English or British or European or Western or Christian cultural superiority and the stereotyping of Muslims as terrorist suspects following 9/11 and 7/7), class (Coleman, 2009 – particularly related to urban regeneration and gentrification – and see Chapter Eight on housing and community in this book) and heterosexuality (Bibbings, 2009 – particularly the continuing dominance of heteronormativity and prevalence of homophobic attitudes, despite the gradually increasing public tolerance of homosexual activity in Britain since the 1980s). At its extreme, disrespect results in demonisation, where the disrespected are seen as inherently evil or depraved, committing acts that are to be unequivocally condemned, and for which they are to be held entirely responsible.

Each of the types of harm arising from the experience of being disrespected is a possible source of grievance on the part of the disrespected people. This can lead to resentment at their treatment and to possible resistance, challenge or threat to the established order in that field. In general, therefore, it can be said that lack of mutual and equal respect and trust is itself indirectly responsible for lack of order. The wide variety of forms that disrespect takes, however, suggests that a correspondingly wide variety of policing practices may be required to remedy the situation.

One general conclusion that can perhaps be made from the consideration of situations of disrespect is that unequal societies result in and are reinforced by unfair policing practices – that is, policing practices tend to reflect and support the power inequalities that already exist. This conclusion is important because it means that we cannot look to policing reform alone as a means to transform these existing power relations (and bearing in mind that 'policing' here does not just mean law enforcement but the whole business of the policy process). It is possible to detect, however, a common mechanism by which policing or policy reform occurs and to identify possible opportunities that such reform offers for more radical change. Prior and Spalek (2008, p 124), for example, in relation to anti-social behaviour, suggest that policies have indeed helped ethnic minority individuals and communities but, at the same time, have reinforced their disadvantaged position within the criminal justice system (as described by Burnett, 2009):

> There are grounds for supposing that the application of anti-social behaviour policies and powers is likely to have a contradictory impact on ethnic minority individuals and communities: providing some additional means of relief in the face of instances of racial harassment and other forms of ethnically motivated abuse, but simultaneously contributing further to the established institutional bias of the criminal justice system against ethnic minorities.

A similar mechanism has been identified in relation to policy and attitudes on homosexuality, where, as Bibbings (2009, p 46) documents, a variety of improvements have occurred, while at the same time:

conceptions of hegemonic heterosexuality continue to underpin the reforms and supposed cultural shifts. As a result, heterosexuality is still prioritised and privileged, while modes of behaviour and identities perceived to be *non*heterosexual continue to be marginalized, discriminated against and in various respects controlled and regulated.

In both cases (of racism and heterosexism), and presumably also for other types of social harm, such as sexism, ageism, classism, disablism and so on, there are nevertheless opportunities for resistance, which have some prospects for success. Bibbings (2009, pp 46–7), for example, points out that legal changes can be interpreted as putting an end to 'appropriate' sexuality as being exclusively hetero, for example, with the recognition of same-sex civil partnerships. The message here seems to be that we have come a long way since the criminalisation of homosexual acts and, although we still have a long way to go towards equal valuing of homosexuals and heterosexuals, considerable progress along this road is still possible. Policing practices will continue to be racist, sexist, ageist, heteronormative and so on, but this can be changed, and has been changed to some extent.

Returning to the key question of what forms of policing practice are needed, it is now clear that actual forms of both public self-policing and policing practices will be deeply infected by the harms discussed above, so how are the 'right' forms of policing practice to be developed? This is a question that I tried, perhaps unsuccessfully, to answer in Somerville (2009b), with particular reference to the public police. In that article, I conceived of policing practitioners acting as street-level bureaucrats, exercising a high degree of discretion in the organisation of their work, but being accountable upwards to their political and administrative masters, across to their peers, and downwards through forms of participatory citizenship (Somerville, 2009b, p 268). The emphasis of this approach is on allowing policing practitioners, individually and collectively, to develop their own ways of working in partnership with community members, working towards common aims and objectives, with everyone learning to trust one another, and including all citizens in decision-making forums of police practitioner and community representatives (see Shiner et al, 2004, pp 45–6, for an illustration of how this can work in practice). Over the course of time, it is envisaged that a double transformation can take place, affecting public self-policing and policing practices simultaneously. The balance of policing practice is to be shifted away from upwards accountability and more towards horizontal and downwards accountability (Somerville, 2009b, p 270), while public self-policing is to become more democratic, more inclusive and more respectful. This is to be achieved by means of structural coordination between public self-policing and policing practices at a number of different levels – strategic, tactical and individual. It has to be admitted, however, that the agenda looks utopian, and it is difficult to see how to move it forward in the currently existing context of widespread social injustice and system-determined harms. This is an issue that will be discussed in the next section of this chapter.

Governmental approaches

Governmental approaches to community order are, in one sense, dualistic, in that there are policies for the 'law-abiding' and policies for the 'others' – we have 'civil renewal' and 'active citizenship' for the former, and 'civilising offensives' (Flint and Powell, 2009) for the latter. Government approaches are not dualistic, however, in that they are not *either* about welfare *or* about control – they are often about *both* care *and* control, or even about care *through* control or control *through* care. The so-called 'welfare state', for example, has always been also a 'warfare state' – the Labour government that established the National Health Service, free secondary education, national assistance and so on was the same one that introduced Britain's nuclear deterrent and attempted to re-establish Britain's global military role. The welfare state itself has always been as much about control (for example, through compulsory schooling of children, policing of families by social workers and so on) as it has been about welfare.

This point has long been recognised by historians (see references in Neocleous, 2000), and by philosophers such as Foucault (with his concepts of disciplinary power, governmentality and pastoral power, for example), but it seems not to have been understood by some influential writers. Garland (2001, p 175), for example, writes in relation to offenders:

> The welfare mode, as well as becoming more muted, has become more conditional, more offence-centred, more risk conscious … The offenders … are now less likely to be represented in official discourse as socially deprived citizens in need of support. They are depicted instead as culpable, undeserving and somewhat dangerous individuals who must be carefully controlled for the protection of the public and the prevention of further offending. Rather than clients in need of support they are seen as risks who must be managed.

It is true that, ever since Michael Howard became Home Secretary in 1993 (with his famous statement that 'prison works'), government policy has shifted towards a more punitive approach towards offending behaviour. In relation to young offenders, this shift became particularly pronounced after a report by the Audit Commission (1996), followed shortly afterwards by a policy paper from the Home Office (1997). Garland, however, misrepresents this as a shift of focus from the 'welfare' of the offender to the 'control' of the offender. He therefore misses the point that the criminal justice system has always been about the detection and apprehension (and thus control) of offenders, and their welfare has been considered only to the extent required to prevent them from reoffending (so-called 'rehabilitation' or 'resettlement').

The New Labour government had a distinctive approach to community order, which is sometimes said to be encapsulated in the slogan: 'Tough on crime, tough on the causes of crime' (Labour Party Manifesto, 1997). This slogan certainly expresses the overriding emphasis on enforcement ('tough'), and also serves rhetorically to link policing (tackling crime) with policy (tackling the causes of crime). It also goes well beyond crime itself to include all forms of rule breaking (and the causes of rule breaking) in which the government might take an interest. So what occurred here was the announcement of a more authoritarian, joined-up approach. In practice, however, the approach has not always looked particularly joined up because of the way in which policy/policing has been infected by stereotypical assumptions about 'them' (offenders) and 'us' (decent folk), leading to different policies for each of the two groups.

A key aim of New Labour's approach was to strengthen its own version of public self-policing – to promote strong, safe, cohesive communities (see Chapter Four). In a revealing speech to the party faithful, Blair said:

> One day when I am asked by someone whose neighbourhood is plagued with anti-social behaviour; or whose local school is failing; or whose hospital is poor, 'what are you going to do about it?', I want to be able to reply: 'We have given you the resources. We have given you the powers. Now tell me what you are going to do about it.' (Blair, 2005)

This quote not only clearly links policy with policing but also vividly illustrates what New Labour meant by 'government through community' (Rose, 1996). The basic idea was that local communities on the scale of a neighbourhood should be responsible for policing what goes on in those communities, and should be given the necessary powers and resources to discharge that responsibility.[11] This was therefore a clear expression of New Labour's communitarian agenda.

Another interesting point about this quote is that it assumes that the complainant has a genuine grievance – that is, that she or he is a member of that decent, law-abiding, respectable majority whom New Labour aimed to support and whose votes it sought to attract. The policies that New Labour wanted to develop were therefore geared towards the needs of this group, which is precisely the 'public' who were to police themselves as far as possible.

A final point about the quote is that it also reveals quite starkly the neo-colonial character of New Labour's approach. Here, as we saw in Chapter Two, government was to be positioned outside and above communities, providing the framework that is required for the communities to govern themselves. The ultimate purpose was to prepare these communities for independence. This independence was envisaged as a form of public self-policing, but the precise nature of this form was not specified. It probably rested on something like Sayer's (2005) notion of lay morality. Blair simply assumed that people would act respectfully to one another and that public services would respect the public that they served, so if these services did not, then the public needed to be able to ensure that they did. In reality, however, life is not so simple. In particular, Blair's vision glosses over the inequalities that may and do exist between different sections of the community, and between service professionals and service users.

So one strand of New Labour's approach to community order focused on the allegedly law-abiding and 'respectable'. The other concentrated on those who deviate, transgress, or are otherwise seen as in need of care and control. Broadly speaking, the first group were interpellated as 'the policers' ('Us'), who were assumed to be responsible for maintaining community order, while the second group were interpellated as 'the policed' ('Them'), who were typically the target of policing interventions (they were seen as being potentially if not actually 'out of order' and in need of being kept 'in order' or 'restored' to order – so this could refer to, for example, health and social service interventions as well as policing interventions in the more usual narrow sense). Ultimately, New Labour wanted the former to deal with the latter. In the meantime, it wanted communities to cooperate actively with policing agencies in securing community order (see Home Office, 2006, p 15).

The New Labour government employed a vast repertoire of policing interventions, targeted at specific individuals, groups and/or communities or simply at certain kinds of behaviour. As a result of this, it came to be known disparagingly as the 'nanny' state. Interventions included practically all the policies discussed in previous chapters, particularly related to health, education and young people. Taken as a whole, this repertoire can be regarded as a 'civilising offensive' (Flint and Powell, 2009, p 221), a term that neatly incorporates the ambivalence of neo-colonialism (that is, as both aggressive and causing offence) as seen from the viewpoint of those at its receiving end.

There seems to be some uncertainty, however, about what exactly were Labour's aims for those who might be termed 'uncivilised'. The first, and most obvious, option was that the government wanted them (or their groups or communities or areas) to become 'civilised' – that is, to change their behaviour (or their community or environment) so that it would become indistinguishable from that of the so-called decent, law-abiding majority.[12] The second option, which overlaps with but is subtly different from the first, is known as the 'eliminative ideal' (Rutherford, 1997) – Labour sought the elimination of uncivilised or transgressive behaviours (these can include anything from spitting in the street to rough sleeping, prostitution, binge drinking, noisy neighbours, to crime of any kind).[13] This could be achieved either through internal change, as in the first option, or through the exclusion, eviction, banishment, exile or extermination of those responsible for these behaviours and/or the destruction of their communities (for example, through so-called 'regeneration' – see Chapters Two and Eight). To call this second option 'civilising' may sound strange, but historically, according to Elias (1978), civilising has precisely involved the removal from public view of certain practices and people seen as embarrassing or shameful, for example, bodily functions, punishments, people with mental health problems and learning difficulties, and so on. Where the first option was found not to work (in that the 'uncivilised' could not or would not change their behaviour), the second option might become the preferred one.[14]

Moore (2008) provides an interesting illustration of a civilising offensive in relation to a street-life community. First of all, he explains the phenomenon as follows:

> The increase of street-life people may be linked to the decline in large-scale institutions and the development of the alternative model of reform of community care that increasingly led to people with a range of social and mental difficulties becoming more visible in public places. (Moore, 2008, p 186)

He goes on to describe how public meetings in the area where street-life people gathered demanded that action be taken against them (specifically, removing them from the area), but the local policing agencies (public police and council officers) became aware that moving them on from one place to another was not resolving the problem:

It became fairly obvious to the police and officials that they were engaged in a pointless task, because the majority of the street-life people did not actually present a significant crime problem. Furthermore, there was a realisation that it was not unreasonable to see the street-life people as victims themselves – often of sexual abuse when children, of marital disharmony, of mental illness, of drug and alcohol dependency – rather than necessarily as aggressive troublemakers. (Moore, 2008, p 194)

So the public in this area were dutifully following New Labour's second option (attempts to change their behaviour had met with fairly robust rejection from members of the street-life community!) but it did not appear to be working. It was the public, not the police, who were pressing for elimination of the 'problem', as they saw it. Moore therefore concluded that:

New Labour's community-led agenda has prevented the development of more reasoned policies and the police feel constrained to continue a punitive line against the street-life people that they may privately disagree with. The outcome of handing power to the community is that punitive voices are heard and, rather than drawing people into the community as government rhetoric would have it, processes of social exclusion develop. (Moore, 2008, p 195)

Box 9.1: New Labour's 'eliminative ideal' – to discipline the 'respectable'?

New Labour's eliminative ideal related not only to the 'uncivilised' but also to certain 'irresponsible' behaviours of the otherwise 'civilised' (of course it did not want to eliminate the 'civilised', as they were crucial to the success of its project!). One type of behaviour that New Labour wanted to eliminate was occasional excessive drinking and drug taking for recreational purposes – what Measham and Moore (2008, p 277) call 'contemporary cultures of intoxication'. To this end, a number of amendments to recent legislation were made – especially the Drugs Act 2005. The policies involved viewed intense intoxication and determined drunkenness as inherently problematic and gave priority to withdrawal and abstinence for both (Measham and Moore, 2008, p 282).

Measham and Moore contrast this approach with that adopted towards those who might count as the 'uncivilised' – that is, dependent and chaotic drug and alcohol users. Here the emphasis was on *diversion* from the criminal justice system to treatment interventions aimed at the minimisation of harm. Actually, this may not be contradictory, as Labour wanted to see abstinence as the goal for these people as well, but recognised that this was likely to take much longer than in the case of recreational users.

Measham and Moore (2008, p 284) conclude that: 'Legislative changes ... have been essentially political decisions in response to developments in popular culture and perceived social threat rather than evidence-based responses to medical harm or police concerns about crime-related problems relating to these specific drugs, and together they form the crest of a new wave of criminalisation of contemporary cultures of intoxication and an increasingly repressive regime of governance.'

The criticism of New Labour's approach by Moore (2008) is one that appears time and time again – see, for example, similar patterns in relation to the policing of sex workers (Sanders, 2005; Phoenix, 2008; Sanders et al, 2009).[15] By identifying the community with its so-called law-abiding majority, the approach serves to exclude 'deviant' minorities from that community. Consequently, rather than civilising behaviour and solving a problem of community order, New Labour's civilising offensive risked being counter-productive, making the problem worse or even creating a problem where none previously existed. This is perhaps most clearly seen in relation to its Respect Agenda. Here the government started with an approach that was inherently disrespectful because it stated that respect is not freely given but has to be earned (Respect Task Force, 2006, p 30). It follows that those who, for whatever reason, have not managed to 'earn' the respect of others are not entitled to be respected and can be disrespected with impunity (see Somerville, 2009a, for further discussion). Labour therefore failed even to begin to build a foundation for the mutual respect that is required for an orderly community. It is this inherent disrespect that is then reflected in the views of the so-called 'respectable' people in Moore's study. As Somerville (2009a, p 150) states:

> the Respect Agenda actually encourages disrespectful behaviour by people who believe themselves to be respectable. The Respect Agenda is part of a wider culture and politics that encourages people to complain about others, report their transgressions to the authorities, 'take a stand', and so on, rather than attempt to communicate, mediate, negotiate, and so on. In short, it encourages people to adopt the status of a victim rather than a citizen.

Neoliberalism is another aspect to government approaches to community order. Beck (2002), for example, sees global capitalism as radicalising social inequalities and changing the character of the state so that it becomes increasingly disrespectful (as argued above in relation to New Labour's Respect agenda). This inevitably leads to increasing rather than diminishing disorder. Again, this seems rather paradoxical and the mechanisms by which this might occur are unclear. Given Gamble's (1994) argument that a free economy requires a strong state, implying that the greater the extent of liberalisation, the more powerful the state has to be, one would have thought that New Labour's deepening interventionism might be quite appropriate as a way of keeping order in what has become (arguably) a less secure, less stable, less predictable society. Perhaps the problem, then, lies not with strong state interventionism in itself but with New Labour's particular version of it.[16]

Box 9.2: New Labour's neoliberal ideal – 'responsible consumption'

Running parallel with New Labour's repression of intoxication was its support for alcohol consumption 'in moderation'. This support was based on the neoliberal idea of consumer freedom, according to which individuals should be as free as possible to choose what they consume and when and where they consume it. Norris and Williams (2008), however, argue that there is a contradiction in government policy here, that the focus in recent policies on reducing harm and limiting alcohol-related disorder is 'myopic' (p 257), and that neoliberalisation in terms of the relaxation of licensing laws and favourable treatment of the drinks and leisure industry has encouraged excessive alcohol consumption (p 269).

Norris and Williams therefore take a different view from Measham and Moore (2008) (see **Box 9.1**). For them, it appears, intoxication is something to be reduced rather than to be managed in terms of harm reduction and the policing of alcohol-related disorder. Yet this raises questions about whether it is desirable to attempt to reduce intoxication and, if so, for whom (for example, at what age) and how it is to be done.

It may be questioned whether there is any real contradiction in Labour's approach to consumption. The mass of citizens are here interpellated as 'responsible consumers' and the evidence cited by Norris and Williams themselves (for example, Loveday, 2005; Hobbs, 2003) indicates that huge numbers of people do drink responsibly. Hundreds of thousands are out drinking every weekend, many of whom are drinking to get drunk, and yet: 'Given the lack of police and transport, and the number of people who are supposedly drunk, perhaps we should be surprised that there is not even more trouble and that, in the circumstances, the *majority*, although noisy and drunk, are generally well-behaved' (Norris and Williams, 2008, p 263 – my italics). Admittedly, there will be some people who drink irresponsibly and make a nuisance of themselves, but is it right to restrict the liberties of the well-behaved majority because of the bad behaviour of a minority? Also, to what extent is it reasonable or fair to hold the government responsible for reducing the health risks taken by an irresponsible minority? It is the government's role to police in order to prevent harm to others, but is it its role to prevent people from enjoying themselves, just in case this enjoyment might result in harm of one kind or another?

Perhaps, however, Norris and Williams (2008) are wanting to argue only that stricter measures are required to police the drinks and leisure industry to ensure that it (also) behaves responsibly, particularly in promoting cheap alcoholic drinks to young people.

Box 9.3: How governments maintain order: traffic control

Where the law is clear, the government is in a strong position to enforce it. Take, for example, the case of a legal speed limit in an area being set at 30mph and clearly signposted as such. The highway authorities and the police use a variety of methods to secure compliance with the speed limit. One of these could be the installation of speed cameras, another could be police vehicles parked at the side of the road using radar to measure the speed of passing vehicles. One unintended consequence of such a policy is that motorists cooperate more with one another, for example, by flashing their lights at oncoming cars to warn them of the presence of such cameras and vehicles. The consequence of this unintended consequence is that more motorists comply with the speed limit, at least in the vicinity of the cameras/vehicles, thus ensuring the apparent success of the government's speed reduction aim.

This simple example serves to illustrate a number of important points about how governments keep order and how community responses to government efforts serve to create and reinforce an illusion of government efficacy. First, the government establishes a clear rule to be followed by people within its territory. At the same time, it prescribes sanctions or penalties for breaking that rule. Then, to assess compliance with the rule, it introduces policing mechanisms or techniques or technologies (in this case, camera technology or police presence) to monitor the behaviour of the relevant population (in this case, motorists). (Note that people are more likely to comply if they accept the rule as just or legitimate or reasonable, but acceptance is not essential for compliance – and indeed is not sufficient for compliance either.) If the monitoring process then finds that large numbers of people are failing to comply with the rule, the government has what can be called a policing problem. On its own, it can deal with this problem only by increasing the amount of monitoring (more speed cameras, more speed cops) and increasing the penalties for non-compliance. It is at this point that the community (in this case, the community of motorists – activated by the rule itself) appears to come to the government's rescue because, by signalling to one another about the imminent risks of being detected, it ensures a perceived higher level of compliance and therefore makes it seem as if the government's policy is working. The twist in the tail, however, is that speed reduction may occur only in the vicinity of the monitoring technologies while elsewhere non-compliance with the speed limit may be endemic. The upshot of all this is that the government is inclined to believe that we are a law-abiding society when it may well be that we are not.

This example highlights a general problem with governmental authority, namely that it prevents the possibility of mutual and equal respect between government and citizens (Somerville, 2009a, p 151). Instead, what we have is a 'cat and mouse' game where the government pretends to catch rule-breakers, and citizens pretend to comply with the rule.

This example also provides a robust riposte to Anglo-Foucauldian writers such as Garland (1997, p 182) who argue that: 'Power is not a matter of imposing a sovereign will.' The sovereign has limited power to impose its will but nevertheless imposing a sovereign will is precisely what much, if not most, law-making and law-enforcing power is about. Moreover, imposing a sovereign will can be justified in order to prevent harm to others, which is typically the reason for having speed limits.

The decivilisation thesis

Rodger (2008) argues that in recent decades a process of 'decivilisation' has occurred in certain areas. Decivilisation involves three processes: 'a shift in the balance between constraints by others and self-restraint in favour of constraints by others' (I take this to mean an emphasis on others constraining themselves more and restraining oneself less); 'the development of a social standard of behaviour and feeling which generates the emergence of a less even, all-round, stable and differentiated pattern of self-restraint' (I take this to mean a less consistent, less predictable, possibly erratic pattern of behaviour); and 'a contraction in the scope of mutual identification between constituent groups and individuals' (I take this to mean a decline in social solidarities) (Fletcher, 1997, p 83, cited in Rodger, 2008, p 31).

Rodger (2008, p 31) goes on to say:

> The issue today is one of the bifurcation of Western societies into mainstream sectors connected with work, the consumer society and the global network, and their relationship to the marginalised communities within their territories that are left outside and disconnected from the arteries that facilitate economic, cultural and interactive nourishment. As interdependence weakens between core and marginal communities, movement towards de-civilisation is facilitated.

Much of what Rodger has to say about the processes of economic, social and political marginalisation and polarisation that have taken place in advanced capitalist countries since the 1970s is fair comment. It is difficult to argue, for example, with the statement that:

> The seismic shifts in the occupational structure of post-industrial economies since the early 1980s have resulted in the creation of residualised communities without sources of secure employment, reliant on community resources that are externally imposed rather than organically grown from local people's priorities and poor life chances. (Rodger, 2008, p 58)

These residualised communities would indeed appear to be identical with the encapsulated communities discussed in Chapter One of this book. The problem, however, is that he goes too far in labelling these residualised or encapsulated communities as decivilised. Indeed, his thesis is very reminiscent of Charles Murray's (1990) concept of the underclass, which attaches similar significance to the effects of long-term worklessness, family breakdown and decline in moral standards, including a sense of duty to others. It goes too far in at least two respects: first, it tars all people in the same community with the same brush; and, second, it equates residualisation (or encapsulation) with moral degeneration. It ignores all the literature (much of it cited elsewhere in this book, for example, Leonard, 2004, MacDonald et al, 2005, and Kintrea et al, 2008) that suggests a more complex picture of what is happening in residualised communities, such as simultaneous processes of decivilisation and recivilisation, changes in the balance of social capital functions, territorialisation (which is uniquely associated with public violence) and different combinations of intergenerational continuity and change. Perhaps the main problem with the decivilisation thesis is that it is a gross and simplistic generalisation that is based on flimsy and one-sided evidence, such as the interviews with young people by Hall and Winlow (2005) (see also Hall et al, 2008) (as if young people alone could be taken to be representative of a community).

Some of Rodger's thesis smacks of a nostalgia for a form of social solidarity and state control that probably never existed except, perhaps, during the Second World War (and maybe not even then):

> The central problem is that 60 years of state welfare, including 25 years of creeping marketisation in the field of social policy, has inevitably destroyed the sense of mutualism and social solidarity that existed prior to the establishment of the welfare state project in the period after 1945. (Rodger, 2008, p 160)

Indeed, Rodger seems very keen on having a strong state:

> The most fundamental premise of Elias' theory, and the theoretical thesis he builds around the civilising process, is that a strong monopoly state power which exercises its authority on a national scale must be maintained to ensure order and maximise solidarity and social interdependence across all social divisions. (Rodger, 2008, p 169)

This Hobbesian view of the basis of social order can of course be criticised on a number of grounds but, first and foremost, what it lacks is a clear concept of the nature and foundation of state power itself. This returns us to the earlier discussion of the state as the source of both policy and policing. As such, the state can function as an overriding authority within a territory, it can work with and on forms of public self-policing, it can even increase social solidarity (for example, through forms of redistribution), but it is also perfectly capable of destroying both public self-policing and social solidarity. So the fundamental question is not so much how strong (or weak) we want the state to be, but what exactly we want the state to do and how we ensure that it does that.

Community safety and anti-social behaviour

'Community safety' is a term signifying a certain governmental approach to community order. It is based loosely on partnership among policing agencies at a local level. Its origins lie in 'crime prevention' (see Hughes, 1998; Hughes et al, 2002; Squires, 2006) but in recent years the community safety agenda has become dominated by issues of anti-social behaviour. The term 'anti-social behaviour' is another governmental term, defined as 'behaviour which causes or is likely to cause harassment, alarm or distress to one or more people who are not in the same household as the perpetrator' (Home Office, 2003, p 5). In other words, anti-social behaviour is whatever is perceived as such by members of the community. This appears to include anything that might be found offensive by the 'decent, law-abiding, respectable' majority discussed above. In essence, therefore, it refers to any behaviour that is deemed to be 'out of order' by this majority.

The term 'anti-social behaviour' itself originates from the policing of housing estates, and arises in particular from the common-law requirement in tenancy agreements that tenants should not cause nuisance or annoyance to their neighbours. As a housing officer from 1975 to 1984, I well remember investigating numerous complaints of such 'neighbour nuisance', as it was commonly called in those days. Such experience taught me many things: that there are two sides to every story; that most complaints are resolvable through communication and negotiation; that in only very exceptional cases is it worthwhile even to attempt to apportion blame; and that complaints vary considerably, but it is possible to fit most of them into certain categories, for example, noise, swearing, litter, children's misbehaviour, obstructive car parking, harassment and intimidation, and disputes over boundaries and shared spaces and facilities. At that time, however, few housing organisations gave any priority to the investigation of tenant complaints – it was considered much more important to collect rents, to recover arrears, to respond to requests for repairs, to get properties let when they came empty, to ensure that tenants looked after their homes and gardens, and generally to see that the communal areas of the estates were kept reasonably tidy and in good order. Consequently, in most housing organisations, neighbour disputes were hardly investigated at all. Even in the organisations that I worked for, in the few cases where a particularly problematic family caused serious upset for their neighbours (for example, burning their house down – perhaps unintentionally), I do not recall any enforcement action being taken.

This somewhat laissez-faire attitude began to change in the 1980s. One reason for the change, very rarely mentioned now, was that housing authorities began to treat the problem of racial harassment with increasing seriousness. Rather than simply rehousing the victims of racist neighbours, as they had done until then, they started to take enforcement action against the perpetrators (this action was pioneered by authorities such as Tower Hamlets, Newham and Leeds). Although this led initially to a sharp increase in racist incidents (at one time, one in four black and minority ethnic people in Newham reported being racially harassed in the previous year), the resolve of the authorities remained strong and, after the eviction of a number of racist tenants, order began to be restored (or rather a new order of racially mixed communities began to be accepted). The success of the new enforcement approach attracted the attention of other housing organisations, and so the Social Landlords Crime and Nuisance Group was born. This group has acted primarily as a campaigning organisation to persuade the government to take the issue of anti-social behaviour more seriously.

A second reason, quite different from the first, for the shift towards a more enforcement-focused approach, was the increasing (Thatcherite) emphasis in the 1980s on so-called 'customer service'. This was interpreted by housing organisations as meaning that they should be more responsive to the demands and wishes of their tenants in particular. Giving more priority to dealing with tenants' complaints, including complaints about their neighbours, therefore seemed a logical development. Since the 1980s the emphasis given by government to tenant involvement has continued to increase, as we saw in Chapter Eight, as part of its more general development of 'active consumer-citizens'.

Running parallel with these policy developments relating to housing estates in the 1980s, there was a growing concern about the safety of town and city centres left desolate by the deindustrialisation of the 1970s. The main community safety response to this was quite different to that for housing estates. It involved, quite simply, the installation of vast numbers of CCTV cameras in the 1990s, based on virtually no reliable evidence of effectiveness (Goold, 2004). The situation here is well summarised by Squires (2006, p 3):

> The Local Government Management Board survey of local authority community safety initiatives in 1996 found that the most common community safety investment involved CCTV projects (LGMB, 1996). Virtually all such CCTV schemes were in town centres, where a commercial interest in 'safer shopping' (an orderly and crime-free retail and business environment) appeared a more obvious objective than community safety itself. Subsequent research has pointed to the fact that, for almost 10 years, public CCTV camera schemes accounted for approximately 75% of the entire Home Office crime prevention budget.

So, even before New Labour came to power, the main government priorities for community safety were: first, to make cities safe for shopping; and second, to get more local authorities to enforce good behaviour by their tenants and residents generally. These remain, by and large, the priorities for government today.[17] If, as the Audit Commission (2006b), Rodger (2008) and many others have noted, the incidence of anti-social behaviour continues to be high, then tackling it is likely to remain a government priority.[18]

The distinctive contribution of New Labour in relation to anti-social behaviour was perhaps its emphasis on the role of community, as is evident from the definition of anti-social behaviour itself as whatever the community finds unacceptable or intolerable. We saw this earlier in the discussion of Moore's (2008) study of street-life people. This study also highlighted how it was the community of the 'respectable', not that of the street-life people, that New Labour had in mind as bearing the power and responsibility for maintaining community order. This assumption ran right through the Respect Agenda: the 'respectable' do not have to earn respect, they are entitled to respect, they are the 'active citizens' that New Labour wanted to cultivate as its natural constituency, they are the ordinary, hard-working people that Gordon Brown was always talking about. This construction of a 'respectable community', however, is purely rhetorical, and does not correspond to any living reality – or, if it does, it seems to evoke the narrow-minded, intolerant, uncaring outlook of the 'community' in Moore's study. New Labour's approach to anti-social behaviour, and to community safety generally, essentially involved the subordination of the needs of the individual to the needs of this 'respectable community' – an approach that is very far removed from the ideal of the beloved community.

When it comes to New Labour's policies on anti-social behaviour, much media and academic attention has focused on the Anti-Social Behaviour Order (ASBO), which was introduced in the Crime and Disorder Act 1998. Other policies, however, have been just as, if not more, important. Most notable have been the changes in policing powers and practices, such as the growth of what is known as 'plural policing', involving new types of uniformed policing agents, such as police community support officers, neighbourhood wardens and private security officers (Crawford et al, 2005), and the shift towards reassurance policing and neighbourhood policing (Tuffin et al, 2006). As stated in the earlier quote from Blair, the general emphasis has been on getting individuals, organisations and communities to assume responsibility for managing their own crime risks, with policing organisations being increasingly expected to support that management by being responsive and contractually accountable to those individuals, organisations and communities (Crawford, 1997; Loader, 2000, p 331; Spalek, 2008, p 94). To this end, increasing powers of policing have been made available to local communities – for example, under the Anti-Social Behaviour Act 2003 (for example, fixed penalty notices, penalty notices for disorder and so on). At the same time, New Labour has introduced new mechanisms of discipline and regulation to help the police and local authorities to ensure order, of which the ASBO is just one, others being parenting orders, housing injunctions, individual support orders, drug testing and treatment orders, demoted tenancies, closure orders, control orders, sex offender orders, dog control orders and dispersal orders.[19] As mentioned before, partnerships among policing agencies were also a crucial piece in New Labour's jigsaw for community safety. There has also occurred what might be called 'pseudo-contractualisation', where a hierarchy of 'contracts' between policing agencies and individuals has developed (such as Acceptable Behaviour Contracts, pioneered by the London Borough of Islington, and Acceptable Behaviour Agreements), designed progressively to 'grip' anti-social individuals at an early stage and to prevent them from deviating from the straight and narrow path that leads to 'respectability' – or to restore them to that path if they do deviate from it.

A number of writers have pointed to the importance of social capital (see Chapter Two) or collective efficacy (Sampson et al, 1997) or local social structure (Bursik and Grasmick, 1993) as being the most important factor affecting the level of anti-social behaviour. The argument relating to these ideas tends to be circular, in that it is claimed that x, for example, causes a reduction in anti-social behaviour, but when one asks what it is about x that has this effect, the answer tends to be in terms of something that is part of the effect itself. Part of the meaning of collective efficacy, for example, is precisely that it produces a reduction in crime and anti-social behaviour. If we question more closely what is meant by collective efficacy, its interpretation is likely to be qualified so that it refers to the capacity to act of the pro-social majority (acting against the anti-social minority). This then leads to the banal conclusion that, in order to reduce anti-social behaviour, it is necessary to boost the capacities (or local social structure or social capital) of those who want to reduce anti-social behaviour. In contrast, the discussion of public self-policing earlier in this chapter claimed only that it *can* maintain community order, not that it necessarily does so, and identified a number of conditions in which it can fail and others in which it can actually be harmful.

Although these concepts (social capital and so on) do not explain anti-social behaviour, the argument remains that there may be certain factors commonly associated with that behaviour. The most obvious such factor is the attitude of the government and of 'respectable' people to anti-social behaviour itself. Here I want to argue that, as in the case of the research by Moore (2008), it is the unholy alliance between so-called 'respectable' people and government that is itself partly responsible for provoking anti-social behaviour, because of the disrespect these allies have shown and continue to show to their fellow citizens and because of the misguided and counter-productive policies they have imposed upon them.

First of all, one could admit that building the social capital of poorer communities while at the same time reducing the harm caused to those communities is a reasonable and worthwhile aim for government (as argued in Chapter Two), and was indeed explicitly set out in Labour's strategy for civil renewal (Blunkett, 2003). In practice, however, community safety and civil renewal policies often adopt solutions 'that at best undermine social capital and at worst actually weaken social capital and trust' (Rodger, 2008, p 166). A good example of this comes from Prior (2005), where the government's policy was actually to arouse suspicion among neighbours (for example, by encouraging the reporting of anti-social behaviour) rather than trust. We are back to the usual problem with New Labour's approach, namely that people are crudely constructed as either trustworthy or not – a construction that clearly divides people rather than bringing them together. The inevitable effect of such a policy is to reduce trust and therefore reduce social capital, running counter to the government's express aim.

Another, and related, example is that of the profligate use of CCTV – which has been, as we have seen, the main instrument of Labour's community safety policy. Rodger (2008, p 186) describes how the deployment of such technology involves the substitution of what he calls a 'thin trust' in 'abstract systems' for the 'thick trust' that exists between people, leading to a decline of trust in strangers, the exaggeration of 'stranger danger', a corresponding increase in fear and territoriality, and consequently an escalating spiral of 'respectable fears' (Pearson, 1983) about crime and disorder:

> The clamour by politicians, the media, and the local community itself for evidence of 'something being done' about incivility ironically tends to weaken generalised trust by campaigning for the abstract systems of surveillance that contribute little to embedding security in relationships between people. This typically alerts the media to the presence of a social malaise. It is the weakening of generalised reciprocity, or *reciprocal trust*, in marginal communities that has been associated with the problem of anti-social behaviour and which the civil renewal strategy was designed to address. A prominent feature of this development is ... the decline in the trust of strangers. The openness to people who are not local and who might establish a connection between one neighbourhood and another has been replaced by fear and territoriality as a filtering mechanism to identify who is and is not a threat. This has also had consequences for trust

in neighbours and those who live in the same community. In a social environment of mistrust, no one can be relied upon. (Rodger, 2008, p 186)

This argument implies that the installation of CCTV has an effect that is equivalent to the infamous 'broken windows' syndrome (Wilson and Kelling, 1982) – it is interpreted as a signal of disorder rather than, as presumably intended, a signal of order. Labour's flagship community safety policy is therefore shown to be almost entirely wasteful and counter-productive. Rather than supporting public self-policing, it tends to undermine and damage it. And where the public self-policing is itself based on fear, intimidation and lack of mutual and equal respect, there is little evidence that CCTV makes any significant difference to the situation.

In relation to ASBOs, there are problems with the order itself, as well as with how it has been implemented. Critics of the order are right to point out that it involves an unacceptable abandonment of legal clarity and due process, resulting inevitably in unequal treatment and injustice. Stephen (2008, p 325), for example, claims that: 'the encouragement of subjective notions of acceptable conduct, the admission of hearsay evidence and the absence of due process within the safeguards of criminal law further encourage climates of suspicion and exclusion, especially in already strained neighbourhoods'. Given that breaches of an ASBO can result in prison sentences of up to five years, this is a particularly damning criticism. Thus, although it appears that some policing organisations are strongly in favour of ASBOs in practice, on the grounds that they achieve positive behavioural change in certain cases (see, for example, Matthews et al, 2007; see also National Audit Office, 2006b), the more significant effect of ASBOs as a policy may be a corrosion of principles of natural justice, resulting in declining trust in the impartiality of the criminal justice system as a whole, with corresponding untold damage being done to social and community order.

Critics have also noted that ASBOs have been disproportionately imposed on young people, contrary to what the government originally envisaged. Defenders of ASBOs, however, have pointed out that more widely used sanctions against anti-social behaviour, such as housing-based anti-social behaviour injunctions, have been imposed entirely on adults (see Somerville et al, 2006, pp 245–6), so it is not the case that ASBOs involve the demonisation of young people in particular – or, perhaps, they do not involve the demonisation *only* of young people (as alleged, for example, by Card, 2006, and by Carr and Cowan, 2006). Rather, Labour intended anti-social behaviour sanctions to be used more promiscuously, to hit a wide variety of targets – 'whatever works'! For Labour, it was the disreputable 'other' that was to be demonised, irrespective of their age or gender or race or whatever. Here again, however, it is the arbitrariness of the process that is its own undoing, as can be seen, for example, from the large number of people with mental health problems and learning difficulties who have received ASBOs (see, for example, Nixon et al, 2007).

Evidence from those who have been the subject of ASBOs reveals a fairly consistent picture. Rather than seeing them as a 'badge of honour', as is so often alleged (Squires, 2008, p 24), those receiving ASBOs have tended to view them as a significant burden, restricting their movements and making it difficult, if not impossible, for them to maintain their usual social contacts (family and friends) and perform their normal everyday activities (Solanki et al, 2006; Goldsmith, 2006, 2008; McIntosh, 2008), thus depriving them of what Burney (2008, p 146) calls the 'normal routes to socialisation', including access to employment or education opportunities. As a consequence, and also because of their lack of understanding of what the ASBO involved, they almost all breached their ASBOs (Wain, 2007; Goldsmith, 2008). In general, young people subjected to ASBOs viewed them negatively (McIntosh, 2008), reported a range of harmful effects on their families (Wain, 2007) and felt angry about what they saw as the injustice of having ASBOs served upon them (Goldsmith, 2008, p 229). They also resented the routine surveillance by CCTV and stopping by the police that they commonly experienced in the areas where they lived, on which Goldsmith (2008, p 234) concluded: 'this policing and practice, by damaging relationships with young people who would grow up to be adults on the estate, appeared deeply flawed' (see Karn, 2006, for similar findings with regard to young people's experience of the policing of dispersal orders). Rather than helping young people to grow up, such practices merely reinforced their vulnerability, leading to some of them taking to drink or drugs (Solanki et al, 2006; Burney, 2008). Once again, therefore, this serves to demonstrate the counter-productive character of government policy on this issue: rather than encouraging young people to put their trust in policing agencies and work with them towards improving community safety, the effect of these policies is exactly the opposite, namely to promote in young people feelings of distrust of the authorities and to increase the likelihood of challenge and resistance to those authorities.

No discussion of ASBOs can be complete without mention of the fact that more than two-thirds of ASBOs are now imposed after a criminal conviction (known as CrASBOs) (see discussion in Burney, 2008). These were introduced under the Police Reform Act 2002, as an add-on to the sentence passed by the court. Such orders can be seen to be particularly unjust, precisely because they impose additional restrictions on the offender, over and above the punishment that is supposed to fit the crime.

A continuing influential strand in the explanation of anti-social behaviour is the one that focuses on so-called 'risk factors' such as poor parenting, poor schooling, peer-group pressure and the social environment generally (Graham and Bowling, 1995; Farrington, 2002). Sampson and Groves (1989, p 799), for example, state: 'Our empirical analysis established that communities characterised by sparse friendship networks, unsupervised teenage peer groups, and low organisational participation had disproportionately high rates of crime and delinquency.' All this tells us, however, is that growing up is more risky in some environments (for example, encapsulated or residualised or marginalised communities – whatever you like to call them) than in others. It tells us nothing about how any particular individual is likely to behave in any given environment. Its only advantage, therefore, is to point to the need to improve the environments that give rise to this individual vulnerability – in other words, the need for effective social policy (on the family, schools and community development generally). Not only does this tell us nothing that we did not know already but it also suggests, in an insidious way, that the policy focus should be on the vulnerable individual and their parents/carers (to steer them away from a future life of crime) rather than on the social institutions that are causing the individual and their carers to be vulnerable in the first place – truly, a criminalisation of social policy.[20]

This Orwellian distortion of focus was the key flaw in much of Labour's policy on anti-social behaviour. In addition to ASBOs, it infected its whole approach to parenting, as revealed in parenting orders and in family intervention projects (FIPs). It is actually well known that only the 'authoritative parenting'[21] style really works in ensuring 'balanced', well-behaved children (see Rodger, 2008, pp 105–6; Roberts et al, 2009), yet Labour's approach clearly risked undermining that authoritativeness by superimposing governmental authority upon parents. Rodger (2008, pp 118–22) provides a useful review of family intervention projects, which aim to 'grip' particularly problematic anti-social families (Parr and Nixon, 2008, p 165) and transform them into active, self-governing, responsibilised citizens (Nixon, 2007, p 548). This is to be achieved through a range of support measures backed up by sanctions such as loss of their tenancies.

It is not clear what skills or authority the 'professionals' in FIPs have that qualify them to work with these families, but it is interesting that they do not see themselves as 'gripped' by government to undertake this role. Rather, they see themselves as 'plugging a gap' in the services that currently exist (Parr and Nixon, 2008, p 170), apparently oblivious to the fact that, if they had not been 'gripped', the gap would surely have continued. In effect, they are civil servants subordinated to a governmental project, and they would appear to lack the authority or discretion of, for example, the police. They are not merely plugging a gap in services, however; they are exercising authority, which comes from government and which overrides the parents' authority over their children. As Nixon (2007, p 547) states, FIPs 'can clearly be located as part of the development of [governmental] technologies to control conduct'. In these circumstances, the 'positive assessments' (Rodger, 2008, p 121) given by parents in FIPs have to be treated with a certain degree of scepticism, as it is in parents' interests to make such assessments, if only for the sake of their children (this point is made by Garrett, 2007, p 562, in his response to Nixon, 2007). Nixon (2007) argues that pastoral rather than penal power is at work here, but the element of coercion in FIPs is surely an indication of penal power, whether the family is being placed in a 'core unit' or is the target of 'outreach work'. One wonders, for example, what the process was that led to these parents being targeted for FIPs – what discussions were held with them, did they understand what was involved, did they take part willingly? The balance in FIPs between pastoral and penal power, between care and control, or between welfare and punishment, remains unclear, as does the extent to which they really succeed in meeting their aims.[22]

As Holt (2008) points out, similar arguments apply to the use of parenting orders. The basic approach is coercive, but there is also room for the exercise of pastoral power 'in creating a space for new subjectivities to emerge', as a result of which some parents 'may discover new ways of "being" through the space provided by parenting programmes' (Holt, 2008, p 214 – see examples on pp 214–16).

Conclusion

Community order, therefore, can be seen as a form of social integration within habitus, which exists in tension with the 'order of positions' characteristic of governmental or system order. In simple terms, community order can be identified with the patterns established by everyday processes of 'going on', and these processes are challenged by the institutional context within which they take place. In this chapter, we have seen how forms of public self-policing, as expressions of these processes, can interact with forms of policing practices in different contexts to produce different kinds of social order. Community policing can then be understood as the maintenance of community order through an integration of policing practices with public self-policing.

The chapter has distinguished between ideal and real forms of community policing, related to the concept of the beloved community and what forms of policing practice are required to support a beloved community. It has argued that the existence and maintenance of community order necessitates that everyone respects everyone else equally. It has acknowledged that current public self-policing and policing practices all leave very much to be desired in this respect. Nevertheless it has argued that there is hope for public self-policing, for example, as seen in the public response in the event of disasters. What is needed to achieve more effective and long-lasting community order is a clearer analysis and evaluation of the social harms that currently prevent such order. These harms involve mainly forms of institutionalised disrespect related to social inequalities of class, race, gender, age, sexuality, disability and so on.

It is particularly important to understand the governmentality of community order if we are to develop community policing that moves more towards the beloved community ideal. This chapter has argued that there are characteristic governmental approaches to this issue. Broadly speaking, as Foucault recognised, these can be identified with two kinds of governmentality. The first is that of a *sovereign* state, which requires or seeks or demands compliance, irrespective of acceptance or consent, while the second is that of a *disciplinary* state, which requires acceptance or consent in order to achieve its aims. The sovereign state was clearly illustrated in **Box 9.3**, where compliance is achieved through technologies that monitor the behaviour of the governed population and trigger enforcement action in the event of non-compliance. The disciplinary state, in contrast, works to establish and maintain legitimacy in the eyes of its citizens, and it does this through a system of keeping order that is seen to be fair and just by the vast majority of those citizens. In the disciplinary state, citizens are constructed, first and foremost, as 'responsible' (as illustrated in **Box 9.2**).

There are problems with both of these kinds of governmentality. The oppressiveness of the sovereign state, for example, results in a strictly partial compliance, with widespread non-compliance going undetected by the monitoring technologies. The disciplinary state, on the other hand, runs the risk of sharpening divisions between those who are recognised as 'responsible' and those who are thought to be 'irresponsible'. Wherever there exists a favoured majority, whether this majority be understood in terms of class, race, sexuality or any other form of social, cultural or moral distinction, then there will also exist an abject minority. In attempting to make the system fairer (so as to make its rule more legitimate), the disciplinary state may improve the treatment of these minorities, but at the cost of reinforcing their subordinate position within the state itself. At the same time, the disciplinary state will tend to reward those whom it judges to be acting 'responsibly', and (like the sovereign state) punish those whom it judges to be acting 'irresponsibly'.

As for New Labour's approach to community order in particular, this chapter has interpreted it as involving a strengthened emphasis on governmentality of both kinds. Arguably, this is the significance of the famous expression 'tough on crime, tough on the causes of crime', with 'tough on crime' meaning a stronger sovereign state, and 'tough on the causes of crime' a stronger disciplinary state. In combination with New Labour's neo-colonial communitarianism, this results in a stronger demarcation between the 'respectable' majority (the 'community' whom New Labour wants to act as policers) and the 'out of order' or 'anti-social' minority, who are the target of policing interventions. New Labour acted primarily as a disciplinary state in relation to the majority, for example, persuading, promoting, cajoling, encouraging, supporting, stimulating, challenging them to take on a range of policing roles (under the broad umbrella of 'active citizenship'), and primarily as a sovereign state in relation to the minority, for example, through numerous coercive 'Orders'. Ultimately, New Labour wanted to eliminate any behaviour that the 'respectable' majority regarded as 'offensive', irrespective of the amount of actual harm that it might be causing anyone. The harm that New Labour might itself be causing as a result of such action was not even considered. This chapter has provided several examples to illustrate these arguments – on ASBOs, the use of CCTV and family intervention projects. In each case, coercive interventions were targeted at generally less powerful and more vulnerable individuals to get them to change their behaviour, with little evident understanding of the nature of the behaviour itself, let alone the causes of it. The *context* in which the behaviour occurred, which is crucial for interpreting and dealing with it, was typically ignored.

Notes

[1] Neocleous (2000), for example, following Marx, identifies and describes a feudal order, which is a divinely ordained or natural universal order, and a bourgeois order, which is a self-regulating man-made order fabricated from below, founded on property rights and wage-labour.

[2] Lockwood (1958) made a useful distinction between two ways in which a society can be held together: social integration and system integration. Social integration has to do with the relationships among persons, while system integration is about the relationships between institutions. Using this terminology, it can be said that community order is about social integration within habitus.

[3] This happens also in the case of community economic development, community learning, community health, housing and so on, as discussed in previous chapters, but the problem is confronted head on only in this chapter.

[4] Millie (2009) suggests that what is in or out of order (or place) is also a matter of aesthetic judgement (p 205), and in modern society this judgement is based primarily on its economic value (p 206).

[5] Some might say that this lay attitude continues, in that one in four African-Americans gets sent to prison and their unpaid prison labour produces a significant quantity of US manufactured goods; while little public concern, in either the UK or the US, has been expressed about the loss of life resulting from the invasions of Afghanistan and Iraq.

[6] Bauman (2001, p 4) says: 'Missing community means missing security; gaining community, if it happens, would soon mean missing freedom. Security and freedom are two equally precious and coveted values which could be better or worse balanced, but hardly ever fully reconciled or without friction.' This conceptualisation views freedom and security (or order) as to some extent contradictory, but in the beloved community they are two sides of the same coin – there can be no freedom for all without order and there can be no order without freedom for all.

[7] Incidentally, this finding shows that lawlessness and instability are not necessarily incompatible with public self-policing. Rather, it is 'law enforcement' itself that can, paradoxically, undermine social order. Neocleous (2000) has much that is useful to say about how the wide discretion typically allowed to so-called 'law enforcers' is precisely a power that is *outside* the law: 'the constable is an officer of order rather than an officer of the law' (Neocleous, 2000, p 113).

[8] This process of 'othering', with its associated disposition towards clear binary oppositions, is unfortunately all too common in human societies – see Levi-Strauss (1963). For recent critiques of this kind of thinking, see Young (1999, 2007).

[9] One thinks, for example, of the expression: 'There but for the grace of God go I.'

[10] 'Research from many countries suggests a reputation for violence to be a necessary component of successful participation in street culture' (Squires, 2009, p 255). See also Kintrea et al's (2008) comments on territoriality reported in Chapter One.

[11] This basic idea was elaborated in detail in Blears (2003).

[12] As Rodger (2008, p xvi) states: 'the trend has been to seek solutions to social disorder by developing policies aimed at "civilising" the "kinds of people" who behave in an uncivil way'.

[13] The policing approach that corresponds most closely to this ideal is that of 'zero tolerance', where all transgressive behaviours, no matter how trivial, are not to be tolerated, on the grounds that, if condoned, they would make more serious transgressions more likely – the so-called 'broken windows' syndrome.

[14] A third possible option for government is to attempt to anticipate the *risks* presented by 'uncivilised' behaviour and to *manage* that behaviour in such a way as to protect the 'civilised'. In principle, this was not favoured by New Labour because it appears to give up on the possibility of behaviour transformation while retaining (partial) responsibility for the consequences of the uncivilised behaviour. How far the *community* can take responsibility for such risk management remains an open question – consider the debate about 'Sarah's Law'.

[15] New Labour's Coordinated Prostitution Strategy was explicitly eliminative. Prostitution was seen as a public nuisance and as associated with male criminality. Sex workers were seen as victims, requiring coercive counselling and support to exit their profession.

[16] We may never know if this is true now, because the Conservatives are not great believers in state intervention.

[17] LGMB (1996) also revealed the existence of local community safety activity in relation to young people, substance misuse and fear of crime. These were not necessarily priorities for government at the time.

[18] Interestingly, however, the British Crime Survey has recently reported that concern about high levels of anti-social behaviour has reached an all-time recorded low, at 15% (Home Office, 2010).

[19] Note that an order (by a court) is precisely intended to create order.

[20] Rodger (2008, pp 101–2) provides a summary of the 'received wisdom' on this vexed topic. This amounts to: (1) the younger that children start transgressing, the more likely it is that they will commit crime as adults; (2) those who transgress as children follow a different path through life from those who do not, that is, they are more likely to transgress as adults; and (3) the factor most strongly associated with transgression is family environment, in particular parental supervision, disciplinary practices and child–parent attachment – that is, lack of caring, authoritative parenting. *Quelle surprise!*

[21] An 'authoritative parent' is one who scores high both on responsiveness to the child and on demandingness from the child.

[22] Comparisons can be made with Sure Start (see Chapter Six) – how can such projects be sustained in the community? For further trenchant criticism of FIPs, see Gregg (2010).

Summary

This chapter has focused largely on governmental approaches to community order. The dualism associated with New Labour ('tough on crime, tough on the causes of crime') seems likely to be continued under the current coalition government, with an increased emphasis on the 'law abiding' governing themselves (the 'Big Society') and the prospect of more initiatives in relation to those judged to be 'deviant'. It will be interesting to see how the new government addresses the uncertainty bequeathed by its predecessor about how best to deal with the 'deviant' – that is, how much effort to put into 'civilising' them before deciding to 'eliminate' them or remove them from public view. The impression so far is that the effort will be rather less than under New Labour, perhaps resulting in a movement even further away from the ideal of a beloved community.

Governments have not yet sufficiently understood that 'conditional inclusion', whereby people are respected by government only on condition that they first act in a certain way, inevitably results in the *exclusion* of those who fail (for whatever reason) to act in that way. A more respectful approach is one where people are always given the benefit of any doubt and trusted to act with due care and consideration for others until such time as evidence is produced that shows otherwise. Even then, action is to be taken on a case-by-case basis that takes full account of the circumstances of the individual transgression, not on the basis of stereotypical and simplistic judgements of the transgressor.

Moving from government to state, the chapter goes on to draw a distinction between the sovereign state and the disciplinary state. Whereas the sovereign state is about securing compliance, the disciplinary state is broadly about consensual *'citizen-shaping'*, that is, deploying different techniques in different fields in an effort to induce or encourage or persuade citizens to act in what are deemed to be 'appropriate' ways. Under New Labour, the sovereign state has emerged more strongly, through the introduction of numerous coercive 'Orders'. It remains to be seen how far this more coercive approach will be continued by the coalition government.

Questions for discussion

- What are the necessary conditions for a beloved community to exist?

- How can these conditions be satisfied?

- What is community policing? Can it be achieved?

- Is there anything wrong with talking about 'decent, law-abiding, respectable folk'?

- How can we 'civilise' the state? In other words, how can we get the state to respect us and treat us equally and fairly? How can we get it to accept and work towards the ideal of a beloved community?

- Does a beloved community really need a state at all?

Further reading

Rodger, J.J. (2008) *Criminalising social policy: Anti-social behaviour and welfare in a de-civilised society*, Cullompton: Willan Publishing.

Somerville, P. (2009) 'Understanding community policing', *Policing: An International Journal of Police Strategies and Management,* vol 32, no 2, pp 261-77.

Conclusion

The coverage of this book has been very wide, and yet it seems to have hardly begun to address the issues surrounding the idea of community. For example, on the concept of community as meaningful interconnectedness, there is a need to look more closely at its *imagined* nature. It might be thought that an imagined community can be reduced to attachments (such as to a place or social group or way of life or some other characteristic shared with other people). Yet the concept of attachment is itself ambiguous. It is possible to distinguish between feeling attached and being attached, between attachment as a mental process and attachment as a state of existence. A feeling of attachment could be a *desire*, for example to possess or be close to an object or person, and it could also mean having a sense of *obligation* to oneself or to others, to an organisation or institution or community or country or humankind or the planet or whatever. The attachments we share with others that give rise to an imagined community, however, are not reducible to either desires or obligations. This is because these attachments are part of the conditions of our lived experience: what we may desire or what obliges us lies beyond the desires and obligations themselves. In this sense, community transcends our everyday understanding and can be described as having a spiritual quality – hence the use of the term '*community spirit*'. Community is not to do with desire, as some have suggested (for example, Brent, 2004), but with a sense of who *we* are, a shared recognition of what we have in common. So the kind of attachment that is characteristic of community is not to do with being 'tied down' in some way but, on the contrary, is the condition for our liberation, through others.

Much of the literature on spirituality focuses on distinguishing attachment from desire, and from the 'ego' generally (see, for example, Tolle, 1999, 2005). What is most strongly criticised is the tendency to indulge our desires and to 'cling' to objects, persons, places and so on, of whatever kind. This criticism echoes the criticism of 'belonging' made earlier in this book. The point of this literature, however, is to show that one can be 'attached' in some sense to things or people or places without any sense of desire or craving for them. 'Letting go' all these things, therefore, in the sense of giving up one's desire for them, does not necessarily mean that one becomes 'detached' from them. The *imagined* community, to which one may be attached, is not an *imaginary* community, which would be detached from reality. As an imagined community, therefore, the beloved community is not really a desired end state (that is, an object of desire) but is rather a guide to action. Community development is then not about transforming the world according to one's desires, not least because such transformation will never happen, given the limitations of one's capacities for action in comparison with the ways of the world itself.[1] Rather, it is about changing the world (which includes ourselves) according to clear principles of freedom, equality and justice.

At the risk of losing my readers altogether, I would say that these arguments are well supported in Buddhist literature (see, for example, Stryk, 1968). In the context of a discussion of community, the Four Noble Truths, which lie at the heart of Buddhist teachings, can be interpreted as follows:

(1) *Dukha*. Often translated as 'sorrow', this really means an absence of community, a loss of meaningful interconnectedness.
(2) *Samudaya*. The cause of dukha is identified as the existence of desire or craving.
(3) *Nirodha (or nirvana)*. This is the cessation of desire, which is interpreted here as the beloved community.
(4) *Magga*. This is the Eightfold Path, to realise the beloved community.

So what we can learn from Buddhism is, first, that the main problem in the world today is a lack of community, in the sense of a lack of spiritual interconnectedness, a lack of recognition of our common humanity, of our shared and equal involvement in the world; second, that the cause of this problem is our own desires, our craving for consumer goods, for recognition from others, for social status, for fame and fortune, for glory, for meaning, for oblivion even; third, that the problem is to be solved by 'letting go', in the sense of allowing the development of individuals through free cooperation with others on the basis not of desire but of mutual and equal respect; and the fourth Noble Truth, the Eightfold Path, can probably be summed up as: recognise what is right and act accordingly. Similar sentiments can be found in other world religions, but perhaps less systematically expressed, and overlain by (arguably unnecessary) theistic interpretations.[2]

Each chapter in this book is, in its own small way, a contribution to this attempt to make sense of the world as (potential) community. Individuals are seen as flourishing only through community, by recognising others as of equal value to themselves, thus knowing their own value. This mutual valuing negates desire and replaces it with respectful thought and action. Each chapter then contains a critique of current forms of disrespectful thought and action (in Buddhist terms, recognising what is right) and points to how these might be reformed or transformed (in Buddhist terms, suggesting what might count as right action).

Unsurprisingly, the path to enlightenment is not at all straightforward. Each aspect of community examined in this book has involved simultaneous interacting and overlapping processes of enabling and disabling of the beloved community. The processes themselves are typically difficult to distinguish, and the relationship between them is complex and difficult to analyse, and varies considerably from one context to another. Chapter Two, for example, concluded that community development could be explained in terms of specific combinations of economic, social, cultural and symbolic capital, perhaps supplemented by specific interventions by government and outside activists. But we must now question how useful such an explanation is: if the combinations of explanatory factors vary according to the context of the development, how can we know which combination fits any given context? And even if we could know the answer to this question, what could it tell us about how to achieve the beloved community?

Fortunately, all is not lost because we know, from Chapter Two, that even very small changes, for example on funding, can bring about a big boost in 'community spirit'. True, for the long-term sustainability of such change, more radical, transformative action is required, particularly on the part of government, and Chapter Three suggests that citizens will have to be well organised, and on a very different basis from that which currently exists, in order for such transformation to take place. This might seem unrealistic, even utopian, but actually it is no more unrealistic than that which is currently being expected by government from its citizens. Here I am referring in particular to the government's expectations in relation to citizen or community participation (see Chapters Three and Four).

From the standpoint of the beloved community, humans are autonomous beings who should be free to develop in their own way. Participation in community life is integral to their development but they should, so far as possible, be free to choose how they participate in that community life and what else they might take part in.[3] So, not only is it unreasonable and unrealistic to expect everyone to participate directly in governmental projects that might affect their lives, but also such an expectation appears to be incompatible with the principle of individual freedom that is required for a beloved community. A *right* to participate seems essential (in order to ensure equality of voice in decision making), but a *duty* to participate seems to place the needs of the community above the needs of all its members.

However, given the importance of ensuring that decision-making processes are completely democratic in a political community, more consideration needs to be given to the question of *representation*, whereby the voices of those who do not participate directly in the policy process are expressed indirectly through their representatives. A beloved political or policy community could be characterised as a democratic one, in which the voices of all the members carry the same weight. In practice, as is well known, representation is a messy process, and the connection between the decisions taken by an elected representative and the views of those whom they represent is often very tenuous (see, for example, Somerville, 2005, on the problem of so-called 'democratic deficit'). In principle, however, electoral reform to achieve a closer relationship between representatives and represented is always possible. In this sense, the movement towards a beloved community is one that has no end, because neither total direct participation nor total identity between represented and representative is practicable. Some people's voices will always count for more than others, either because they participate more (in terms of time, expertise, money and so on) or because the decisions made by their representatives coincide more with their own than with others' views (because they are more powerful or influential or supportive of the powerful and influential or just lucky) – or because they are representatives themselves and/or even in government! In these circumstances, the best that can be hoped for is a continuous process of improving the quality of representation, a process that has to be driven from the bottom upwards – hence the importance of social movements.

Chapters Five, Six, Seven, Eight and Nine have all explored the nature of community in relation to key dimensions of everyday life and the social system: the economy, education, health, housing and general social order. This is not to say that these are the only such dimensions – others that could usefully be explored include food, transport, sport, art, music and literature. In all of these cases, the purpose of the book has been to show the utility of the concept of community in throwing light on the nature of practices of different kinds.

With regard to the economy, the book has highlighted the potential role of community entrepreneurship and community enterprise in transforming capitalism into a system that facilitates rather than undermines the beloved community. Currently, the development of such economically, socially and environmentally sustainable enterprises looks like the only clear way forward for communities generally. Examples such as Hill Holt Wood (discussed in **Box 5.1**) have shown that, far from being a utopian dream, the creation of such enterprises is a reasonable and appropriate response to contemporary economic, social and environmental problems and pressures.

To continue the Buddhist analogy, the desire for profit can be seen as the cause of lack or loss of community, whereas the creation of community enterprise involves the abandonment of this desire and its replacement by free and open cooperation on the basis of mutual equal respect.

In relation to education, the book has emphasised how far away we are at present from being a learning community or communities. We do not even understand *that* we might be meaningfully interconnected, let alone *how* we might be so connected. This is tantamount to alienation on a grand scale, and appears to present us with a task of Herculean proportions. In contemporary society, the education system has become increasingly geared towards the needs of capital rather than the needs of community, and arguably now represents one of the greatest obstacles to the beloved community, particularly through its emphasis on creating 'successes' and 'failures'. This book has shown, however, that it would not be too difficult to reverse this trend, for example, by changing schools into hubs for community learning and giving more priority to community-led learning initiatives. In Buddhist terms, the lack of community is caused by the desire for individual success (for example, to be 'top of the class', to become part of the elite and so on) and the restoration of community involves recognising that learning is fundamentally a collaborative process in which everyone is equal and there are no winners or losers.

A healthy community essentially has the characteristics of a beloved community, namely the flourishing of its members in cooperation with one another on the basis of mutual and equal respect. In a sense, then, the other dimensions affecting community (the economy, education, housing and so on) can all be assessed in terms of their contribution to the health of a community. This centrality of health was recognised in the Alma Ata Declaration in 1975, which contained a clear vision of a global beloved community, based on communities and health professionals working and learning together, not only in developing community services but also in tackling the causes of poor health. Unfortunately, however, this vision remains far from realisation, and indeed has faded to some extent, largely due to the activities of capitalists (banks, insurance companies, 'big pharma' and so on) and their governmental allies, who have, for example, caused the imposition of user charges as a condition for debt repayments. Today, 35 years later, governmental health services remain heavily bureaucratised, centralised and largely unresponsive and insensitive to community needs. Ironically, therefore, in view of the centrality of health to the beloved community, health policy seems to be the furthest away from what is required for the beloved community. The cause of this would seem to lie in a combination of the desire for profit (as already mentioned) and the self-interested power exerted by the medical profession, which is overwhelmingly committed to a biomedical approach and tends to see community as a challenge to its authority. The elimination of this cause would then require the cessation of profit-seeking from health, the ending of professional monopolies, and widespread collaboration along the lines of the Alma Ata model.

The relationship between housing and community is less well understood and perhaps much misunderstood. Indeed, it may be that one should speak here of *residence* rather than housing. Common residence in an area is often assumed to be a basis for community but this should not be taken for granted. Also, much of the collective action around housing, as explored in this book, is not compatible with the vision of a beloved community, being based on narrow self-interest and the desire to hold on to what one already has. Again, the increasing commercialisation of residence, with housing increasingly being seen as an investment asset rather than as a means of shelter and a site for various forms of activity, seems to make it less conducive to the beloved community ideal, according to which people would own and manage their homes cooperatively, on an equal basis. To use the Buddhist analogy once more, residential community is being undermined and destroyed by the desire for profit in the housing market, both for those seeking profit and for those harmed by their search. The ending of this desire would be associated with an acceptance of a common stake in housing and of sharing in a common wealth of residence – not just among members of, say, a particular housing cooperative, but across the whole world.

Finally, the issue of community order is perhaps the most complex of all, and strikes at the heart of the role of the state in contemporary society. Chapter Nine has argued that equal valuing of one another is a crucial condition for order in the world today because without it those who are valued less will harbour a sense of injustice that will result in law breaking, rebellion and disorder. Justice must not only be done but be seen to be done, according to due process and with due recognition of the equal rights of all those involved. Such justice is, of course, also characteristic of a beloved community. Despite the complexity, however, the chapter has taken the view that community order can be achieved to a large extent by allowing the community (interpreted in the widest possible sense as 'the public') to police itself – whilst at the same time recognising that this course of action incurs certain risks. This position amounts to a form of 'letting go' under certain conditions, with these conditions including a clear framework of law, everyday commonly understood rules of engagement, and a capacity within the community for specific interventions directed at specific breaches of the law where this is seen to be appropriate, for example, for enforcement of the law or prevention of the breach. What is being 'let go' here is the desire to control or to be in control, so that order is maintained without (for the most part) being willed by any particular individual.

Unfortunately, community order cannot be left entirely to the vagaries of everyday practice, and Chapter Nine explicitly mentions the harms that cause and are caused by disrespect, for example, racism, sexism, Islamophobia, heterosexism, classism and so on. Each of these harms requires its own ameliorative response, which adds to the difficulties of 'policing' community order. The responses themselves, however, while alleviating the harms involved, also tend to reinforce the inequalities with which those harms are associated, thus underlining their intractability. For this reason, what a Buddhist might call 'right policing' seems like a utopian project. It seems unlikely that any government would give up its desire to control, yet that seems to be what must happen for a beloved community to exist. For some years now, however, the trend of government policy and practice has been towards increasing both the breadth and depth of control, to the detriment of traditional civil liberties (let alone the freedom to flourish that is characteristic of a beloved community). Even the most basic entitlement to respect has been rejected on the totally spurious grounds that respect has to be earned (Respect Task Force, 2006, p 30). The consequence of such disrespect is of course an increased likelihood of disorder, which is precisely the opposite of what the government intends.

Chapter Nine raises the fundamental question of what we want governments to do and how we ensure that they do what we want. This takes the discussion back to Chapter Three because it is about the nature of our political community (who are 'we'?) and how to make it as democratic as possible. It may be difficult to accept, for example, that the government's priorities for community order (as measured by the amount of money spent), namely to make the city safe for shopping and to crack down on anti-social behaviour on social housing estates, may actually reflect the priorities of the electorate, but it is possible that this is really the case. If it is, then it means that the government is indeed doing what 'we' (that is, the majority) want, but the problem is that what it does may not turn out to be the most effective or productive use of public resources, the mass installation of CCTV cameras being perhaps the most extreme example of this. This suggests that government decision making needs to be far better informed both about the needs of communities (which are hugely variable) and about what might best satisfy these needs. Currently, it appears to do little more than pander to the prejudices of the 'respectable' majority (who now perhaps populate the 'Big Society'), thus disrespecting the allegedly 'deviant' minority and tending to exacerbate disorder rather than alleviate it.

At the time of writing, the substance of the Conservatives' Big Society idea is not entirely clear, though the term itself seems to mean something remarkably similar to New Labour's idea of 'community', that is, as a term that invokes a form of collective responsibility outside the state. In some respects, it constitutes a continuation and further development of New Labour's approach – for example, the emphasis on active citizenship, the third sector, mutualisation, communities taking over public services and so on. There is a more explicit emphasis on neighbourhood governance, with proposed new powers for neighbourhood groups to own and run community amenities and assets and be better supported by enhanced access to information and funding (Conservative Party, 2010, p 5). This clearly has potential for developing communities in a number of areas. There is also a commitment to provide extra funding for neighbourhood groups in the poorest areas and to train community organisers to help such groups to form (Conservative Party, 2010, p 7).

It is not yet clear, however, how far the Conservatives are committed to 'active government' in support of communities.[4] For example, does their rejection of the 'nanny state', that is, of Labour's top-down 'micro-management' of everyday community affairs, involve throwing out the baby as well, namely, the attempt to achieve effective coordination of mainstream public services at neighbourhood community level? The decision to protect Sure Start funding for now is a good sign but the Big Society idea seems to imply that such 'big government' is not seen as the way forward for the future. The aim to devolve real power to poorer neighbourhoods is also commendable, but what will happen to neighbourhood groups that actively disagree with government and campaign accordingly?

Notes

[1] In any case, the greater one's capacities for action, the greater the significance of the unintended consequences of that action; so one should beware of what one wishes for because it may come true!

[2] By theism I mean the current of thought that interprets spirit in terms of a being that transcends the world as we know it. The nature and existence of such a being are inherently unknowable, so the only reasonable position to adopt is one of agnosticism. Broadly following the thinking of Spinoza, my argument would be that our experience and understanding of spirit indicates that it is immanent in our world rather than transcendent – for further reading on immanence, see Deleuze (2001), Deleuze and Guattari (1994, 2004) and Agamben (1993).

[3] Such autonomy is the basis of what is now called 'empowerment' (Somerville, 1998).

[4] For further discussion, see Bochel (2011).

references

Adamson, D. and Bromiley, R. (2008) *Community empowerment in practice: Lessons from Communities First*, York: Joseph Rowntree Foundation.

Advisory Group on Citizenship (1998) *Education for citizenship and teaching of democracy in schools*, London: QCA.

Aeron-Thomas, D., Nicholls, J., Forster, S. and Westall, A. (2004) *Social return on investment: Valuing what matters*, London: New Economics Foundation.

Agamben, G. (1993) *The coming community*, trs M. Hardt, Minneapolis, MN: University of Minnesota Press.

Agur, M. and Low, N. (2009) *2007–08 Citizenship survey: Empowered communities topic report*, London: DCLG.

Albert, M. (2003) *Parecon: Life after capitalism*, London: Verso.

Aldridge, S. and Halpern, D. (2002) *Social capital: A discussion paper*, London: Performance and Innovation Unit, Cabinet Office.

Allen, C. (2008) *Housing market renewal and social class*, London: Routledge.

Allen, L. and Martin, J. (2002) *Governing education for community regeneration*, London: New Local Government Network/IDeA.

Allnock, D. et al (2005) *Implementing Sure Start Local Programmes: An in-depth study. Part Two – A close up on services*, London: DCSF.

Allport, G. (1979) *The nature of prejudice (25th anniversary edition)*, New York: Basic Books.

Althusser, L. (1970) 'Ideology and ideological state apparatuses', in *Lenin and philosophy and other essays*, trs B. Brewster, Monthly Review Press. Available online at: www.marxists.org/reference/archive/althusser/1970/ideology.htm.

Amin, A., Cameron, A. and Hudson, R. (2002) *Placing the social economy*, London: Routledge.

Amion Consulting (2004) *Evaluation of the Residents' Consultancy Pilots Initiative*, Research Report 10, London: Neighbourhood Renewal Unit.

Anderson, B. (1983) *Imagined communities: Reflections on the origin and spread of nationalism*, London: Verso.

Anderson, E. (1999) *The code of the street: Decency, violence and the moral life of the street*, New York: Norton.

Anning, A., Stuart, J., Nicholls, M., Goldthorpe, J. and Morley, A. (2007) *Understanding variations in effectiveness among Sure Start Local Programmes*, NESS Report 024, London: HMSO.

Anwar, M. (1985) *Pakistanis in Britain: A sociological study*, London: New Century.

Appiah, K. (1996) 'Cosmopolitan patriots', in J. Cohen (ed), *For love of country: Debating the limits of patriotism*, Boston: Beacon, pp 21–9.

Aristotle (1976) *Ethics*, Harmondsworth: Penguin.

Atkinson, R. (2006) 'Padding the bunker: strategies of middle-class disaffiliation and colonisation in the city', *Urban Studies*, vol 43, no 4, pp 819–32.

Atkinson, R. and Moon, G. (1994) *Urban policy in Britain: The city, the state and the market*, Basingstoke: Macmillan.

Audit Commission (1996) *Misspent youth*, London: Audit Commission.

Audit Commission (2003) *Economic and community regeneration: Learning from inspection*, London: Audit Commission.

Audit Commission (2006a) *More than the sum: Mobilising the whole council and its partners to support school success*, London: Audit Commission. Available online at: www.audit-commission.gov.uk/Products/NATIONAL-REPORT/79BCF4AB-DF36-47d8-8EEC-4C1B2621990F/MoreThanThe%20Sum.pdf.

Audit Commission (2006b) *Neighbourhood crime and anti-social behaviour: Making places safer through improved local working*, London: Audit Commission.

Avis, M., Bulman, D. and Leighton, P. (2007) 'Factors affecting participation in Sure Start programmes: a qualitative investigation of parents' views', *Health and Social Care in the Community*, vol 15, no 3, pp 203–11.

Bailey, N. and Livingston, M. (2007) *Population turnover and area deprivation*, Bristol: The Policy Press.

Ball, S.J. (2008) *The education debate*, Bristol: The Policy Press.

Ballinger, A. (2009) 'Gender, power and the state: same as it ever was?' in R. Coleman, J. Sim, S. Tombs and D. Whyte (eds) *State, power, crime*, London: Sage, pp 20–34.

Banks, S. (2007) 'Working in and with community groups and organisations: processes and practices', in H. Butcher, S. Banks, P. Henderson with J. Robertson *Critical community practice*, Bristol: The Policy Press, pp 77–96.

Bannister, J. and Kearns, A. (2009) 'Tolerance, respect and civility amid changing cities', in A. Millie (ed) *Securing respect: Behavioural expectations and anti-social behaviour in the UK*, Bristol: The Policy Press, pp 171–91.

Barnes, J. and Baylis, G. (2004) *Place and parenting: A study of four communities*, London: Institute for the Study of Children, Families and Social Issues, University of London.

Barnes, M., Newman, J. and Sullivan, H. (2007) *Power, participation and political renewal: Case studies in public participation*, Bristol: The Policy Press.

Barnes, M., Stoker, G. and Whiteley, P. (2004) *Delivering civil renewal: Some lessons from research*, ESRC Seminar Series – Mapping the public policy landscape, Swindon: Economic and Social Research Council. Available online at: www.esrc.ac.uk.

Barnes, M., Skelcher, C., Beirens, H., Dalziel, R., Jeffares, S. and Wilson, L. (2008) *Designing citizen-centred governance*, York: Joseph Rowntree Foundation.

Barnes, M., Sullivan, H. and Matka, E. (2001) *Building capacity for collaboration: The national evaluation of Health Action Zones*, Birmingham: University of Birmingham/Department of Health.

Barr, A. and Hashagen, S. (2000) *ABCD handbook: A framework for evaluating community development*, London: Community Development Foundation.

Bauman, Z. (2001) *Community: Seeking safety in an insecure world*, Cambridge: Polity Press.

Bauwens, M. (2005) *The political economy of peer production*. Available online at: www.ctheory.net/articles.aspx?id=499.

Beck, U. (2002) 'The cosmopolitan society and its enemies', *Theory, Culture & Society*, vol 19, nos 1/2, pp 17–44.

Becker, G.S. (1964, 1993, 3rd edn) *Human capital: A theoretical and empirical analysis, with special reference to education*, Chicago: University of Chicago Press.

Begum, H. (2003) *Social capital in action: Adding up local connections and networks*, London: NCVO and CCS.

Benzeval, M. (2003) *The final report of the Tackling Inequalities in Health module of the national evaluation of Health Action Zones*, London: Health Research Group, Department of Geography, Queen Mary, University of London.

Bevir, M. (2005) *New Labour: A critique*, London: Routledge.

Bibbings, L. (2009) 'The heterostate: hegemonic heterosexuality and state power', in R. Coleman, J. Sim, S. Tombs and D. Whyte (eds) (2009) *State, power, crime*, London: Sage, pp 35–48.

Bickle, R. (2006) 'Co-operation and social enterprise in the West Midlands', MSc dissertation, University of Birmingham.

Blair, T. (2005) Speech to Labour Party Conference, September.

Blake, G., Diamond, J., Foot, J., Gidley, B., Mayo, M., Shukra, K. and Yarnit, M. (2008) *Community engagement and community cohesion*, York: Joseph Rowntree Foundation.

Blakey, H., Pearce, J. and Chesters, G. (2006) *Minorities within minorities: Beneath the surface of South Asian participation*, York: Joseph Rowntree Foundation.

Blears, H. (2003) *Communities in control: Public services and local socialism*, London: Fabian Society.

Blunkett, D. (2003) *Civil renewal: A new agenda*, London: Home Office Communication Directorate.

Bochel, H. (ed) (2011, forthcoming) *The Conservative Party and social policy*, Bristol: The Policy Press.

Bogdanor, V. (ed) (2005) *Joined up government*, Oxford: Oxford University Press.

Boudreau, J.-A. and Keil, R. (2001) 'Seceding from responsibility? Secession movements in Los Angeles', *Urban Studies*, vol 38, no 10, pp 1701–31.

Bourdieu, P. (1984) *Distinction: A social critique of the judgement of taste*, London: Routledge.

Bourdieu, P. (1986) 'The forms of capital', in J. Richardson (ed) *Handbook of theory and research for the sociology of education*, New York: Greenwood Press.

Bourdieu, P. (1990) *The logic of practice*, Cambridge: Polity Press.

Bourdieu, P. (1998) *Practical reason*, Cambridge: Polity Press.

Bourdieu, P. (2005) *The social structures of the economy*, Cambridge: Polity Press.

Bourdieu, P. and Wacquant, L. (1992) *An invitation to reflexive sociology*, Cambridge: Polity Press.

Bovaird, T. (2007) 'Beyond engagement and participation – user and community co-production of services', *Public Administration Review*, vol 67, no 5, pp 846–60.

Boyle, D., Conisbee, M. and Burns, S. (2004) *Towards an asset-based NHS: The missing element of NHS reform*, London: New Economics Foundation. Available online at: www.neweconomics.org.

Boyle, D., Clark, S. and Burns, S. (2006) *Hidden work: Co-production by people outside paid employment*, York: Joseph Rowntree Foundation. Available at: www.jrf.org.uk.

Brent, J. (2004) 'The desire for community: illusion, confusion and paradox', *Community Development Journal*, vol 39, no 3, pp 213–23.

Bretherton, J. and Pleace, N. (2009) *Residents' views of new forms of high density affordable living*, Coventry: Chartered Institute of Housing/Joseph Rowntree Foundation.

Bridgen, P. (2004) 'Evaluating the empowerment potential of community-based health schemes: the case of community health policies in the UK since 1997', *Community Development Journal*, vol 39, no 3, pp 288–301.

Bridgen, P. (2006) 'Social capital, community empowerment and public health: policy developments in the UK since 1997', *Policy & Politics*, vol 34, no 1, pp 27–50.

Brownill, S. and Darke, J. (1998) *Rich mix? Inclusive strategies for regeneration*, Bristol: The Policy Press.

Bruegel, I. (2005) 'Social capital and feminist critique', in J. Franklin (ed), *Women and social capital*, London: Families & Social Capital ESRC Research Group, London South Bank University, pp 4–17

Buonfino, A. with Thomson, L. (2007) *Belonging in contemporary Britain*, London: Commission for Integration and Cohesion.

Burnett, J. (2009) 'Racism and the state: authoritarianism and coercion', in R. Coleman, J. Sim, S. Tombs and D. Whyte (eds) (2009) *State, power, crime*, London: Sage, pp 49–61.

Burney, E. (2008) 'The ASBO and the shift to punishment', in P. Squires (ed) *ASBO nation: The criminalisation of nuisance*, Bristol: The Policy Press, pp 135–48.

Burns, D. and Taylor, M. (1998) *Mutual aid and self-help: Coping strategies for excluded communities*, Bristol: The Policy Press.

Bursik, R. and Grasmick, H. (1993) 'Economic deprivation and neighbourhood crime rates 1960–1980', *Law and Society Review*, vol 27, no 2, pp 265–83.

Butcher, H. (1993) 'Introduction', in H. Butcher, A. Glen, P. Henderson, and J. Smith (eds) *Community and public policy*, London: Pluto Press.

Butcher, H. (2007a) 'What is critical community practice? Case studies and analysis', in H. Butcher, S. Banks, P. Henderson with J. Robertson *Critical community practice*, Bristol: The Policy Press, pp 33–50.

Butcher, H. (2007b) 'Towards a model of critical community practice', in H. Butcher, A. Banks, P. Henderson with J. Robertson *Critical community practice*, Bristol: The Policy Press, pp 51–76.

Butcher, H., Banks, S., Henderson, P. with Robertson, J. (2007) *Critical community practice*, Bristol: The Policy Press.

Butcher, H., Glen, A., Henderson, P. and Smith, J. (eds) (1993) *Community and public policy*, London: Pluto Press.

Butler, T. (1997) *Gentrification and the middle classes*, Aldershot: Ashgate.

Cabinet Office (2007) *The future role of the third sector in social and economic regeneration: Final report*, London: Cabinet Office.

Campbell, B. (1993) *Goliath: Britain's dangerous places*, London: Methuen.

Cantle, T. (2008) *Community cohesion: A new framework for race and diversity* (2nd edn), Basingstoke: Palgrave Macmillan.

Card, P. (2006) 'Governing tenants: from dreadful enclosures to dangerous places', in J. Flint (ed) *Housing, urban governance and anti-social behaviour: Perspective, policy and practice*, Bristol: The Policy Press, pp 37–56.

Carr, H. and Cowan, D. (2006) 'Labelling: constructing definitions of anti-social behaviour?' in J. Flint (ed) *Housing, urban governance and anti-social behaviour: Perspective, policy and practice*, Bristol: The Policy Press, pp 57–78.

Casey, T. (2004) 'Social capital and regional economies in Britain', *Political Studies*, vol 52, pp 96–117.

Centre for Cities (2009) *Public sector cities: Trouble ahead*, London: Centre for Cities.

Centre for Local Economic Strategies (CLES) (2008) *Evaluating regeneration projects and programmes*, Manchester: CLES.

CFMEB (Commission on the Future of Multi-Ethnic Britain) (2000) *The future of multi-ethnic Britain: The Parekh report*, London: Profile Books for the Runnymede Trust.

Cheshire, P. (2007) *Segregated neighbourhoods and mixed communities: A critical analysis*, York: Joseph Rowntree Foundation

CIC (Commission on Integration and Cohesion) (2007) *Our shared future*, London: CIC. Available online at: www.integrationandcohesion.org.uk.

Clarke, J. (2009) 'Community, social change and social order', in G. Mooney and S. Neal (eds) *Community: Welfare, crime and society*, Maidenhead: Open University Press, pp 65–97.

Clarke, S., Gilmour, R. and Garner, S. (2007) 'Home, identity and community cohesion', in M. Wetherell, M. Laflèche and R. Berkeley (eds) *Identity, ethnic diversity and community cohesion*, London: Sage, pp 87–101.

CLG (Communities and Local Government) (2004) *Firm foundations: The government's framework for community capacity building*, London: CLG. Available online at: www.communities.gov.uk/index.asp?id=1502531.

CLG (2006a) *The community development challenge*, London: CLG.

CLG (2006b) *Promoting effective citizenship and community empowerment*, London: CLG.

CLG (2006c) *From decent homes to sustainable communities*, London: CLG.

CLG (2007a) *An action plan for community empowerment: Building on success*, London: CLG.

CLG (2007b) *Tenant empowerment: A consultation paper*, London: CLG.

CLG (2007c) *Index of multiple deprivation*, London: CLG.

CLG (2008a) *The government's response to the Commission on Integration and Cohesion*, London: CLG.

CLG (2008b) *Communities in control: Real people, real power*, London: CLG.

CLG (2008c) *How to develop a local charter: A guide for local authorities*, London: CLG.

CLG (2008d) *Guidance on meaningful interaction: How encouraging positive relationships between people can help build community cohesion*, London: CLG.

CLG (2008e) *Giving more people a say in local spending. Participatory budgeting: A national strategy*, London: CLG.

CLG (2008f) *No one left out: Communities ending rough sleeping*, London: CLG.

CLG (2009) *Transforming places, changing lives: Taking forward the regeneration framework*, London: CLG.

CLG (2010) *Cohesion delivery framework 2010*, London: CLG.

Cole, I. and Furbey, R. (1994) *The eclipse of council housing*, London: Routledge.

Coleman, J.S. (1988) 'Social capital in the creation of human capital', *American Journal of Sociology*, vol 94, Supplement, pp S95–S120.

Coleman, R. (2009) 'Policing the working class in the city of renewal: the state and social surveillance', in R. Coleman, J. Sim, S. Tombs and D. Whyte (eds) *State, power, crime*, London: Sage, pp 62–75.

Coleman, R., Sim, J., Tombs, S. and Whyte, D. (eds) (2009) *State, power, crime*, London: Sage.

Coles, A. (2009) 'Mutual respect', *ROOF*, May/June, p 36.

Commission on Families and the Wellbeing of Children (2005) *Families and the state: Two-way support and responsibilities*, Bristol: The Policy Press.

Community Development Exchange (2001) *A strategic framework for community development*. Available online at: www.cdx.org.uk.

Comptroller and Auditor General (C&AG) (2009) *Building the capacity of the Third Sector*, HC (2008-09) 132, London: C&AG.

Confederation of Co-operative Housing (CCH) (2010) *Community Gateway*. Available online at: http://cch.coop/gateway.index.html (accessed 9 February 2010).

Connelly, P. and Healy, J. (2004) 'Symbolic violence, locality and social class: the educational and career aspirations of 10–11 year old boys in Belfast', *Pedagogy, Culture and Society*, vol 12, no 1, pp 15–33.

Connor, W. (2004) 'Nationalism and political illegitimacy', in D. Conversi (ed) *Ethnonationalism in the contemporary world*, London: Routledge.

Conservative Party (2010) *Building a Big Society*. Available at: www.conservatives.com (published and accessed 19 May 2010).

Conversi, D. (2007) 'Homogenisation, nationalism and war: should we still read Ernest Gellner?' *Nations and Nationalism*, vol 13, no 3, pp 371–94.

Conversi, D. (2008a) 'Democracy, nationalism and culture. The limits of liberal mono-culturalism', *Sociology Compass*, vol 1, no 3, pp. 1–27.

Conversi, D. (2008b) '"We are all equals!" Militarism, homogenization and "egalitarianism" in nationalist state-building (1789–1945)', *Ethnic and Racial Studies*, vol 31, no 7, pp 1286–314.

Cook, D. (1989) *Rich law, poor law: Different responses to tax and supplementary benefit fraud*, Milton Keynes: Open University Press.

Cook, D. (2005) 'The sundered totality of system and lifeworld', *Historical Materialism*, vol 13, no 4, pp 55–78.

Cook, D. (2006) *Criminal and social justice*, London: Sage.

Copeland, S. (2004) *Consultation for PPI forums: Powers and support*, London: Department of Health.

Copus, C. (2001) 'Citizen participation in local government: the influence of the political party group', *Local Governance*, vol 27, no 3, pp 151–63.

Cornwall, A. and Coelho, V. (eds) (2006) *Spaces for change? The politics of citizen participation in new democratic arenas*, London: Zed Books.

CPPP (Commission on Poverty, Participation and Power) (2000) *Listen hear: The right to be heard*, Bristol: The Policy Press.

Craig, G. (2007) 'Community capacity-building: something old, something new...?', *Critical Social Policy*, vol 27, pp 335–59.

Craig, G. et al (2007) *Sure Start and Black and minority ethnic populations*, Nottingham: DfES.

Crawford, A. (1997) *The local governance of crime: Appeals to community and partnerships*, Oxford: Oxford University Press.

Crawford, A., Lister, S., Blackburn, S. and Burnett, J. (2005) *Plural policing: The mixed economy of visible security patrols*, Bristol: The Policy Press.

Crispin, T., Milliken, D. and Bews, K. (2005) *Armbands in deep water: A summary of research into Home Start's home-visiting volunteers*. Available online at: www.home-start.org.uk.

Crossley, N. (2002) *Making sense of social movements*, Buckingham: Open University Press.

Crow, G. and Allan, G. (1994) *Community life: An introduction to local social relations*, Hemel Hempstead: Harvester Wheatsheaf.

Crowther, D., Cummings, C., Dyson, A. and Millward, A. (2003) *Schools and area regeneration*, Bristol: The Policy Press/Joseph Rowntree Foundation.

Cummings, C., Dyson, A., Muijs, D., Papps, I., Pearson, D., Raffo, C., Tiplady, L. and Todd, L. with Crowther, D. (2007) *Evaluation of the full service extended schools initiative: Final report*, London: Department for Education and Skills.

Cunninghame, P. (2008) 'Whither autonomism as a global social movement?' paper presented at Panel 8: Global Challenges. RC47: 'Globalization, social movements and experience'. First ISA Forum of Sociology: Sociological Research and Public Debate, Barcelona, Spain, September 5–8. Available online at: www.isarc47.org/Files/Cunighame.pdf.

Davies, J. (2007) 'The limits of partnership: an exit-action strategy for local democratic inclusion', *Political Studies*, vol 55, pp 779–800.

Davies, J. (2009) 'The limits of joined-up government: towards a political analysis', *Public Administration*, vol 87, no 1, pp 80–96.

Davis, S., Porteous, J. and Skidmore, C. (2009) *Housing, health and care*, Coventry: Chartered Institute of Housing.

Day, G. (2006) *Community and everyday life*, Abingdon: Routledge.

DCSF (Department for Children, Schools and Families) (2009a) *Trust Schools toolkit*, London: DCSF.

DCSF (2009b) *Guidance on the duty to promote community cohesion*, London: DCSF.

Dean, C., Dyson, A., Gallanaugh, F., Howes, A. and Raffo, C. (2007) *Schools, governors and disadvantage*, York: Joseph Rowntree Foundation. Available online at: www.jrf.org.uk/bookshop/eBooks/1994-schools-governors-disadvantage.pdf.

Dearling, A. with Melzer, G. (2003) *Another kind of space: Creating ecological dwellings and environments*, Lyme Regis: Enabler Publications.

DeFilippis, J., Fisher, R. and Shragge, E. (2006) 'Neither romance nor regulation: re-evaluating community', *International Journal of Urban and Regional Research*, vol 30, no 3, pp 673–89.

Delanty, G. (2003) *Community*, London: Routledge.

Deleuze, G. (2001) *Pure immanence*, trs A. Boyman, New York: Zone Books.

Deleuze, G. and Guattari, F. (1994) *What is philosophy?*, trs G. Burchell and H. Tomlinson, London: Verso.

Deleuze, G. and Guattari, F. (2004) *A thousand plateaus*, trs B. Massumi, London and New York: Continuum.

Dennis, N. (1970) *People and planning: The sociology of housing in Sunderland*, London: Faber.

De Vos, P., De Ceukelaire, W., Malaise, G., Pérez, D., Lefèvre, P. and Van der Stuyft, P. (2009) 'Health through people's empowerment: a rights-based approach to participation', *Health and Human Rights: An International Journal*, vol 11, no 1, pp 23–35.

DfES (Department for Education and Skills) (2005) *Extended Schools: Access to opportunities and services for all*, London: DfES.

DH (Department of Health) (2005) *A short guide to NHS Foundation Trusts*, London: Department of Health. Available online at: www.dh.gov.uk.

DH (2006) (White Paper) *Our health, our care, our say: A new direction for community services*, London: Department of Health.

DH (2009a) *Transforming community services: Enabling new patterns of provision*, London: Department of Health.

DH (2009b) *Tackling health inequalities: 10 years on*, London: Department of Health.

DH and HM Treasury (2002) *Tackling health inequalities*, London: Department of Health/HM Treasury.

Dobson, A. (2006) 'Thick cosmopolitanism', *Political Studies*, vol 54, pp 165–84.

Donzelot, J. (1979) *The policing of families*, New York: Random House.

Dorling, D. et al (2007) *Poverty and wealth across Britain 1968–2005*, York: Joseph Rowntree Foundation.

Dreier, P. (2005) *ACORN and progressive politics in America*, http://comm-org.wisc.edu/papers2005/dreier.htm.

Duncan, S. and Edwards, R. (1999) *Lone mothers, paid work and gendered moral rationalities*, London: Macmillan.

Dunleavy, P. (1981) *The politics of mass housing in Britain: A study in corporate power and professional influence in the welfare state*, Oxford: Clarendon Press.

Durkheim, E. (1984 [orig 1893]) *The division of labour in society*, trs W.D. Halls, London: Macmillan.

Edwards, C. (2003) 'Disability and the discourses of the Single Regeneration Budget', in R. Imrie and M. Raco (eds) *Urban renaissance? New Labour, community and urban policy*, Bristol: The Policy Press, pp 163–80.

Edwards, M. (2004) *Civil society*, Cambridge: Polity Press.

Elias, N. (1974) 'Foreword – towards a theory of communities', in C. Bell and H. Newby (eds) *The sociology of community: A selection of readings*, London: Frank Cass.

Elias, N. (1978) *The civilising process: Volume 1. The history of manners*, Oxford: Blackwell.

Elias, N. and Scotson, J. (1994) *The established and the outsiders: A sociological enquiry into community problems* (2nd edn), London: Sage.

Ellis, B. (2003) *White Paper: Life-long self-learning*. Available online at: http:// ezinearticles.com/ (accessed 17 August 2009).

Ellis, B. (2005) *The Gaian paradigm Part 3: Cooperative life-long self-learning*. Available online at: http://ezinearticles.com/ (accessed 17 August 2009).

Emmel, N. (2004) *Towards community involvement: Strategies for health and social care providers. Guide 2: The complexity of communities and lessons for community involvement*, Leeds: Nuffield Institute for Health.

Emmel, N. and Conn, C. (2004) *Towards community involvement: Strategies for health and social care providers. Guide 1: Identifying the goal and objectives of community involvement*, Leeds: Nuffield Institute for Health.

Etzioni, A. (1995) *The spirit of community: Rights, responsibilities and the communitarian agenda*, London: Fontana Press.

Farrington, D. (2002) 'Understanding and preventing youth crime', in J. Muncie, G. Hughes and E. McLaughlin (eds) *Youth justice: Critical readings*, London: Sage.

FCWTG (Federation of Community Work Training Groups) (2002) *Reach out: Sharing community development training ideas – learning from practice*, Sheffield: FCWTG.

Fine, R. (2007) *Cosmopolitanism*, London: Routledge.

Fisher, R. (1994) *Let the people decide: Neighbourhood organizing in America* (2nd edn), New York: Twayne Publishers.

Flint, J. (2004) 'The responsible tenant: housing governance and the politics of behaviour', *Housing Studies*, vol 19, no 6, pp 893–910.

Flint, J. and Powell, R. (2009) 'Civilising offensives: education, football and "eradicating" sectarianism in Scotland', in A. Millie (ed) *Securing respect: Behavioural expectations and anti-social behaviour in the UK*, Bristol: The Policy Press, pp 219–38.

Forrest, R. and Murie, A. (1990) *Selling the welfare state* (2nd edn), London: Routledge.

Forrest, R., Murie, A. and Gordon, D. (1996) *The resale of former council homes*, London: HMSO.

France, A. and Meredith, J. (2009) 'Giving respect: the "new" responsibilities of youth in the transition towards citizenship', in A. Millie (ed) *Securing respect: Behavioural expectations and anti-social behaviour in the UK*, Bristol: The Policy Press, pp 75–95.

Franklin, J. (2007) *Social capital: Between harmony and dissonance*, London: Families & Social Capital ESRC Research Group, South Bank University, www.lsbu.ac.uk/families.

Fraser, N. (1989) *Unruly practices: Power, discourse and gender in contemporary social theory*, Cambridge: Polity.

Frazer, E. (1999) *The problem of communitarian politics: Unity and conflict*, Oxford: Oxford University Press.

Freire, P. (1996 [orig 1970]) *Pedagogy of the oppressed*, Harmondsworth: Penguin Books.

Frith, K. and McElwee, G. (2009) 'Value adding and value extracting entrepreneurship at the margins', *The Journal of Small Business and Entrepreneurship*, vol 22, no 1, pp 39–53.

Frith, K., McElwee, G. and Somerville, P. (2009) 'Building a "community co-operative" at Hill Holt Wood', *Journal of Co-operative Studies*, vol 42, no 2, pp 38–47.

Fuller, C. and Davies, J.S. (2005) *National evaluation of local strategic partnerships. Issues paper: Local strategic partnerships, multi-level governance and economic development*, London: ODPM. Available online at: www.communities. gov.uk/documents/localgovernment/pdf/143054.pdf.

Fuller, C. and Geddes, M. (2008) 'Urban governance under neoliberalism: New Labour and the restructuring of state-space', *Antipode*, vol 40, no 2, pp 252–82.

Gajardo, M. (1994) 'Ivan Illich', in Z. Morsy (ed) *Key thinkers in education, Volume 2*, Paris: UNESCO Publishing.

Gamble, A. (1994) *The free economy and the strong state: The politics of Thatcherism* (2nd edn), Basingstoke: Palgrave Macmillan.

Garland, D. (1997) '"Governmentality" and the problems of crime', *Theoretical Criminology*, vol 1, no 2, pp 173–214.

Garland, D. (2001) *The culture of control*, Oxford: Oxford University Press.

Garrett, P.M. (2007) '"Sinbin" research and the "lives of others": a rejoinder in an emerging and necessary debate', *Critical Social Policy*, vol 27, no 4, pp 560–64.

Gaventa, J. (2004) *Representation, community leadership and participation: Citizen involvement in neighbourhood renewal and local governance*, London: ODPM.

Gellner, E. (2006 [orig 1983]) *Nations and nationalism*, Oxford: Blackwell.

Giddens, A. (1998) *The Third Way: The renewal of social democracy*, Cambridge: Polity.

Gilchrist, A. (2004) *The well-connected community: A networking approach to community development*, Bristol: The Policy Press.

Gilchrist, A. (2009) *The well-connected community: A networking approach to community development*, (2nd edn), Bristol: The Policy Press.

Glass, N. (2005) 'Surely some mistake?', *Society Guardian*, 5 January, p 2.

Glass, R. (1964) *London: Aspects of change*, London: MacGibbon & Kee.

Glennie, S., Tresder, G., Williams, J. and Williams, M. (2005) *Mini Sure Start Local Programmes: An overview of their early implementation*, Nottingham: DfES. Available online from: www.surestart.gov.uk.

Goldsmith, C. (2006) '"You just know you're being watched everywhere": young people, custodial experiences and community safety', in P. Squires (ed) *Community safety: Critical perspectives on policy and practice*, Bristol: The Policy Press, pp 13–33.

Goldsmith, C. (2008) 'Cameras, cops and contracts: what anti-social behaviour management feels like to young people', in P. Squires (ed) *ASBO nation: The criminalisation of nuisance*, Bristol: The Policy Press, pp 223–37.

Goldthorpe, J., Lockwood, D., Beckhofer, F. and Platt, J. (1969) *The affluent worker in the class structure*, Cambridge: Cambridge University Press.

Goold, B. (2004) *CCTV and policing: Public area surveillance and police practices in Britain*, Oxford: Oxford University Press.

Gore, T., Fothergill, S. Hollywood, E., Lindsay, C., Morgan, K., Powell, R. and Upton, S. (2007) *Coalfields and neighbouring cities: Economic regeneration, labour markets and governance*, York: Joseph Rowntree Foundation.

Gorz, A. (1980) *Farewell to the working class*, London: Pluto Press.

Graham, J. and Bowling, B. (1995) *Young people and crime*, London: Home Office.

Granovetter, M. (1973) 'The strength of weak ties', *American Journal of Sociology*, vol 78, pp 1360–80.

Grayson, J. (1997) 'Campaigning tenants: a pre-history of tenant involvement to 1979', in C. Cooper and M. Hawtin (eds) *Housing, community and conflict: Understanding resident 'involvement'*, Aldershot: Arena, pp 15–65.

Green, A. and White, R. J. (2007) *Attachment to place: Social networks, mobility and prospects of young people*, York: Joseph Rowntree Foundation.

Gregg, D. (2010) *Family intervention projects: A classic case of policy-based evidence*, London: Centre for Crime and Justice Studies, King's College London.

Gret, M. and Sintomer, Y. (2005) *The Porto Alegre experiment: Learning lessons for better democracy*, London: Zed Books.

Gustafsson, U. and Driver, S. (2005) 'Parents, power and public participation: Sure Start, an experiment in New Labour governance', *Social Policy & Administration*, vol 39, no 5, pp 528–43.

Habermas, J. (1974) 'The public sphere: An encyclopedia article (1964)', trs S. Lennox and F. Lennox, *New German Critique* 3: 49–55. Available online at: www.jstor.org (accessed July 2008).

Habermas, J. (2000) *The divided West*, Cambridge: Polity Press.

Halabi, S.F. (2009) 'Participation and the right to health: lessons from Indonesia', *Health and Human Rights: An International Journal*, vol 11, no 1, pp 49–59.

Hall, A. and Midgley, J. (2004) *Social policy for development*, London: Sage.

Hall, J. (2005) *Bringing budgets alive: Participatory budgeting in practice*, Manchester: Community Pride Initiative/Oxfam UK Poverty Programme.

Hall, P.A. (1999) 'Social capital in Britain', *British Journal of Political Science*, vol 29, no 3, pp 417–61.

Hall, S. (2009) 'Preface', in R. Coleman, J. Sim, S. Tombs and D. Whyte (eds) *State, power, crime*, London: Sage, pp xii–xviii.

Hall, S. and Winlow, S. (2005) 'Anti-Nirvana: crime, culture and instrumentalism in the age of insecurity', *Crime, Media, Culture*, vol 1, no 1, pp 31–48.

Hall, S., Winlow, S. and Ancrum, C. (2008) *Criminal identities and consumer culture: Crime, exclusion and the new culture of narcissism*, Cullompton: Willan Publishing.

Hallsworth, S. and Young, T. (2004) 'Getting real about gangs', *Criminal Justice Matters*, vol 55, pp 12–13.

Halpern, D. (2005) *Social capital*, Cambridge: Polity Press.

Handy, C. (2010) 'Mutual housing', *ROOF* Jan/Feb, pp 30–1.

Hardt, M. and Negri, A. (2000) *Empire*, New York: Harvard University Press.

Harris, K. (ed) (2006) *Respect in the neighbourhood: Why neighbourliness matters*, Lyme Regis: Russell House Publishing.

Hastings, A. (2003) 'Strategic, multilevel neighbourhood regeneration: an outward-looking approach at last?', in R. Imrie and M. Raco (eds) *Urban renaissance? New Labour, community and urban policy*, Bristol: The Policy Press, pp 85–100.

Hawdon, J.E., Ryan, J. and Griffin, S.P. (2003) 'Policing tactics and perceptions of police legitimacy', *Police Quarterly*, vol 6, no 4, pp 469–91.

Healthcare Commission (2007) *Caring for dignity: A national report on dignity in care for older people while in hospital*, London: Healthcare Commission. Available online at: www.healthcarecommission.org.uk/_db/_documents/Caring_for_dignity.pdf.

Heap, D. (1991) *An outline of planning law* (10th revised edn), London: Sweet & Maxwell.

Henderson, P. (2007) 'Politics and policy: a critical community practice perspective', in H. Butcher, S. Banks, P. Henderson with J. Robertson *Critical community practice*, Bristol: The Policy Press, pp 117–32.

Heraud, B. (1968) 'Social class and the new towns', *Urban Studies*, vol 5, no 1, pp 33–58.

Hewstone, M., Tausch, N., Hughes, J. and Cairns, E. (2007) 'Prejudice, intergroup contact and identity: do neighbourhoods matter?' in M. Wetherell, M. Laflèche and R. Berkeley (eds) *Identity, ethnic diversity and community cohesion*, London: Sage, pp 102–12.

Hickey, S. and Mohan, G. (2004) 'Relocating participation within a radical politics of development: insights from political action and practice', in S. Hickey and G. Mohan (eds) *Participation: From tyranny to transformation?* London: Zed Books, 159–74.

Hines, F. (2004) *Turning big ideas into viable social enterprise*, Cardiff: University of Cardiff/Triodos Bank. Available online at: www.brass.cf.ac.uk.

HMG (HM Government) (2008) *Fair rules for strong communities*, London: HMG.

HMG (2009a) *Working together: Public services on your side*, London: HMG.

HMG (2009b) *New opportunities: Fair chances for the future*, London: HMG.

HM Treasury (2006) *The future role of the third sector in social and economic regeneration: Interim report*, London: HM Treasury.

HM Treasury (2007) *The future role of the third sector in social and economic regeneration: Final report*, Cm 7189, London: HM Treasury. Available online at: www.hm-treasury.gov.uk.

Hobbs, D. (2003) *The night-time economy*, London: Alcohol Concern Research Forum Papers.

Hoggett, P. (1992) 'A place for experience: a psychoanalytic perspective on boundary, identity and culture', *Environment and Planning D: Society and Space*, vol 10, pp 345–56.

Holmes, C. (2006) *Mixed communities: Success and sustainability*, York: Joseph Rowntree Foundation.

Holt, A. (2008) 'Room for resistance? Parenting Orders, disciplinary power and the production of "the bad parent"', in P. Squires (ed) *ASBO nation: The criminalisation of nuisance*, Bristol: The Policy Press, pp 203–22.

Holt, J. (1964) *How children fail*, London: Pitman Publishing.

Home Office (1997) *No more excuses*, Cm 3809, London: HMSO.

Home Office (2001a) *Community cohesion: A report of the independent review team* (the Cantle Report), London: The Stationery Office.

Home Office (2001b) *The Oldham independent review* (the Ritchie Report), London: The Stationery Office.

Home Office (2001c) *The report of the Burnley Task Force* (the Clarke Report), London: The Stationery Office.

Home Office (2003) *A guide to anti-social behaviour orders and acceptable behaviour contracts*, London: ACPO and the Youth Justice Board, Home Office Communications Directorate.

Home Office (2006) *National Community Safety Plan*, London: Home Office.

Home Office (2010) *British Crime Survey*, London: Home Office.

Honneth, A. (1991) *The critique of power: Reflective stages in a critical social theory*, trs K. Baynes, Cambridge, MA: MIT Press.

Hopper, P. (2003) *Rebuilding communities in an age of individualism*, Aldershot: Ashgate.

Hothi, M. with Bacon, N., Brophy, M. and Mulgan, G. (2007) *Neighbourliness + empowerment = wellbeing*, York: Joseph Rowntree Foundation.

House of Commons Public Accounts Committee (2009) *Building the capacity of the third sector*, 37th report of session 2008–09, London: The Stationery Office.

Housing Corporation (2007) *People first: Delivering change through involvement*, London: The Housing Corporation.

Hughes, G. (1998) *Understanding crime prevention*, Buckingham: Open University Press.

Hughes, G., McLoughlin, E. and Muncie, J. (eds) (2002) *Crime prevention and community safety: New directions*, London: Sage.

ICC (Institute for Community Cohesion) (2009) *Building community cohesion in Britain: Lessons from iCoCo local reviews*, London: ICC.

Illich, I. (1973) *Deschooling society*, Harmondsworth: Penguin.

Ipsos MORI (2007) *'What works' in community cohesion*, London: CLG.

Jacobs, J. (1961) *The death and life of great American cities: The failure of town planning*, Harmondsworth: Penguin Books.

Jessop, B. (2002) *The future of the capitalist state*, Cambridge: Polity.

Jochum, V. (2003) *Social capital: Beyond the theory*, London: NCVO.

Johannisson, B. and Wigren, C. (2006) 'The dynamics of community identity making in an industrial district: the spirit of Gnosjö revisited', in C. Steyaert and D. Hjorth (eds) *Entrepreneurship as social change: A third movement in entrepreneurship book*, Cheltenham: Edward Elgar, pp 188–209.

Johnson, A. (2004) *Communities: How to create a lasting footprint in deprived communities*, London: BASSAC.

Johnson, M. and Schmuecker, K. with Reed, H. (2007) *The sand timer: Skills and employment in the North West*, Newcastle upon Tyne: IPPR North. Available online at: www.ippr.org.uk.

Johnston, G. and Percy-Smith, J. (2003) 'In search of social capital', *Policy & Politics*, vol 31, no 3, pp 321–34.

Jones, C. and Murie, A. (2006) *The Right to Buy: Analysis and evaluation of a housing policy*, Oxford: Blackwell.

Jones, D., Keogh, B. and O'Leary, H. (2007) *Developing the social economy: Critical review of the literature*, Edinburgh: Communities Scotland. Available online at: www.communitiesscotland.gov.uk/stellent/groups/public/documents/webpages/pubcs_017896.pdf.

Jordan, G. and Maloney, W. (2007) *Democracy and interest groups*, Basingstoke: Palgrave Macmillan.

JRF (Joseph Rowntree Foundation) (2006) *Findings: Minorities within minorities: beneath the surface of community participation*, York: JRF.

JRF (2007) *Changing neighbourhoods: The impact of 'light touch' support in 20 communities*, York: JRF.

Kagan, C. (2006) 'Health hazards', *New Start*, 13 January, pp 14–17.

Kapasi, H. (2006) *Neighbourhood play and community action*, York: Joseph Rowntree Foundation.

Karn, J. (2006) *Narratives of neglect: Community, exclusion and the local governance of security*, Cullompton: Willan Publishing.

Katungi, D., Neale, E. and Barbour, A. (2006) *People in low-paid informal work: Need not greed*, Bristol: The Policy Press/Joseph Rowntree Foundation.

Kearns, A. (2004) *Social capital, regeneration and urban policy*, CNR Paper 15. Available online at: www.neighbourhoodcentre.org.uk.

Kearns, A. and Turok, I. (2003) *Sustainable communities: Dimensions and challenges*, London: Office of the Deputy Prime Minister.

King, M.L. (1986) *Testament of hope: The essential writings and speeches of Martin Luther King, Jr*, ed J.M. Washington, New York: Harper Collins.

Kintrea, K., Bannister, J., Pickering, J., Reid, M. and Suzuki, N. (2008) *Young people and territoriality in British cities*, York: Joseph Rowntree Foundation.

Kisby, B. (2007) 'New Labour and citizenship education', *Parliamentary Affairs*, vol 60, no 1, pp 84–101.

Labour Party Manifesto (1997) Available online at: www.bbc.co.uk/election97/background/parties/manlab/labman6.html.

Latane, B. and Darley, J. (1970) *The unresponsive bystander: Why doesn't he help?* New York: Appleton-Century-Crofts.

Laverack, G. (2004) *Health promotion practice, power and empowerment*, London: Sage.

Lawless, P. (2008) *New Deal for Communities: A synthesis of new programme-wide evidence 2006–7*, London: Department for Communities and Local Government.

Lawlor, E. and Nicholls, J. (2006) *Hitting the target, missing the point: How government regeneration targets fail deprived areas*, London: New Economics Foundation.

Lawlor, E., Neizert, E. and Nicholls, J. (2008) *Measuring real value: A guide to social return on investment* (2nd edn), London: New Economics Foundation.

Leadbeater, C. (2000) *Living on thin air: The new economy*, London: Penguin.

Leather, P., Ferrari, E. and Cole, I. (2009) *National evaluation of housing market renewal pathfinders 2005–2007*, London: Department for Communities and Local Government.

Ledwith, M. (2005) *Community development: A critical approach*, Bristol: The Policy Press.

Lehning, P. (1998) 'Towards a multicultural civil society: the role of social capital and democratic citizenship', *Government and Opposition*, vol 33, pp 221–42.

Leonard, M. (2004) 'Bonding and bridging capital: reflections from Belfast', *Sociology*, vol 38, no 5, pp 927–44.

Leunig, T. and Swaffield, J. (2008) *Cities unlimited: Making urban regeneration work*, London: Policy Exchange.

Levi, Y. (2007) 'The notion of nonprofit: ambiguities and a research proposal', *Journal of Co-operative Studies*, vol 40, no 3, pp 41–6.

Levi-Strauss, C. (1963) *Structural anthropology*, trs C. Jacobson, New York: Basic Books.

Levine, R. et al (2002) *Promoting intervention against violent crime: A social identity approach*, Swindon: Economic and Social Research Council. Available at: www1.rhbnc.ac.uk/socio-political-violence-science/vrp/findings/rflevine.pdf.

Ley, D. (1996) *The new middle class and the remaking of the central city*, Oxford: Oxford University Press.

LGA (Local Government Association) (2004) *Community cohesion: An action guide*, London: LGA.

LGA and IDeA (2006) *Community cohesion: A guide for local authority leaders and chief executives*, London: LGA and IDeA.

LGMB (Local Government Management Board) (1996) *Survey of community safety activities in local government in England and Wales*, London: LGMB.

Lindgren, M. and Packendorff, J. (2006) 'Entrepreneurship as boundary work: deviating from and belonging to community', in C. Steyaert and D. Hjorth (eds) *Entrepreneurship as social change: A third movement in entrepreneurship book*, Cheltenham: Edward Elgar, pp 210–30.

Littman, D. (2008) 'Another politics is possible', *Red Pepper*, 160 (June/July), pp 20–2.

Livingston, M., Bailey, N. and Kearns, A. (2008) *People's attachment to place – The influence of neighbourhood deprivation*, York: Joseph Rowntree Foundation.

Loader, I. (2000) 'Plural policing and democratic governance', *Social & Legal Studies*, vol 9, no 3, pp 323–45.

Lockwood, D. (1958) *The blackcoated worker*, London: Allen and Unwin.

Loney, M. (1979) *Community against government: The British Community Development Project 1968–78*, London: Harcourt Education.

Loveday, B. (2005) 'The 2003 Licensing Act: alcohol use and anti-social behaviour in England and Wales', *Police Journal*, vol 78, no 3, pp 178–91.

Loveday, B. (2006) 'The police and community safety', in P. Squires (ed), *Community safety: Critical perspectives on policy and practice*, Bristol: The Policy Press, pp 111–24.

Lowndes, V., Pratchett, L. and Stoker, G. (2006) *Locality matters: Making participation count in local politics*, London: Institute for Public Policy Research.

Lownsbrough, H. and Beunderman, J. (2007) *Equally spaced? Public space and interaction between diverse communities*, London: Demos.

Lupton, R. (2004) *Poverty street*, Bristol: The Policy Press.

McCarthy, T. (1991) 'Complexity and democracy: or the seducements of systems theory', in A. Honneth and H. Joas (eds) *Communicative action: Essays on Jürgen Habermas's 'The theory of communicative action'*, trs J. Gains and D.L. Jones, Cambridge, MA: MIT Press.

MacDonald, R. and Marsh, J. (2005) *Disconnected youth? Growing up in Britain's poor neighbourhoods*, Basingstoke: Palgrave Macmillan.

MacDonald, R., Shildrick, T., Webster, C. and Simpson, D. (2005) 'Growing up in poor neighbourhoods: the significance of class and place in the extended transitions of "socially excluded" young adults', *Sociology*, vol 39, no 5, pp 873–91.

McGregor, A., Glass, A., Higgins, K., Macdougall, L. and Sutherland, V. (2003) *Developing people – regenerating place: Achieving greater integration for local area regeneration*, Bristol: The Policy Press/Joseph Rowntree Foundation.

McInroy, N. and MacDonald, S. (2005) *From community garden to Westminster: Active citizenship and the role of public space*, Manchester: Centre for Local Economic Strategies. Available online at: www.cles.org.uk.

McIntosh, B. (2008) 'ASBO youth: rhetoric and realities', in P. Squires (ed) *ASBO nation: The criminalisation of nuisance*, Bristol: The Policy Press, pp 239–56.

McKee, K. (2008) 'The "responsible" tenant and the problem of apathy', *Social Policy & Society*, vol 8, no 1, pp 25–36.

McLaughlin, E. (2002) '"Same bed, different dreams": postmodern reflections on crime prevention and community safety', in G. Hughes and A. Edwards (eds) *Crime control and community*, Cullompton: Willan Publishing.

Macmillan, R. with Batty, E., Goudie, R., Morgan, G. and Pearson, S. (2007) *Building effective local VCS infrastructure: The characteristics of successful support for the local voluntary and community sector*, Sheffield: NAVCA. Available online at: www.navca.org.uk/publications/belvi.

McPake, B. (2008) *The story of primary health care: From Alma Ata to the present day*. Available online at: www.id21.org – search 'McPake'.

Maguire, K. and Truscott, F. (2006) *Active governance: The value added by community involvement in governance through local strategic partnerships*, York: Joseph Rowntree Foundation. Available online at: www.jrf.org.uk.

Maloney, W., Smith, G. and Stoker, G. (2000) 'Social capital and urban governance: adding a more contextualised "top-down perspective"', *Political Studies*, vol 48, pp 823–41.

Marinetto, M. (2003) 'Who wants to be an active citizen? The politics and practice of community involvement', *Sociology*, vol 37, no 1, pp 103–20.

Marmot, M. and Wilkinson, R.G. (2001) 'Psychosocial and material pathways in the relation between income and health: a response to Lynch et al', *British Medical Journal*, vol 322, no 7296, pp 1233–6.

Marqusee, M. (2009) 'The politics of cancer', *Red Pepper*, 168, pp 56–7.

Marx, K. (1970) *Capital: A critique of political economy*, vol 1, London: Lawrence & Wishart.

Matthews, R., Easton, H., Briggs, D. and Pease, K. (2007) *Assessing the use and impact of ASBOs*, Bristol: The Policy Press.

May, T. and Powell, J.L. (2008) *Situating social theory* (2nd edn), Maidenhead: Open University Press.

May, T., Duffy, M., Few, B. and Hough, M. (2006) *Understanding drug selling in communities: Insider or outsider trading?* York: Joseph Rowntree Foundation.

Mayo, M. and Rooke, A. (2006) *Active learning for active citizenship: Evaluation report*, London: HMSO.

Measham, F. and Moore, K. (2008) 'The criminalisation of intoxication', in P. Squires (ed) *ASBO nation: The criminalisation of nuisance*, Bristol: The Policy Press, pp 273–88.

Measor, L. (2006) 'Young women, community safety and informal cultures', in P. Squires (ed) *Community safety: Critical perspectives on policy and practice*, Bristol: The Policy Press, pp 181–97.

Meen, G., Gibb, K., Goody, J., McGrath, T. and Mackinnon, J. (2005) *Economic segregation in England: Causes, consequences and policy*, Bristol: The Policy Press.

Meighan, R. (ed) (2004) *Damage limitation: Trying to reduce the harm schools do to children*, Nottingham: Educational Heretics Press.

Melhuish, E. et al (2005) *National evaluation report: Early impacts of Sure Start Local Programmes on children and families*, London: DfES.

Melhuish, E. et al (2008) *The impact of Sure Start Local Programmes on three year olds and their families*, London: DCSF.

Melnyk, G. (1985) *In search of community: From Utopia to co-operative society*, Montreal–Buffalo: Black Rose Books.

Merrett, S. (1976) 'Gentrification', in M. Edwards, F. Gray, S. Merrett and J. Swann (eds) *Housing and class in Britain: A second volume of papers presented at the Political Economy of Housing workshop of the Conference of Socialist Economists*, London: The Russell Press.

Midgley, J. and Bradshaw, R. (2006) *Should I stay or should I go? Rural youth transitions*, Newcastle upon Tyne: IPPR North.

Millie, A. (ed) (2009) *Securing respect: Behavioural expectations and anti-social behaviour in the UK*, Bristol: The Policy Press.

Ministry of Justice (2008) *A national framework for greater citizen engagement*, London: Ministry of Justice. Available online at: www.justice.gov.uk/index.htm.

Minton, A. (2009) *Ground control: Fear and happiness in the twenty-first-century city*, Harmondsworth: Penguin.

Misztal, B. (2000) *Informality: Social theory and contemporary practice*, London: Routledge.

Mohan, G. and Mohan, J. (2002) 'Placing social capital', *Progress in Human Geography*, vol 26, pp 191–210.

Mooney, G. (2009) '"Problem" populations, "problem" places', in J. Newman and N. Yeates (eds) *Social justice: Welfare, crime and society*, Maidenhead: Open University Press, pp 97–128.

Mooney, G. and Neal, S. (2009) 'Community: themes and debates', in G. Mooney and S. Neal (eds) *Community: Welfare, crime and society*, Maidenhead: Open University Press, pp 1–33.

Moore, S. (2008) 'Street life, neighbourhood policing and the community', in P. Squires (ed) *ASBO nation: The criminalisation of nuisance*, Bristol: The Policy Press, pp 179–201.

Morgan, A. and Swann, C. (2004) *Social capital for health: Issues of definition, measurement and links to health*, London: Health Development Agency. Available online at: www.nice.org.uk/nicemedia/documents/socialcapital_issues.pdf#.

Morley, A. and Campbell, F. (2003) *People power and health: A Green Paper on democratising the NHS*, London: The Local Government Information Unit/Democratic Health Network.

Mornement, A. (2005) *No longer notorious: The revival of Castle Vale 1993–2005*, Brimingham: Castle Vale Neighbourhood Partnership.

Mulgan, G. and Bury, F. (2006) *Double devolution: The renewal of local government*, London: Smith Institute.

Murray, C. (1990) *The emerging British underclass*, London: Institute for Economic Affairs.

NAO (National Audit Office) (2006a) *Sure Start children's centres*, London: The Stationery Office.

NAO (2006b) *Tackling anti-social behaviour*, London: NAO.

National Assembly for Wales (2005) *Education, Wales: The School Councils (Wales) Regulations 2005*, SI 2005/3200 (W. 236), London: The Stationery Office.

National Statistics Online (2009) *Focus on social inequalities*, www.statistics. gov.uk/focuson/socialinequalities.

NEF (New Economics Foundation) (2003) *Ghost town Britain*, London: NEF.

Neocleous, M. (2000) *The fabrication of social order: A critique of police power*, London: Pluto Press.

Newby, H., Bell, C., Rose, D. and Saunders, P. (1978) *Property, paternalism and power: Class and control in rural England*, London: Hutchinson.

Nixon, J. (2007) 'Deconstructing "problem" researchers and "problem families": a rejoinder to Garrett', *Critical Social Policy*, vol 27, no 4, pp 546–56.

Nixon, J., Hunter, C., Myers, S., Parr, S. and Whittle, S. (2006) *Anti-social behaviour intensive family support projects: An evaluation of six pioneering projects*, London: Department for Communities and Local Government.

Nixon, J., Hodge, N., Barr, S., Willis, B. and Hunter, C. (2007) 'Anti-social behaviour and learning disability in the UK', *People, Place & Policy Online*, vol 2, no 1, pp 37–47.

Norris, P. and Williams, D. (2008) '"Binge drinking", anti-social behaviour and alcohol-related disorder: examining the 2003 Licensing Act', in P. Squires (ed) *ASBO nation: The criminalisation of nuisance*, Bristol: The Policy Press, pp 257–72.

North, D., Syrett, S. and Etherington, D. (2007) *Devolution and regional governance: Tackling the economic needs of deprived areas*, York: Joseph Rowntree Foundation.

Nozick, R. (1980) *Anarchy, state and utopia*, Oxford: Blackwell.

OCR (2009) *Citizenship studies*. Available online at: www.ocr.org.uk/Data/ publications/key_documents/GCSE_Citizenship_Spec.pdf.

ODPM (Office of the Deputy Prime Minister) (2002a) *Review of area based initiatives*, London: ODPM. Available online at: www.gos.gov.uk/ common/docs/239379/236556.

ODPM (2002b) *Tenants managing: An evaluation of tenant management organisations in England*, Housing Research Summary No. 174, London: ODPM.

ODPM (2005) *Citizen engagement and public services: Why neighbourhoods matter*, London: ODPM.

OECD (2006) *Boosting jobs and incomes: Policy lessons from reassessing the OECD Jobs Strategy*, Paris: OECD. Available online at: www.oecd.org/ dataoecd/47/53/36889821.pdf.

Ofsted (2006) *Towards consensus: Citizenship in secondary schools*. Available online at: www.ofsted.gov.uk/Ofsted-home/Publications-and-research/Browse-all-by/Education/Curriculum/Citizenship/Secondary/Towards-consensus-Citizenship-in-secondary-schools.

Oldman, C. (2003) 'Deceiving, theorizing and self-justification: a critique of independent living', *Critical Social Policy*, vol 23, no 1, pp 44–62.

Orton, A. (2009) *What works in enabling cross-community interactions?* London: CLG/National Community Forum.

Page, D. (2000) *Communities in the balance: The reality of social exclusion on housing estates*, York: Joseph Rowntree Foundation.

Page, D. (2006) *Respect and renewal*, York: Joseph Rowntree Foundation. Available online at: www.jrf.org.uk/bookshop/eBooks/1988-neighbourhood-social-regeneration.pdf.

Pandey, G. (2006) *Routine violence: Nations, fragments, histories*, Stanford, CA: Stanford University Press.

Parkinson, M., Evans, R., Meegan, R., Karecha, J. and Hutchins, M. (2006) *New evaluated Manchester: Interim evaluation of New East Manchester*. Available online at: www.communities.gov.uk.

Parr, S. and Nixon, J. (2008) 'Rationalising family intervention projects', in P. Squires (ed) *ASBO nation: The criminalisation of nuisance*, Bristol: The Policy Press, pp 161–77.

Pascal, C. and Bertram, T. (2004) *Sure Start: For everyone. Inclusion pilot projects*, Nottingham: DfES.

Pawson, H., Davidson, E., Morgan, J., Smith, R. and Edwards, R. (2009) *The impacts of housing stock transfers in urban Britain*, Coventry: Chartered Institute of Housing/Joseph Rowntree Foundation.

Pearson, G. (1983) *Hooligan: A history of respectable fears*, Basingstoke: Macmillan.

Peck, J. and Tickell, A. (2002) 'Neoliberalising space', *Antipode* vol 34, no 3, pp 380-404.

Pemberton, S. and Mason, J. (2008) 'Co-production and Sure Start Children's Centres: reflecting upon users' perspectives and implications for service delivery, planning and evaluation', *Social Policy & Society*, vol 8, no 1, pp 13–24.

Percy-Smith, J. (2006) 'What works in strategic partnerships for children: a research review', *Children and Society*, vol 20, no 4, pp 313–23.

Pettit, P. (1997) *Republicanism: A theory of freedom and government*, Oxford: Clarendon Press.

Phillips, D. (2006) 'Parallel lives? Challenging discourses of British Muslim self-segregation', *Environment and Planning D*, vol 24, no 1, pp 25–40.

Phillips, S.K. (1986) 'Natives and incomers: the symbolism of belonging in Muker parish, North Yorkshire', in A.P. Cohen (ed) *Symbolising boundaries: Identity and diversity in British cultures*, Manchester: Manchester University Press.

Phoenix, J. (2008) 'ASBOs and working women: a new revolving door?' in P. Squires (ed) *ASBO nation: The criminalisation of nuisance*, Bristol: The Policy Press, pp 289–303.

Porter, M. (2004) *Competitive advantage*, New York: Free Press.

POWER (2005) *The causes of the decline in 'electoral activity' in Britain*, www.powerinquiry.org.

Pratchett, L., Durose, C., Lowndes, V., Smith, G., Stoker, G. and Wales, C. (2009a) *Empowering communities to influence local decision making: A systematic review of the evidence*, London: CLG.

Pratchett, L., Durose, C., Lowndes, V., Smith, G., Stoker, G. and Wales, C. (2009b) *Empowering communities to influence local decision making: Evidence-based lessons for policy makers and practitioners*, London: CLG.

Prior, D. (2005) 'Civil renewal and community safety: virtuous policy spiral or dynamic of exclusion?' *Social Policy and Society*, vol 4, no 4, pp 357–68.

Prior, D. and Spalek, B. (2008) 'Anti-social behaviour and ethnic minority populations', in P. Squires (ed) *ASBO nation: The criminalisation of nuisance*, Bristol: The Policy Press, pp 117–34.

Prior, D., Farrow, K., Spalek, B. and Barnes, M. (2007) 'Anti-social behaviour and civil renewal', in T. Brannan, P. John and G. Stoker (eds) *Re-energising citizenship: Strategies for civil renewal*, Basingstoke: Palgrave Macmillan.

Purdue, D. (2005) 'Community leadership cycles and the consolidation of neighbourhood coalitions in the new local governance', *Public Management Review*, vol 7, no 2, pp 247–66.

Putnam, R.D. (1993) *Making democracy work: Civic traditions in modern Italy*, Princeton, NJ: Princeton University Press.

Putnam, R.D. (2000) *Bowling alone: The collapse and revival of American community*, New York: Simon and Schuster.

Ranson, S. and Rutledge, H. (2005) *Including families in the learning community: Family centres and the expansion of learning*, York: Joseph Rowntree Foundation.

Ratner, C. (2007) 'The co-operative manifesto: social philosophy, economics and psychology for co-operative behaviour', *Journal of Co-operative Studies*, vol 40, no 3, pp 14–26.

Ray, K., Hudson, M., Campbell-Barr, V. and Shutes, I. (2008) *Public officials and community involvement in local services*, York: Joseph Rowntree Foundation.

Readfearn, G. (2005) 'Growing pains', *New Start*, vol 30, September, pp 12–13.

Reed, H. and Stanley, K. (2005) *Cooperative social enterprise and its potential in public service delivery*, London: Institute for Public Policy Research.

Respect Task Force (2006) *Respect action plan*, London: Home Office.

Rexroth, K. (1974) *Communalism: From its origins to the twentieth century*, New York: Seabury Press.

Richard, D. (2008) *Small business and government: The Richard report*, London: Conservative Party. Available online at: www.conservatives.com.

Richardson, L. (2008) *DIY community action*, Bristol: The Policy Press.

Rifkin, S. (1986) 'Lessons from community participation in health programmes', *Health Policy and Planning*, vol 1, pp 240–9.

Roberts, E. (1995) *Women and families: An oral history, 1940–1970*, Oxford: Basil Blackwell.

Roberts, Y., Brophy, M. and Bacon, N. (2009) *Parenting and well-being: Knitting families together*, London: Young Foundation.

Robertson, D., Smyth, J. and McIntosh, I. (2008) *Neighbourhood identity: People, time and place*, York: Joseph Rowntree Foundation.

Robinson, V. (1986) *Transients, settlers and refugees: Asians in Britain*, Oxford: Clarendon Press.

Robson, B., Parkinson, M., Boddy, M. and Maclennan, D. (1994) *Assessing the impact of urban policy*, London: HMSO.

Robson, T. (2000) *The state and community action*, London: Pluto Press.

Rodger, J.J. (2008) *Criminalising social policy: Anti-social behaviour and welfare in a de-civilised society*, Cullompton: Willan Publishing.

Rogers, B. and Robinson, E. (2004) *The benefits of community engagement*, London: Active Citizenship Centre, Home Office.

Rose, N. (1996) 'The death of the social? Re-figuring the territory of government', *Economy and Society*, vol 25, pp 327–56.

Rutherford, A. (1997) 'Criminal policy and the eliminative ideal', *Social Policy & Administration*, vol 31, no 5, pp 116–35.

Sampson, R. and Groves, W. (1989) 'Community structure and crime: testing social-disorganisation theory', *American Journal of Sociology*, vol 94, no 4, pp 774–802.

Sampson, R.J., Raudenbush, S.W. and Earls, F. (1997) 'Neighbourhoods and violent crime: a multilevel study of collective efficacy', *Science*, vol 277, pp 918–24.

Sanders, T. (2005) *Sex work: A risky business*, Cullompton: Willan Publishing.

Sanders, T., O'Neill, M. and Pitcher, J. (2009) *Prostitution: Sex work, policy and politics*, London: Sage.

Saunders, P. (1990) *A nation of homeowners*, London: Allen and Unwin.

Savage, M. (2005) in T. May et al, 'The future of urban sociology', *Sociology*, vol 39, no 2, pp 343–70.

Savage, M., Bagnall, G. and Longhurst, B. (2005) *Globalisation and belonging*, London: Sage.

Sayer, A. (2005) 'Class, moral worth and recognition', *Sociology*, vol 39, no 5, pp 947–63.

Scherer, J. (1972) *Contemporary community: Sociological illusion or reality?* London: Tavistock.

Scott, J. (1995) *Sociological theory: Contemporary debates*, Aldershot: Edward Elgar.

SDC (Sustainable Development Commission) (2007) *Building houses or creating communities? A review of government progress on sustainable communities*, London: Sustainable Development Commission.

Seabrook, J. (1973) *City close-up*, Harmondsworth: Penguin.

Seddon, J. (2008) *Systems thinking in the public sector*, Axminster: Triarchy Press.

SEU (Social Exclusion Unit) (2001) *A new commitment to neighbourhood renewal: National strategy action plan*, London: The Stationery Office.

Seyfang, G. (2006) 'Sustainable consumption, the new economics and community currencies: developing new institutions for environmental governance', *Regional Studies*, vol 40, no 7, pp 781–91.

Sherbourne, C.D., Hayes, R.D. and Wells, K.B. (1995) 'Personal and psychological risk factors for physical and mental health outcomes and course of depression amongst depressed patients', *Journal of Consulting and Clinical Psychology*, vol 63, no 3, pp 345–55.

Shiner, M., Thom, B. and MacGregor, S. (2004) *Exploring community responses to drugs*, York: Joseph Rowntree Foundation. Available online at: www.jrf.org.uk.

Shinman, S. (2005) *Learning from families: Policies and practices to combat social exclusion in families with young children in Europe*. Available online at: www.home-start.org.uk.

Silver, E. and Miller, L.L. (2004) 'Sources of informal social control in Chicago neighborhoods', *Criminology*, vol 42, no 3, pp 551–83.

Sintomer, Y., Herzberg, C. and Röcke, A. (2008) 'Participatory budgeting in Europe: potentials and challenges', *International Journal of Urban and Regional Research*, vol 32, no 1, pp 164–78.

Skidmore, P. (no date) *Polls apart: Democracy in an age of inequality*, Compass Online at www.compassonline.org.uk.

Skidmore, P., Bound, K. and Lownsbrough, H. (2006) *Community participation: Who benefits?* York: Joseph Rowntree Foundation.

Slater, T. (2008) '"A literal necessity to be re-placed": a rejoinder to the gentrification debate', *International Journal of Urban and Regional Research*, vol 32, no 1, pp 212–23.

Slatter, P. (2010) *Looking sideways: A community asset approach to coproduction of neighbourhoods and neighbourhood services in Birmingham*, Birmingham: Chamberlain Forum.

Small Business Service (2006) *A survey of social enterprises across the UK*, London: SBS with IFF Research.

Smith, G. (2008) *Democratic innovations*, Cambridge: Cambridge University Press.

Smith, N. (1979) 'Toward a theory of gentrification: a back to the city movement by capital not people', *Journal of the American Planning Association*, vol 45, pp 538–48.

Smith, N. (1996) *The new urban frontier: Gentrification and the revanchist city*, London: Routledge.

Smith, T. et al (2004) *National evaluation of the wraparound care pilot project*, Nottingham: DfES. Available online at: www.surestart.gov.uk.

Smith, T. and Lee, C. (2005) *Early stages of the neighbourhood nurseries initiative*, Nottingham: DfES. Available online at: www.surestart.gov.uk.

Social Centre Stories (2008) *What's this place? Stories from radical social centres in the UK and Ireland*. Available online at: http://socialcentrestories. wordpress.com or www.socialcentrestories.org.uk.

Solanki, A.-R., Bateman, T., Boswell, G. and Hill, E. (2006) *Anti-social behaviour orders*, London: Youth Justice Board for England and Wales.

Solnit, R. (2009) *A paradise built in hell: The extraordinary communities that arise in disaster*, New York: Viking.

Somerville, P. (1998) 'Empowerment through residence', *Housing Studies*, vol 13, no 2, pp 235–59.

Somerville, P. (2000) *Social relations and social exclusion: Rethinking political economy*, London: Routledge.

Somerville, P. (2005) 'Community governance and democracy', *Policy & Politics*, vol 33, no 1, pp 117–44.

Somerville, P. (2007) 'Co-operative identity', *Journal of Co-operative Studies* vol 40, no 1, pp 5–17

Somerville, P. (2009a) '"The feeling's mutual": respect as the basis for co-operative interaction', in A. Millie (ed) *Securing respect: Behavioural expectations and anti-social behaviour in the UK*, Bristol: The Policy Press, pp 139–67.

Somerville, P. (2009b) 'Understanding community policing', *Policing: An International Journal of Police Strategies and Management*, vol 32, no 2, pp 261–77.

Somerville, P. (2010, forthcoming) 'Multiscalarity and neighbourhood governance', *Public Policy & Administration*.

Somerville, P. (2011, forthcoming) 'Resident and housing movements', in S.J. Smith (ed) *International Encyclopedia of Housing and Home*, Elsevier.

Somerville, P. and Haines, N. (2008) 'Prospects for local co-governance', *Local Government Studies* vol 34, no 1, pp 61–79.

Somerville, P. and McElwee, G. (2010, forthcoming) 'Situating community enterprise: a theoretical exploration', *Entrepreneurship and Regional Development*.

Somerville, P., Dearling, A. and Newburn, T. (2006) 'Conclusion', in A. Dearling, T. Newburn and P. Somerville (eds) *Supporting safer communities: Housing, crime and neighbourhoods*, Coventry: Chartered Institute of Housing, pp 235–50.

Spalek, B. (2008) *Communities, identities and crime*, Bristol: The Policy Press.

Squires, P. (1990) *Anti-social policy*, Brighton: Harvester Wheatsheaf.

Squires, P. (ed) (2006) *Community safety: Critical perspectives on policy and practice*, Bristol: The Policy Press.

Squires, P. (ed) (2008) *ASBO nation: The criminalisation of nuisance*, Bristol: The Policy Press.

Squires, P. (2009) '"You looking at me?" Discourses of respect and disrespect, identity and violence', in A. Millie (ed) *Securing respect: Behavioural expectations and anti-social behaviour in the UK*, Bristol: The Policy Press, pp 239–65.

SQW (2008a) *Neighbourhood management pathfinders: Final evaluation report*, London: CLG.

SQW (2008b) *Community cohesion and neighbourhood management: A theme report from the neighbourhood management pathfinders national evaluation*, London: CLG.

Stephen, D. (2008) 'The responsibility of respecting justice: an open challenge to Tony Blair's successors', in P. Squires (ed) *ASBO nation: The criminalisation of nuisance*, Bristol: The Policy Press, pp 319–35.

Stephens, L., Ryan-Collins, J. and Boyle, D. (2008) *Co-production: A manifesto for growing the core economy*, London: New Economics Foundation.

Stoecker, R. (2001) *Report to the West Bank CDC: Primer on community organizing*, http://comm-org.wisc.edu/cr/crreporta.htm.

Stolle, D. (2003) 'Sources of social trust: theoretical and empirical insights', in M. Hooghe and D. Stolle (eds) *Generating social capital: Civil society and institutions in comparative perspective*, Basingstoke: Palgrave Macmillan.

Stone, C. (2002) 'Urban regimes and problems of local democracy', Paper presented to workshop 6, 'Institutional Innovations in Local Democracy', at the European Consortium for Political Research conference, Turin, 22–27 March.

Stryk, L. (ed) (1968) *World of the Buddha: A reader – from the three baskets to modern Zen*, New York: Doubleday and Co.

Taylor, M. (2000) *Top down meets bottom up: Neighbourhood management*, York: Joseph Rowntree Foundation.

Taylor, M. (2003) *Public policy in the community*, Basingstoke: Palgrave Macmillan.

Taylor, M. (2006) 'Communities in partnership: developing a strategic voice', *Social Policy & Society*, vol 5, no 2, pp 269–79.

Taylor, M. (2007) *Neighbourhood management and social capital*, Research Report 35, London: Department for Communities and Local Government.

Taylor, M. (2008) *Transforming disadvantaged places: Effective strategies for places and people*, York: Joseph Rowntree Foundation.

Taylor, M. and Wilson, M. (2006) *The importance of the neighbourhood: Tackling the implementation gap*, York: Joseph Rowntree Foundation.

Taylor, M., Wilson, M., Purdue, D. and Wilde, P. (2007) *Changing neighbourhoods: Lessons from the JRF neighbourhood programme*, Bristol: The Policy Press/ Joseph Rowntree Foundation.

Taylor, M., Purdue, D., Carlton, N., Mackridge, R., Syed, A., Ardron, R., Wilson, M., Meegan, R. and Russell, H. (2005) *Making connections: An evaluation of the community participation programmes*, Research Report 15, London: Neighbourhood Renewal Unit, ODPM.

Teague, P. (2007) 'Developing the social economy in Ireland?' *International Journal of Urban and Regional Research*, vol 31, no 1, pp 91–108.

Tebbutt, M. (1995) *Women's talk: A social history of 'gossip' in working-class neighbourhoods, 1880–1960*, Aldershot: Scolar Press.

The Patients' Association (2009) *Patients …, not numbers. People … not statistics*, London: The Patients' Association. Available online at: www.patients-association.org.uk.

Thomson, L. and Caulier-Grice, J. (2007) *Improving small scale grant funding for local voluntary and community organisations*, London: The Young Foundation.

Thornhill, J. (2009) *Transforming estates*, Coventry: Chartered Institute of Housing.

Thornhill, J. and Kent-Smith, J. (2009) *Housing, schools and communities*, Coventry: Chartered Institute of Housing.

Tisdall, K., Wallace, J., McGregor, E., Millen, D. and Bell, A. (2005) *Seamless services, smoother lives*, York: Children in Scotland/Joseph Rowntree Foundation.

Tolle, E. (1999) *The power of now: A guide to spiritual enlightenment*, Novato, CA: New World Library.

Tolle, E. (2005) *A new earth: Create a better life*, Harmondsworth: Penguin.

Tönnies, F. (1988) *Community and society (Gemeinschaft and Gesellschaft)*, New York: Transaction Publishers.

Townsend, P. (1979) *Poverty in the UK: A survey of household resources and standards of living*, London: Penguin and Allen Lane.

Tuffin, R., Morris, J. and Poole, A. (2006) *The national reassurance policing programme: A six-site evaluation*, HORS 296, London: Home Office.

Tunstall, R. and Fenton, A. (2006) *In the mix: A review of mixed income, mixed tenure and mixed communities*, London: Housing Corporation/Joseph Rowntree Foundation/English Partnerships.

Twelvetrees, A. (2002) *Community work* (3rd edn), Basingstoke: Palgrave Macmillan/ Community Development Foundation.

Uguris, T. (2004) *Space, power and participation: Ethnic and gender divisions in tenants' participation in public housing*, Aldershot: Ashgate.

Uitermark, J., Duyvendak, J. W. and Kleinhaus, R. (2007) 'Gentrification as a governmental strategy: social control and social cohesion in Hoogvliet, Rotterdam', *Environment and Planning A*, vol 39, pp 125–41.

Vaitilingam, R. (2009) 'Be well ...', *The Broker*, vol 12, pp 4–8. Available online at: www.thebrokeronline.eu.

Wacquant, L. (2008) 'Relocating gentrification: the working class, science and the state in recent urban research', *International Journal of Urban and Regional Research*, vol 32, no 1, pp 198–205.

Wain, N. with Burney, E. (2007) *The ASBO: Wrong turning, dead end*, London: Howard League for Penal Reform.

Wainwright, H. (2003) *Reclaim the state: Experiments in popular democracy*, London: Verso.

Walby, S. (1990) *Theorising patriarchy*, Oxford: Basil Blackwell.

Walklate, S. and Evans, K. (1999) *Zero tolerance or community tolerance?* Aldershot: Ashgate.

Wallace, E., Smith, K., Pye, J., Crouch, J., Ziff, A. and Burston, K. (2009) *Extended schools survey of schools, pupils and parents: A quantitative study of perceptions and usage of extended services in schools*, London: DCSF.

Wallman, S. (1984) *Eight London households*, London: Tavistock.

Wampler, B. (2007) *Participatory budgeting in Brazil*, Pennsylvania: Pennsylvania State University Press.

Ward, K. (2003) 'Entrepreneurial urbanism, state restructuring and civilising "New East Manchester"', *Area*, vol 35, pp 116–27.

Watt, P. (2006) 'Respectability, roughness and "race": neighbourhood place images and the making of working-class social distinctions in London', *International Journal of Urban and Regional Research*, vol 30, no 4, pp 776–97.

Wayland, C. and Crowder, J. (2002) 'Disparate views of community in primary health care: understanding how perceptions influence success', *Medical Anthropology Quarterly*, vol 16, no 2, pp 231–2.

Webb, J. (2004) 'Organizations, self-identities and the new economy', *Sociology*, vol 38, pp 719–38.

Wemyss, G. (2006) 'The power to tolerate: contests over Britishness and belonging in East London', *Patterns of Prejudice*, vol 40, no 3, pp 215–36.

WHO (World Health Organisation) (1978) *Declaration of Alma-Ata*. Available online at: www.who.int/hpr/NPH/docs/declaration_almaata. pdf.

WHO (2002) *World health report 2002*, Geneva: WHO.

WHO (2008) *Primary health care: Now more than ever*, Geneva: WHO. Available online at: www.who.int.

Wilkinson, D. (1999) 'The social environment', in D. Gordon et al (eds) *Inequalities in health: The evidence*, Bristol: The Policy Press, pp 68–75.

Wilkinson, K. and Noble, M. (2010) *Tackling economic deprivation in New Deal for Communities areas*, London: Department for Communities and Local Government.

Wilkinson, R.G. (1996) *Unhealthy societies: The afflictions of inequality*, London: Routledge.

Wilkinson, R. and Pickett, K. (2009) *The spirit level: Why more equal societies almost always do better*, London: Allen Lane.

Williams, C. and Windebank, J. (2000) 'Helping each other out? Community exchange in deprived neighbourhoods', *Community Development Journal*, vol 35, no 2, pp 146–56.

Williams, F. and Churchill, H. (2006) *Empowering parents in Sure Start Local Programmes*, NESS Report, London: HMSO.

Williams, G. (2004) 'Towards a repoliticisation of participatory development: political capabilities and spaces of empowerment', in S. Hickey and G. Mohan (eds) *Participation: From tyranny to transformation?* London: Zed Books, pp 92–107.

Williams, R. (1985) *The country and the city*, London: The Hogarth Press.

Williamson, H. (2006) 'Growing out of crime? Youth transitions, opportunity structures and social inclusion', in A. Dearling, T. Newburn and P. Somerville (eds) *Supporting safer communities: Housing, crime and neighbourhoods*, Coventry: Chartered Institute of Housing, pp 203–17.

Wills, J. (2001) 'Community unionism and trade union renewal in the UK: moving beyond the fragments at last?' *Transactions of the Institute of British Geographers,* vol 26, pp 465–83.

Wills, J. (2002) Union futures: Building networked trade unionism in the UK, Fabian Ideas pamphlet 602, London: Fabian Society.

Wills, J. (2004) 'Organising the low paid: East London's Living Wage Campaign as a vehicle for change', in G. Healy, E. Heery, P. Taylor and W. Brown (eds), *The future of worker representation*, Oxford: Oxford University Press, pp 246–82.

Wills, J. and Simms, M. (2004) 'Building reciprocal community unionism in the UK', *Capital and Class,* vol 82, pp 59–84.

Wilson, J. and Kelling, G. (1982) 'The police and neighbourhood safety: broken windows', *The Atlantic Monthly*, March, pp 29–38.

Woolcock, M. (1998) 'Social capital and economic development: towards a theoretical synthesis and policy framework', *Theory and Society*, vol 27, pp 151–208.

World Bank (2009) *Empowerment*. Available online at: www.worldbank.org (accessed 13 October 2009).

Yamin, A.E. (2009) 'Suffering and powerlessness: the significance of promoting participation in rights–based approaches to health', *Health and Human Rights: An International Journal*, vol 11, no 1, pp 5–22.

Young, I. M. (1990) *Justice and the politics of difference*, Princeton, NJ: Princeton University Press.

Young, J. (1999) *The exclusive society: Social exclusion, crime and difference in late modernity*, London: Sage.

Young, J. (2007) *The vertigo of late modernity*, London: Sage.

Žižek, S. (1993) *Tarrying with the negative*, Durham, NC: Duke University Press.

Index

Page references for notes are followed by n